The Way of the House Husband

KOUSUKE OONO

9

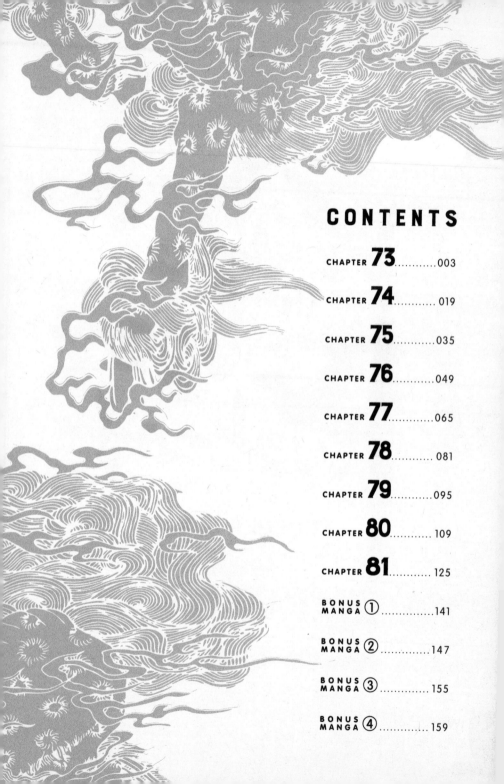

CONTENTS

CHAPTER 73

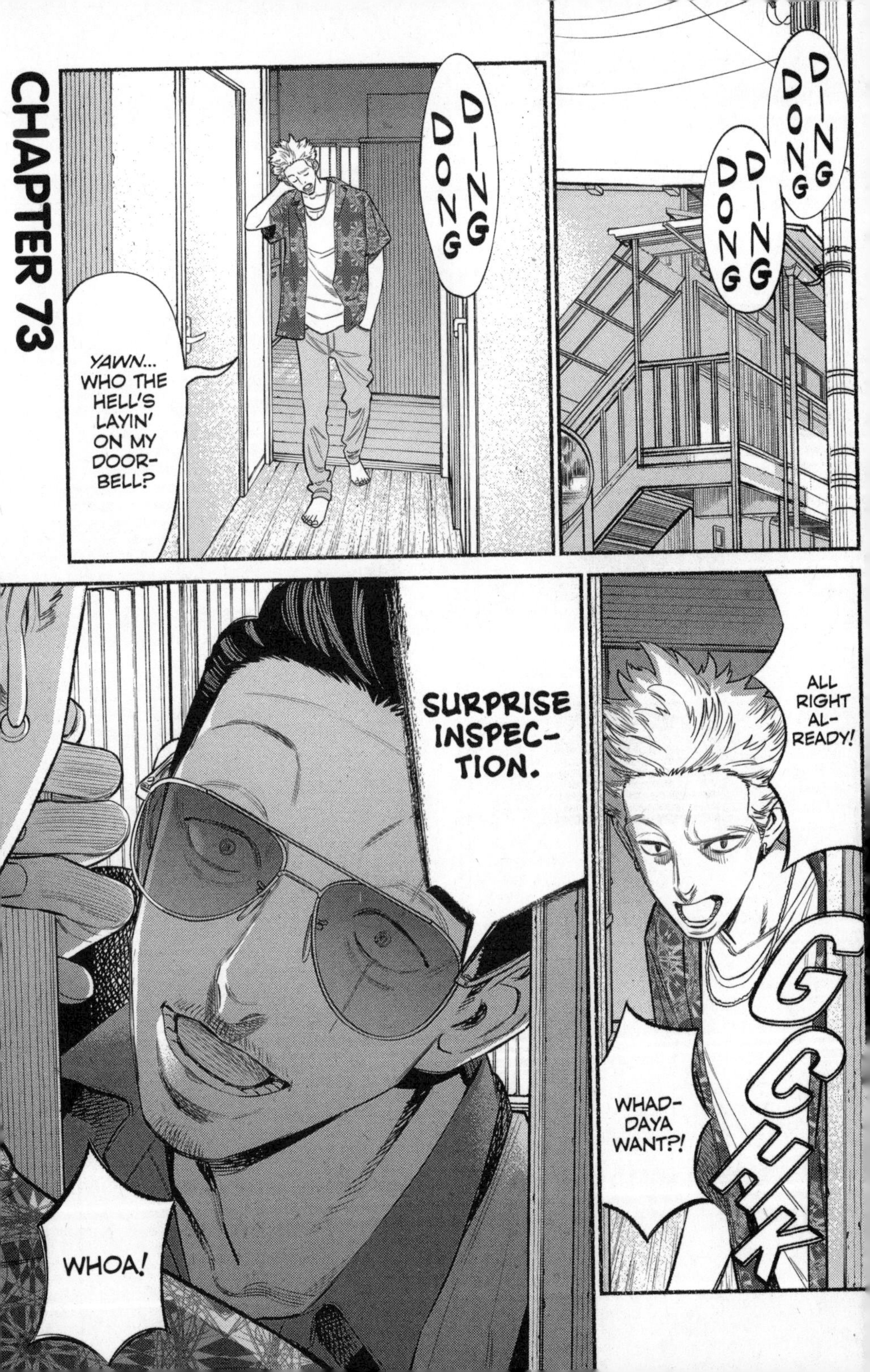
DING DONG
DING DONG
DING DONG
YAWN... WHO THE HELL'S LAYIN' ON MY DOOR-BELL?
ALL RIGHT AL-READY!
GCHK
WHAD-DAYA WANT?!
SURPRISE INSPEC-TION.
WHOA!

RANK.

YOU SCARED ME, BOSS.

HUH?! IS IT?

I WAS PASSIN' THROUGH THE AREA. FIGURED I'D DROP IN, SEE WHETHER YOU'RE KEEPIN' UP ON YER CHORES...

C'MON IN AND I'LL BUST OUT SOME TEA.

OH, THAT'S JUST THE MOISTURE THAT ACCUMULATES BY THE FRONT DOOR. IT'S COOL.

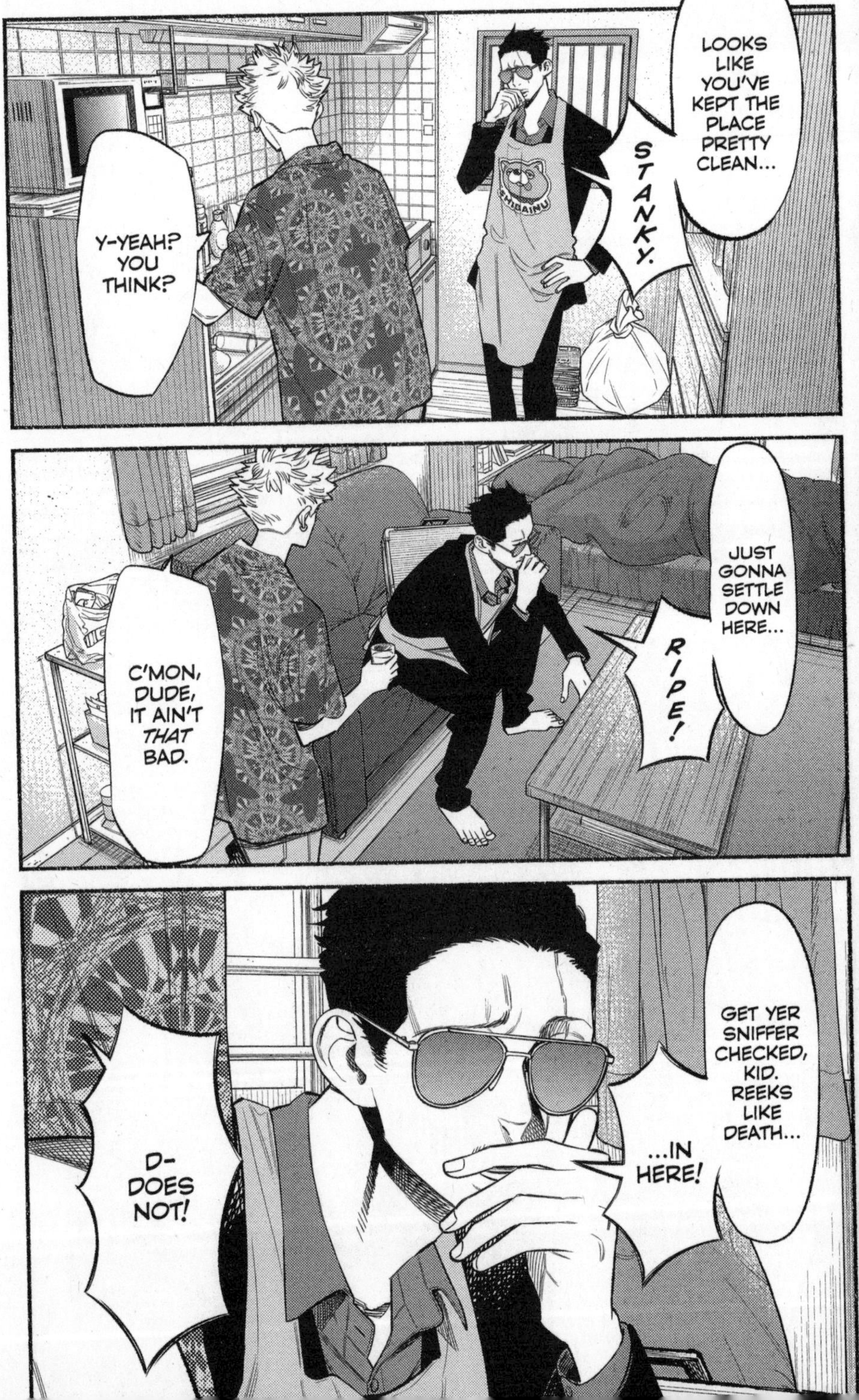
LOOKS LIKE YOU'VE KEPT THE PLACE PRETTY CLEAN...
STANKY.
Y-YEAH? YOU THINK?
JUST GONNA SETTLE DOWN HERE...
RIPE!
C'MON, DUDE, IT AIN'T *THAT* BAD.
GET YER SNIFFER CHECKED, KID. REEKS LIKE DEATH...
...IN HERE!
D-DOES NOT!

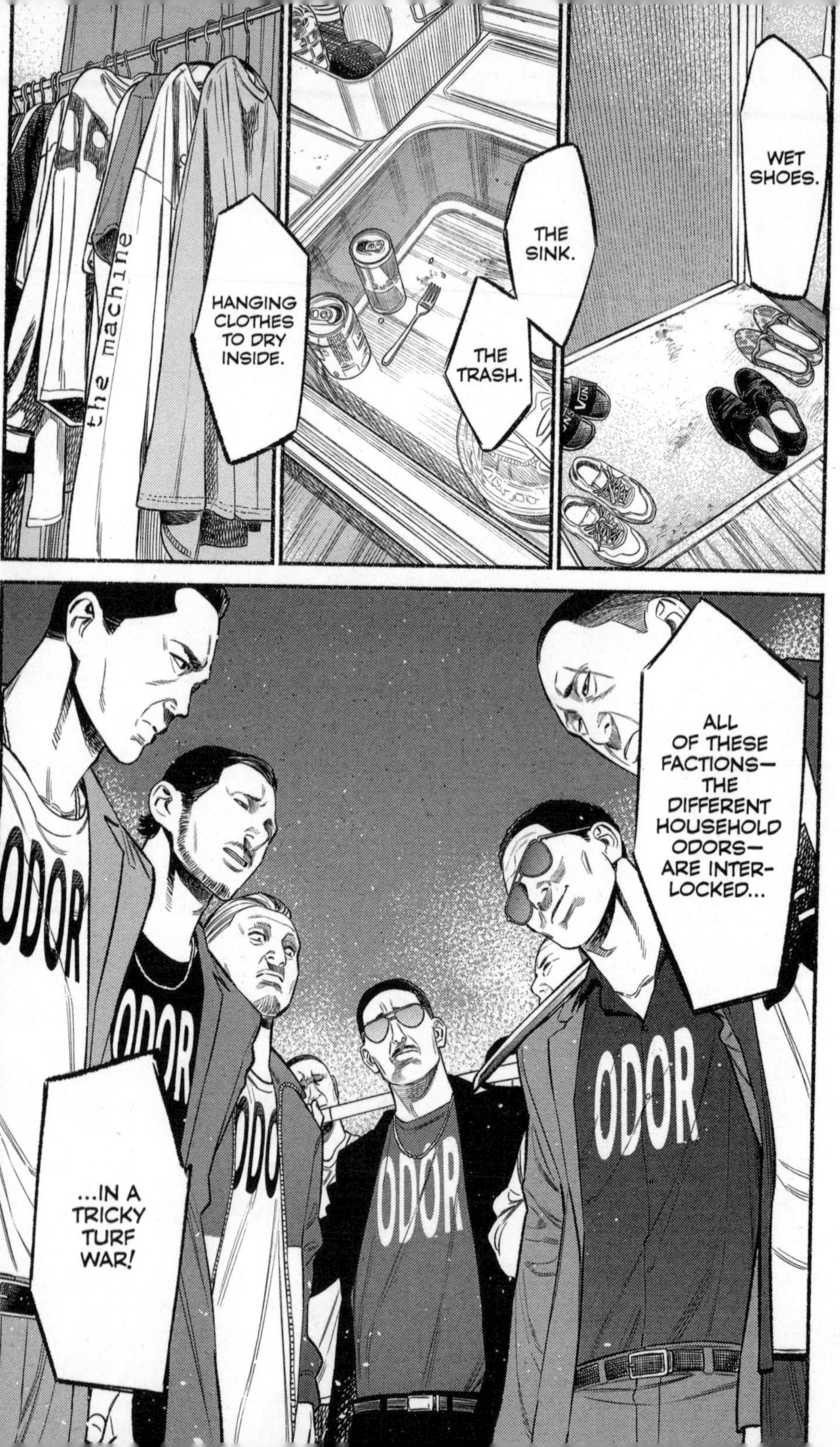
WET SHOES.
THE SINK.
THE TRASH.
HANGING CLOTHES TO DRY INSIDE.
the machine
ALL OF THESE FACTIONS—THE DIFFERENT HOUSEHOLD ODORS—ARE INTER-LOCKED...
ODOR
...IN A TRICKY TURF WAR!

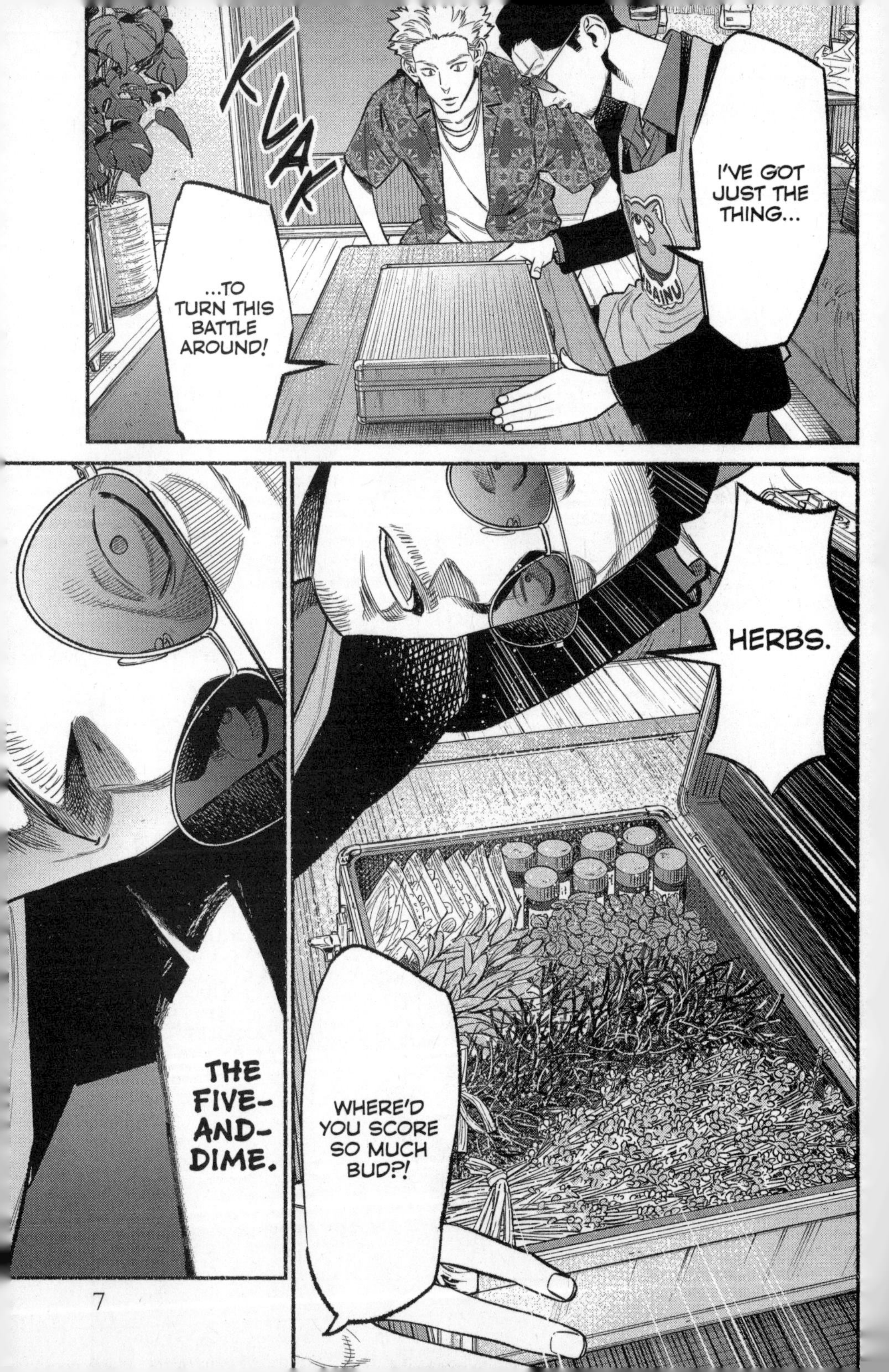
KLAK
I'VE GOT JUST THE THING...
...TO TURN THIS BATTLE AROUND!
HERBS.
WHERE'D YOU SCORE SO MUCH BUD?!
THE FIVE-AND-DIME.

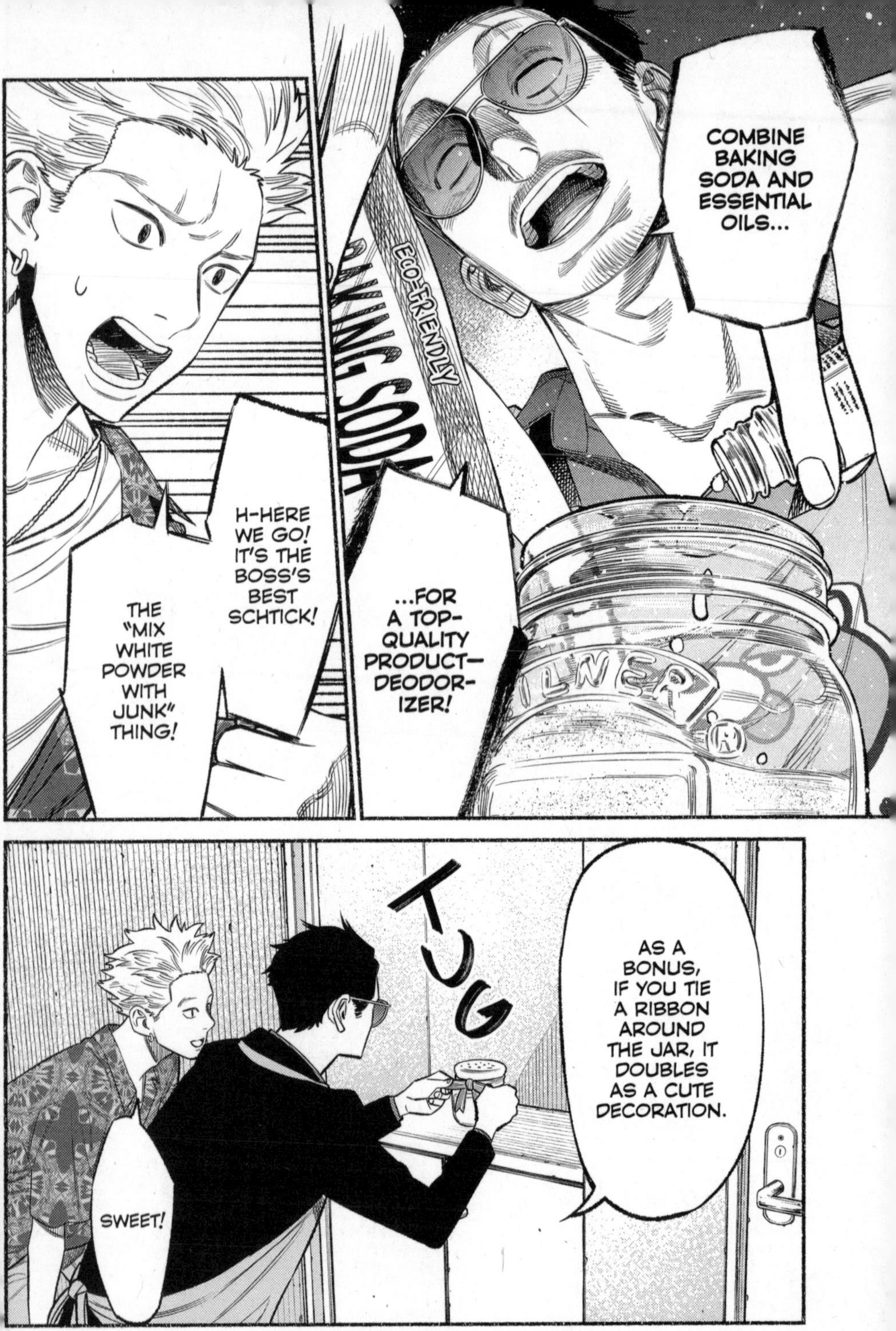
COMBINE BAKING SODA AND ESSENTIAL OILS...
ECO-FRIENDLY
...FOR A TOP-QUALITY PRODUCT-DEODORIZER!
H-HERE WE GO! IT'S THE BOSS'S BEST SCHTICK!
THE "MIX WHITE POWDER WITH JUNK" THING!
AS A BONUS, IF YOU TIE A RIBBON AROUND THE JAR, IT DOUBLES AS A CUTE DECORATION.
TUG
SWEET!

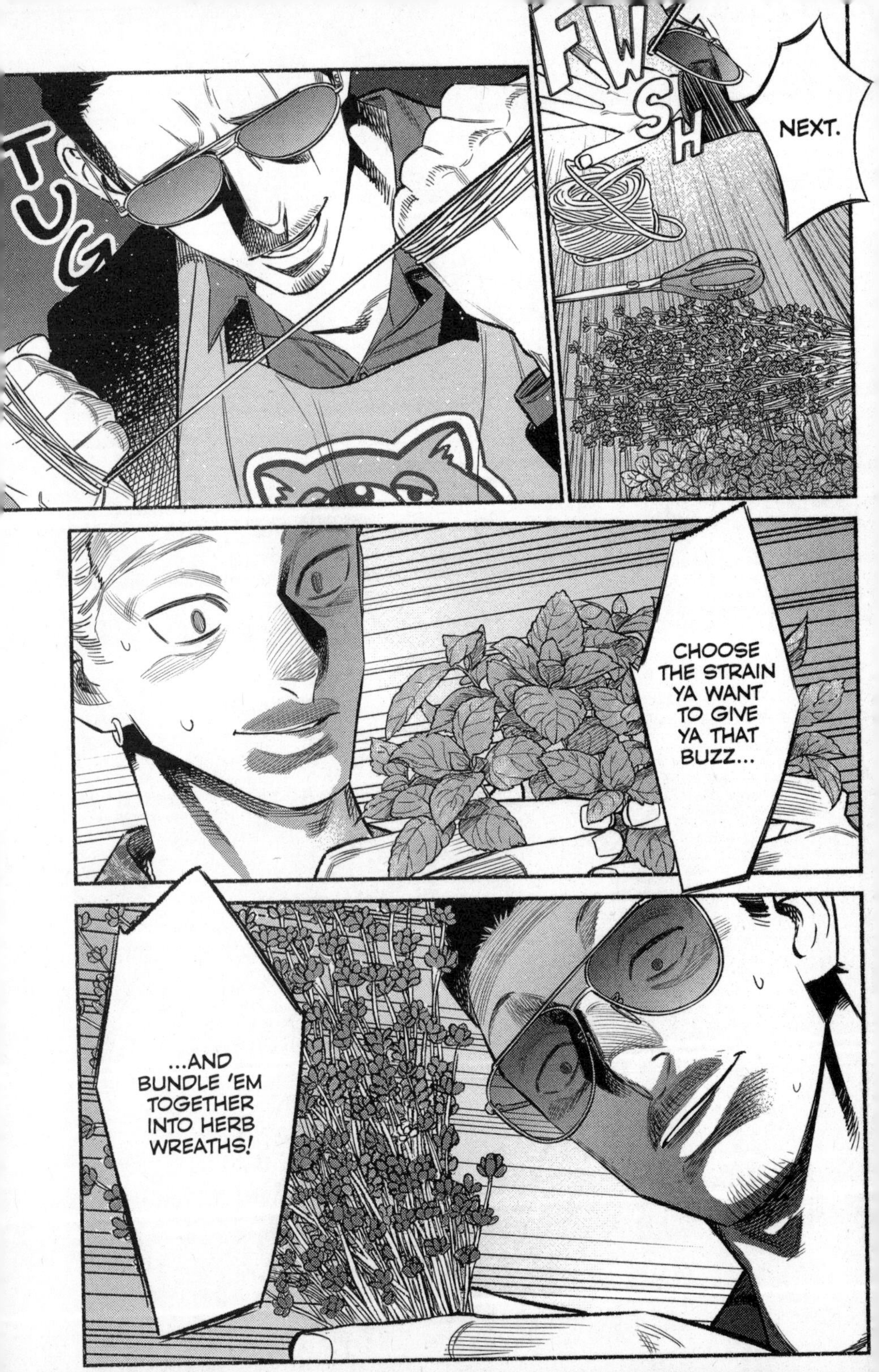
FWSH
NEXT.
TUG
CHOOSE THE STRAIN YA WANT TO GIVE YA THAT BUZZ...
...AND BUNDLE 'EM TOGETHER INTO HERB WREATHS!

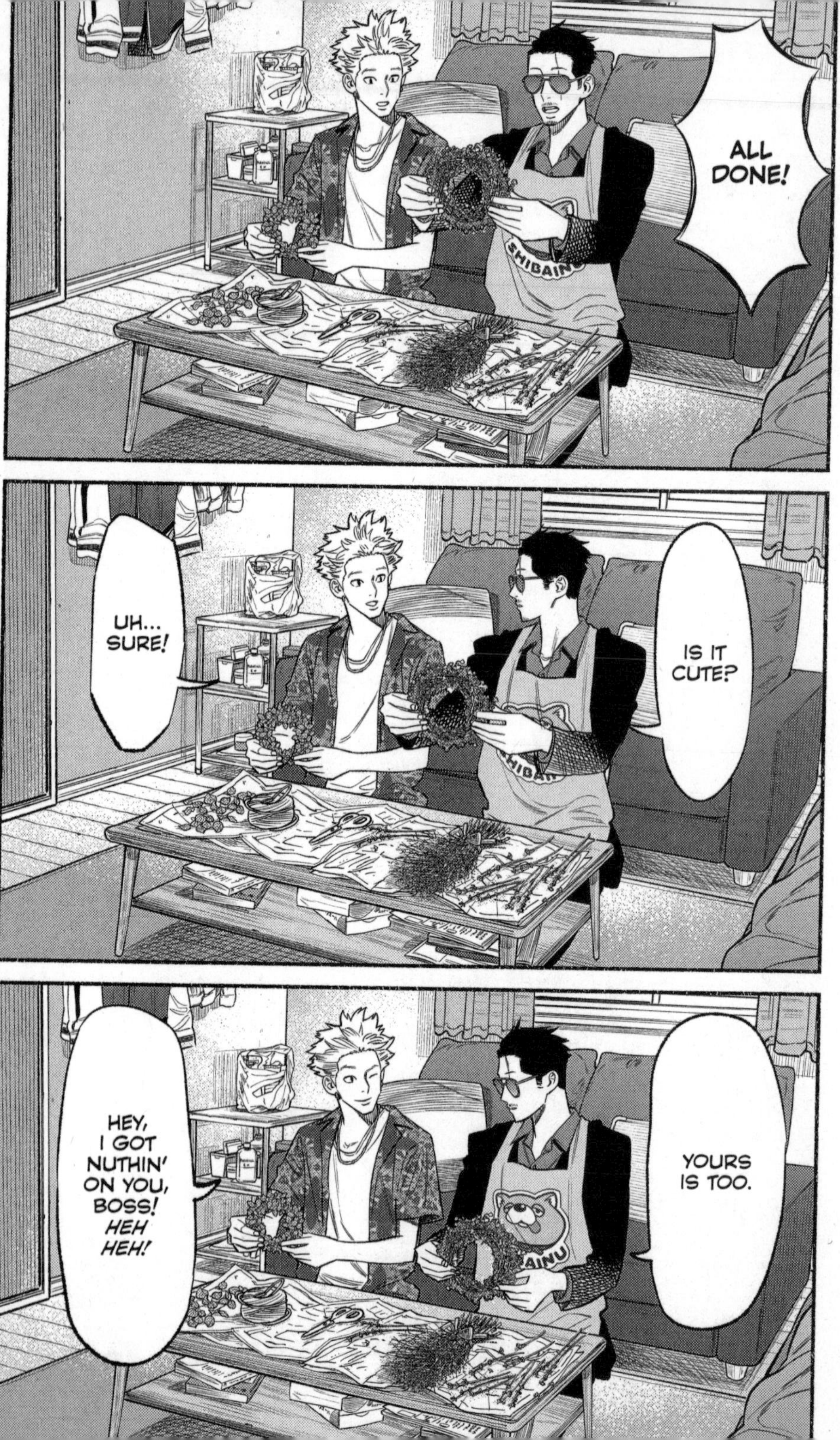
ALL DONE!
IS IT CUTE?
UH... SURE!
YOURS IS TOO.
HEY, I GOT NUTHIN' ON YOU, BOSS! *HEH HEH!*

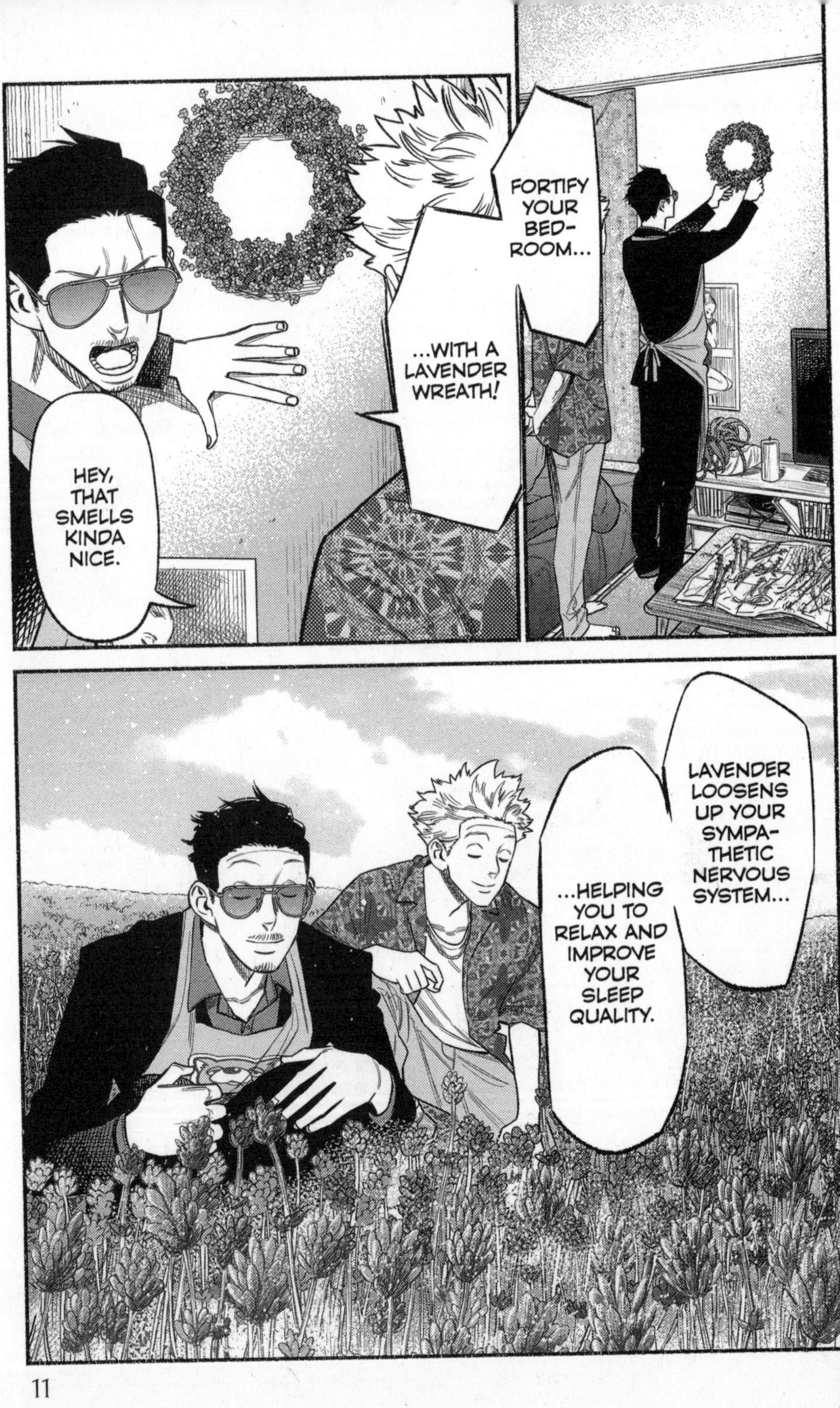
FORTIFY YOUR BED-ROOM...
...WITH A LAVENDER WREATH!
HEY, THAT SMELLS KINDA NICE.
LAVENDER LOOSENS UP YOUR SYMPA-THETIC NERVOUS SYSTEM...
...HELPING YOU TO RELAX AND IMPROVE YOUR SLEEP QUALITY.

12

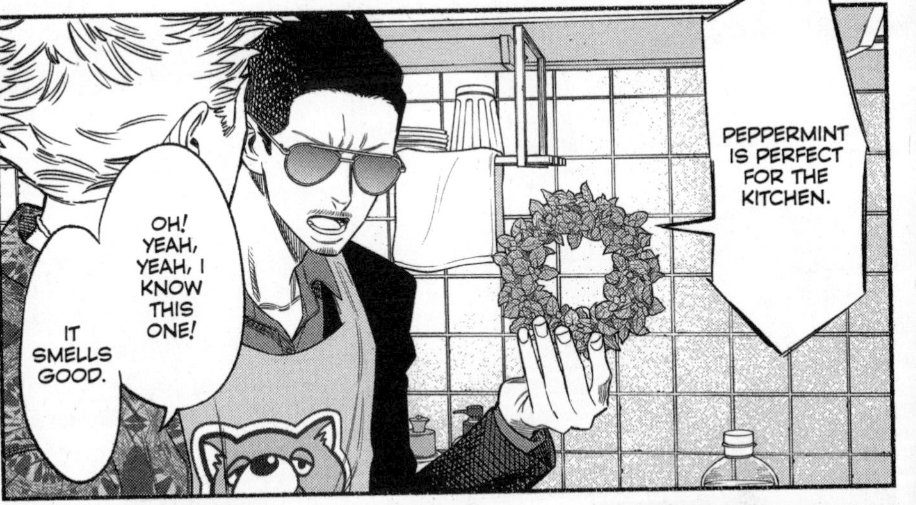
PEPPERMINT IS PERFECT FOR THE KITCHEN.
OH! YEAH, YEAH, I KNOW THIS ONE!
IT SMELLS GOOD.

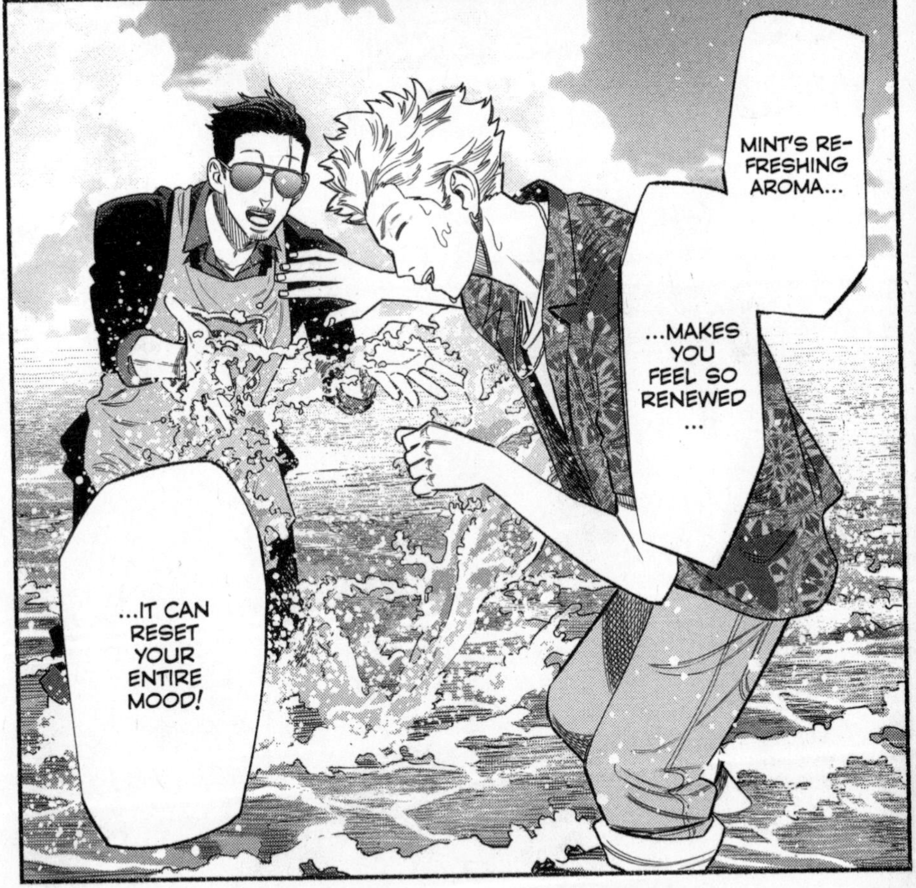
MINT'S RE-FRESHING AROMA...
...MAKES YOU FEEL SO RENEWED ...
...IT CAN RESET YOUR ENTIRE MOOD!

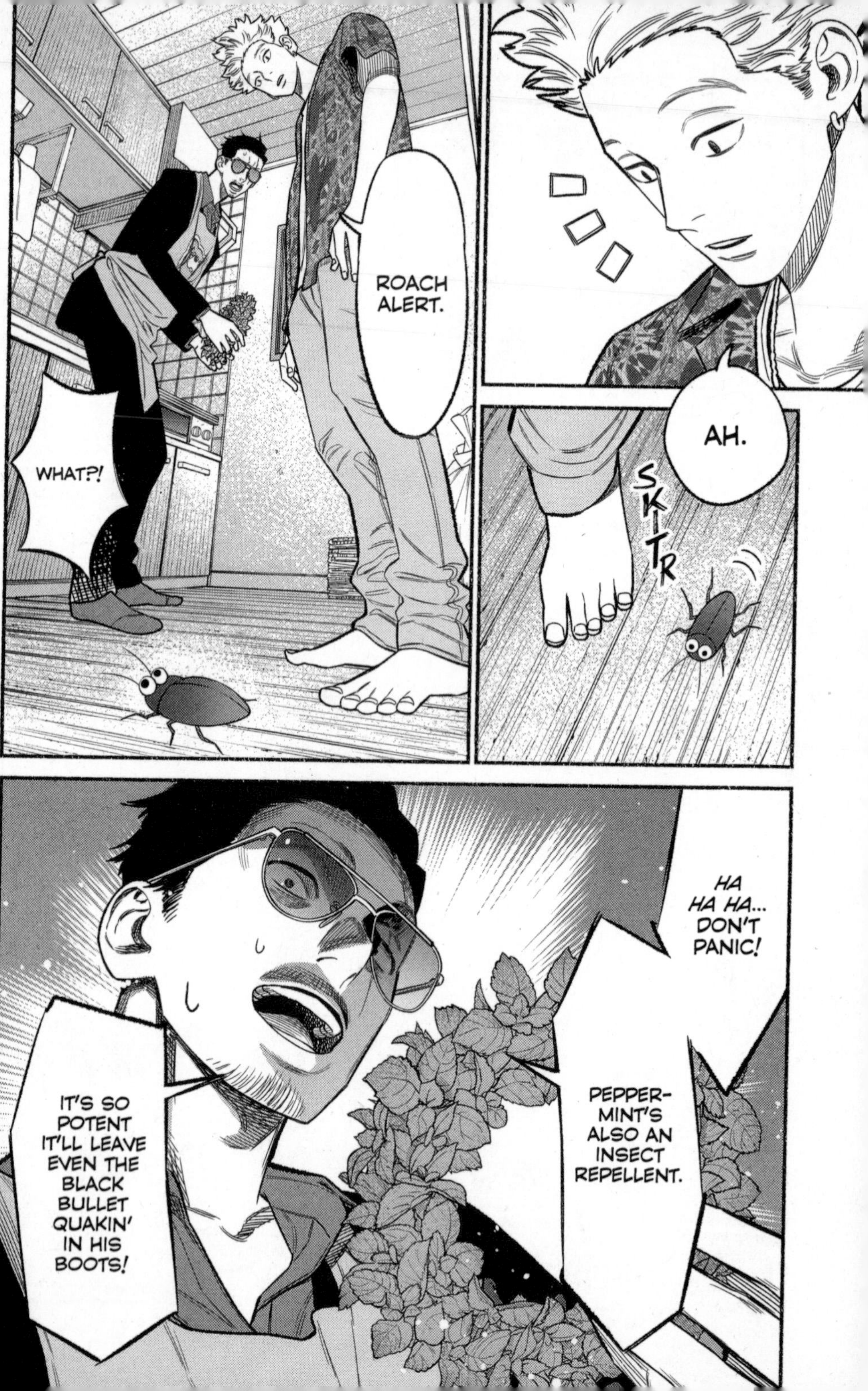
AH.
SKTR
ROACH ALERT.
WHAT?!
HA HA HA... DON'T PANIC!
PEPPERMINT'S ALSO AN INSECT REPELLENT.
IT'S SO POTENT IT'LL LEAVE EVEN THE BLACK BULLET QUAKIN' IN HIS BOOTS!

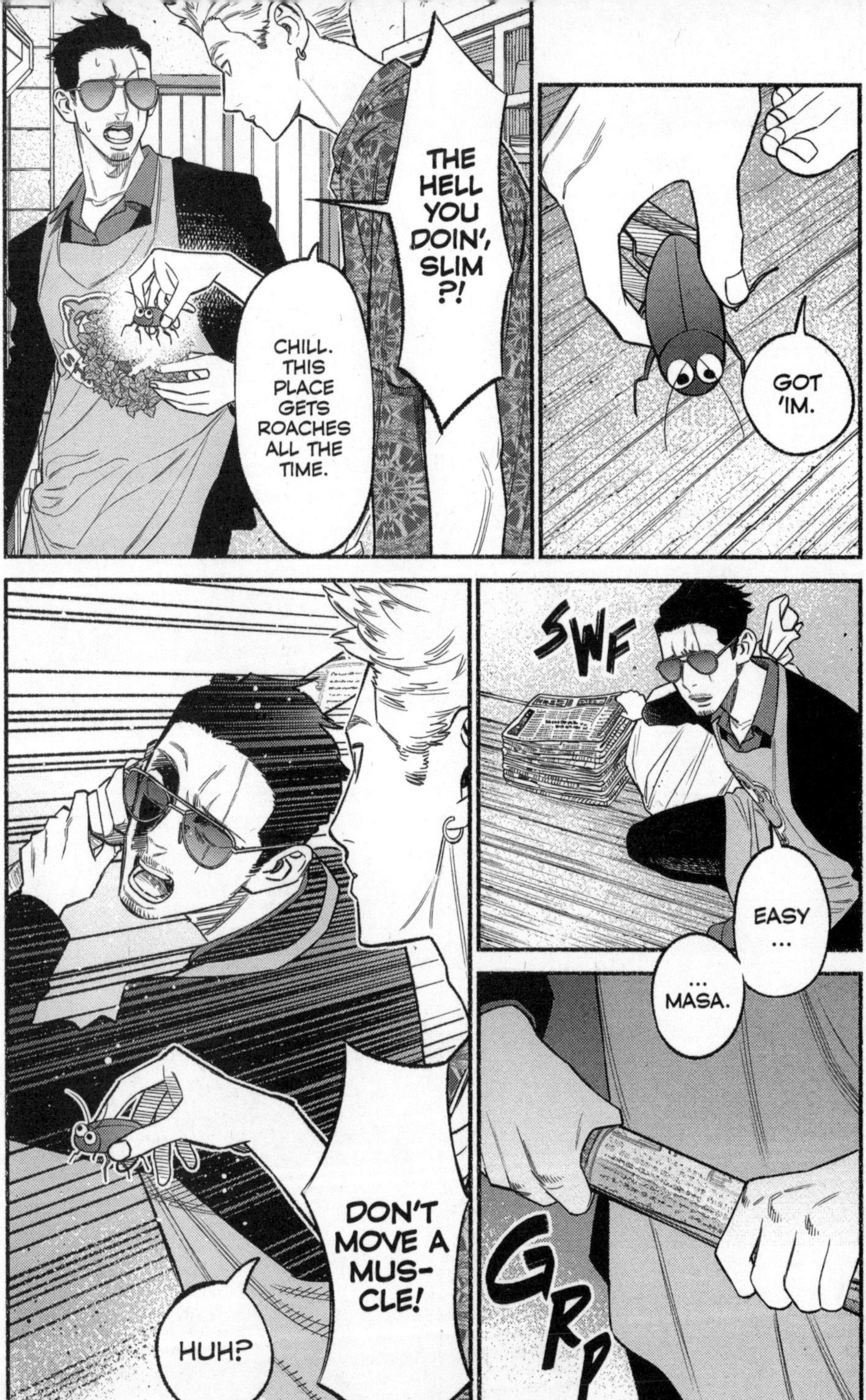
GOT 'IM.
THE HELL YOU DOIN', SLIM?!
CHILL. THIS PLACE GETS ROACHES ALL THE TIME.
SWF
EASY...
...MASA.
GRP
DON'T MOVE A MUS-CLE!
HUH?

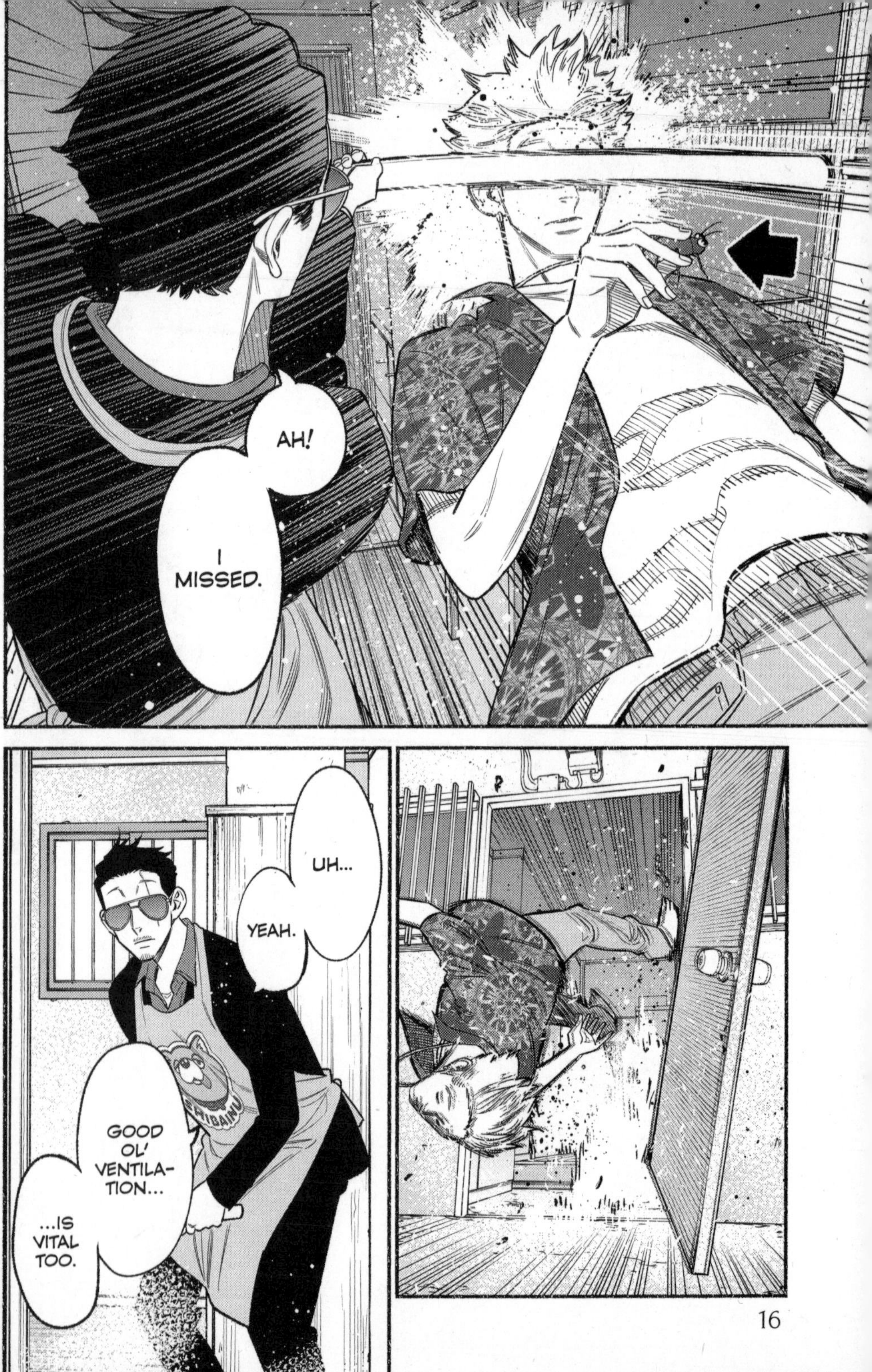
AH!
I MISSED.
UH...
YEAH.
GOOD OL' VENTILATION...
...IS VITAL TOO.

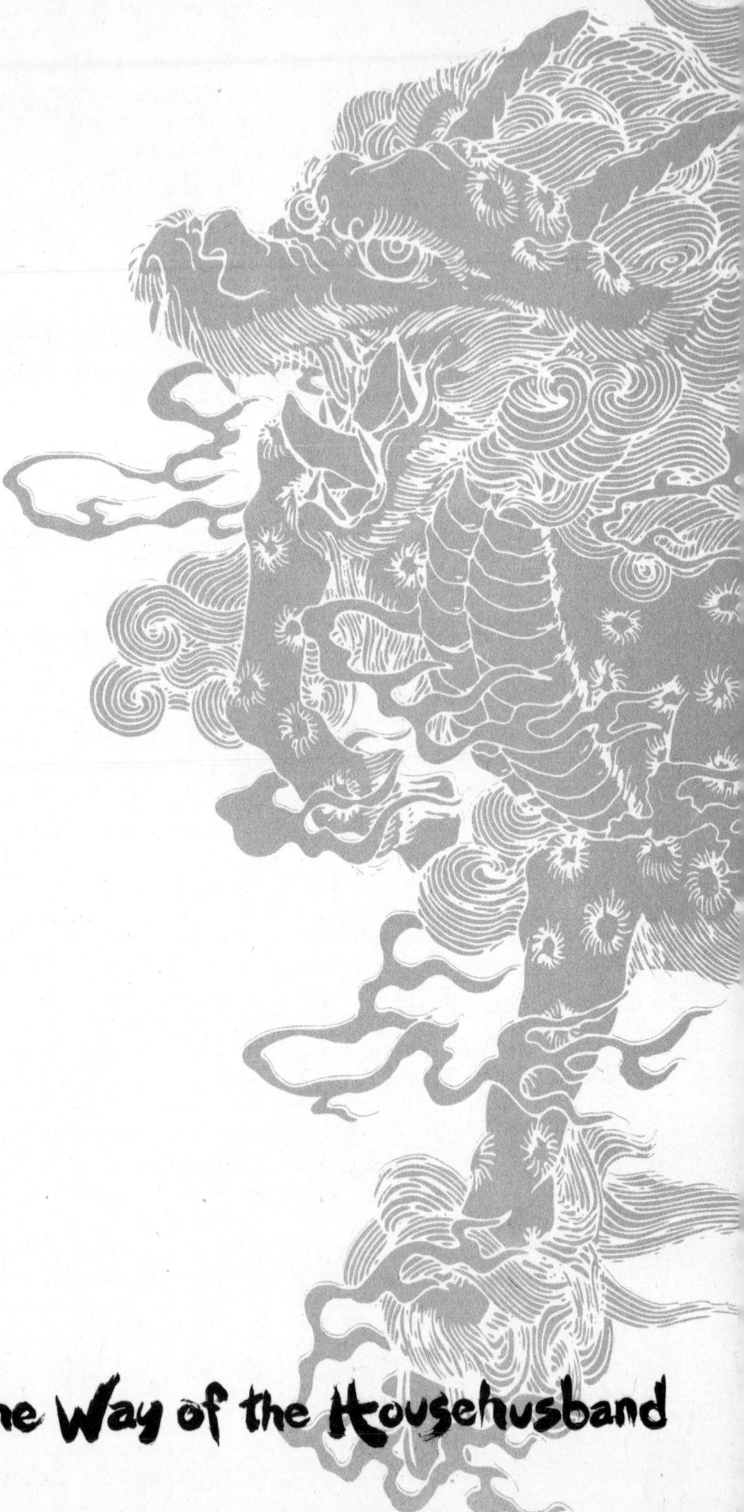

The Way of the Househusband

CHAPTER 74

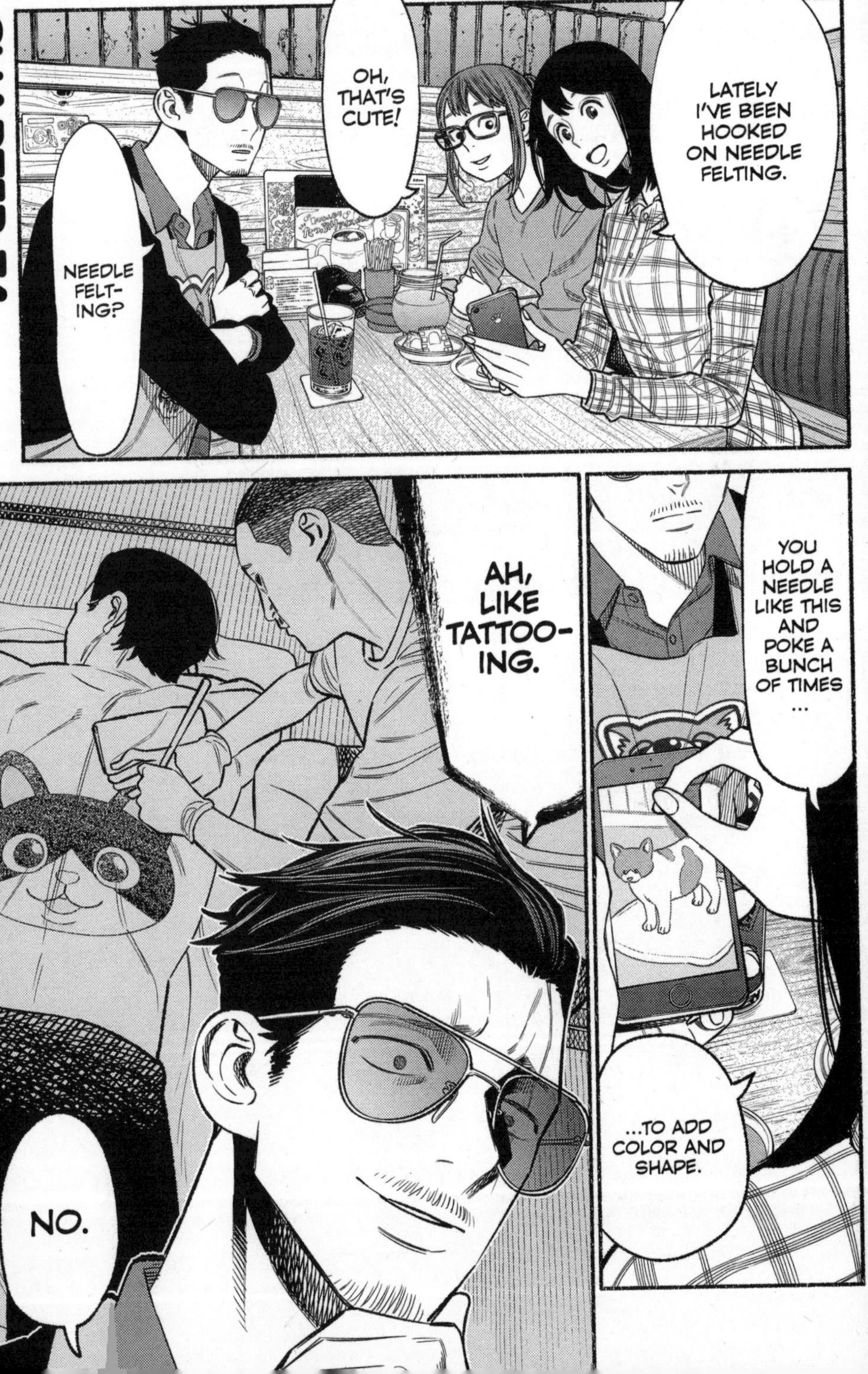
LATELY I'VE BEEN HOOKED ON NEEDLE FELTING.
OH, THAT'S CUTE!
NEEDLE FELT-ING?
YOU HOLD A NEEDLE LIKE THIS AND POKE A BUNCH OF TIMES ...
...TO ADD COLOR AND SHAPE.
AH, LIKE TATTOO-ING.
NO.

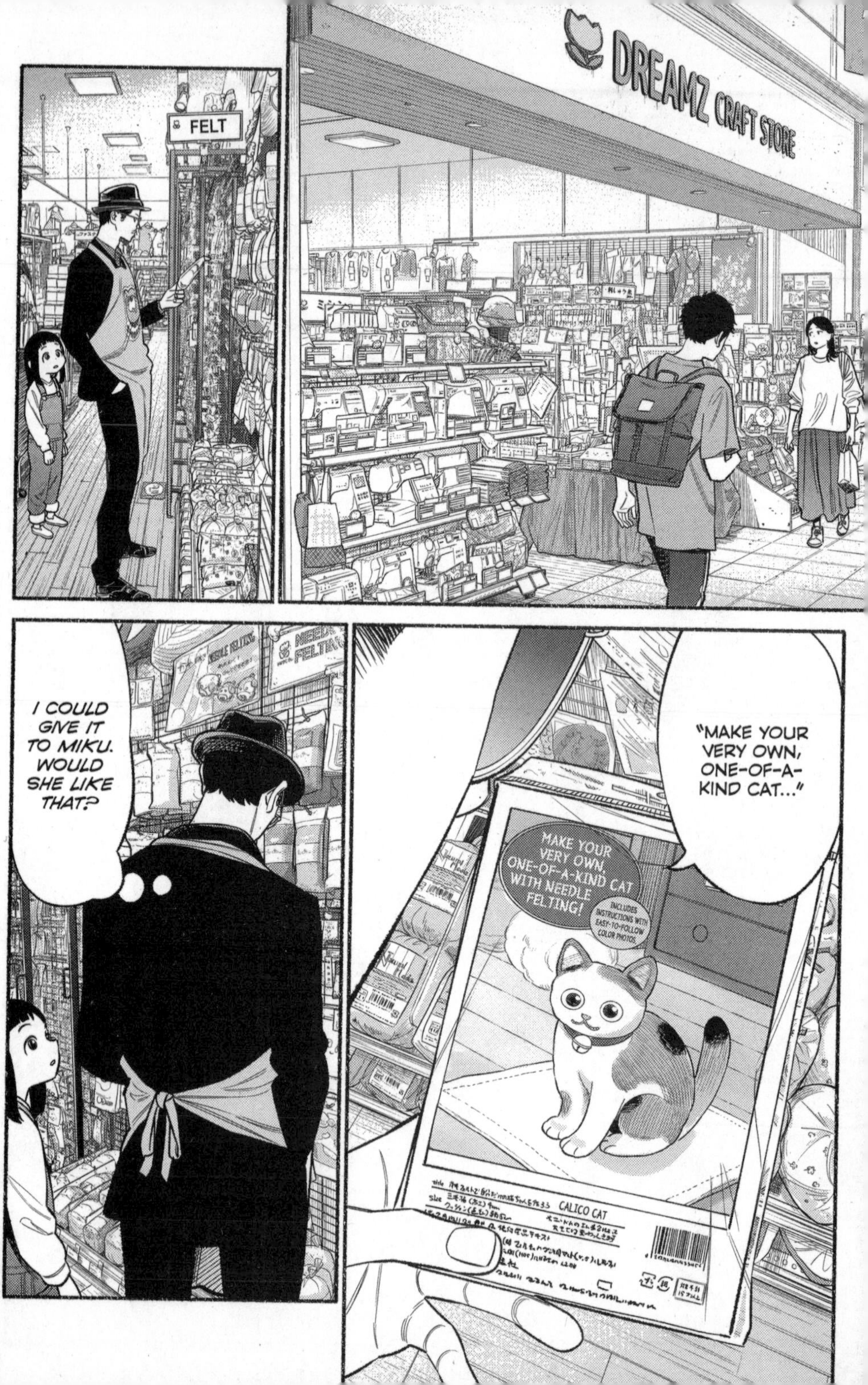
DREAMZ CRAFT STORE
FELT
"MAKE YOUR VERY OWN, ONE-OF-A-KIND CAT..."
MAKE YOUR VERY OWN, ONE-OF-A-KIND CAT WITH NEEDLE FELTING!
INCLUDES INSTRUCTIONS WITH EASY-TO-FOLLOW COLOR PHOTOS.
CALICO CAT
NEEDLE FELTING
I COULD GIVE IT TO MIKU. WOULD SHE LIKE THAT?

WHERE THE HELL...

...IS IT?

!

LOOKING FOR *THIS*, MS. TORII?

MAKE YOUR VERY OWN ONE-OF-A-KIND CAT WITH NEEDLE FELTING!

INCLUDES EVERYTHING YOU NEED WITH EASY-TO-FOLLOW COLOR PHOTOS!

CALICO CAT

THEY'VE GOT TO HAVE A CAT KIT SOME-WHERE.

WHAT MAKES YOU THINK I'D BE INTERESTED IN THAT CRAP?

I-I DON'T KNOW WHAT YOU'RE TALKING ABOUT!

THERE ARE ONLY TWO LEFT.

FINE!

I'LL TAKE THE KID UNDER MY WING!

SWIPE

22

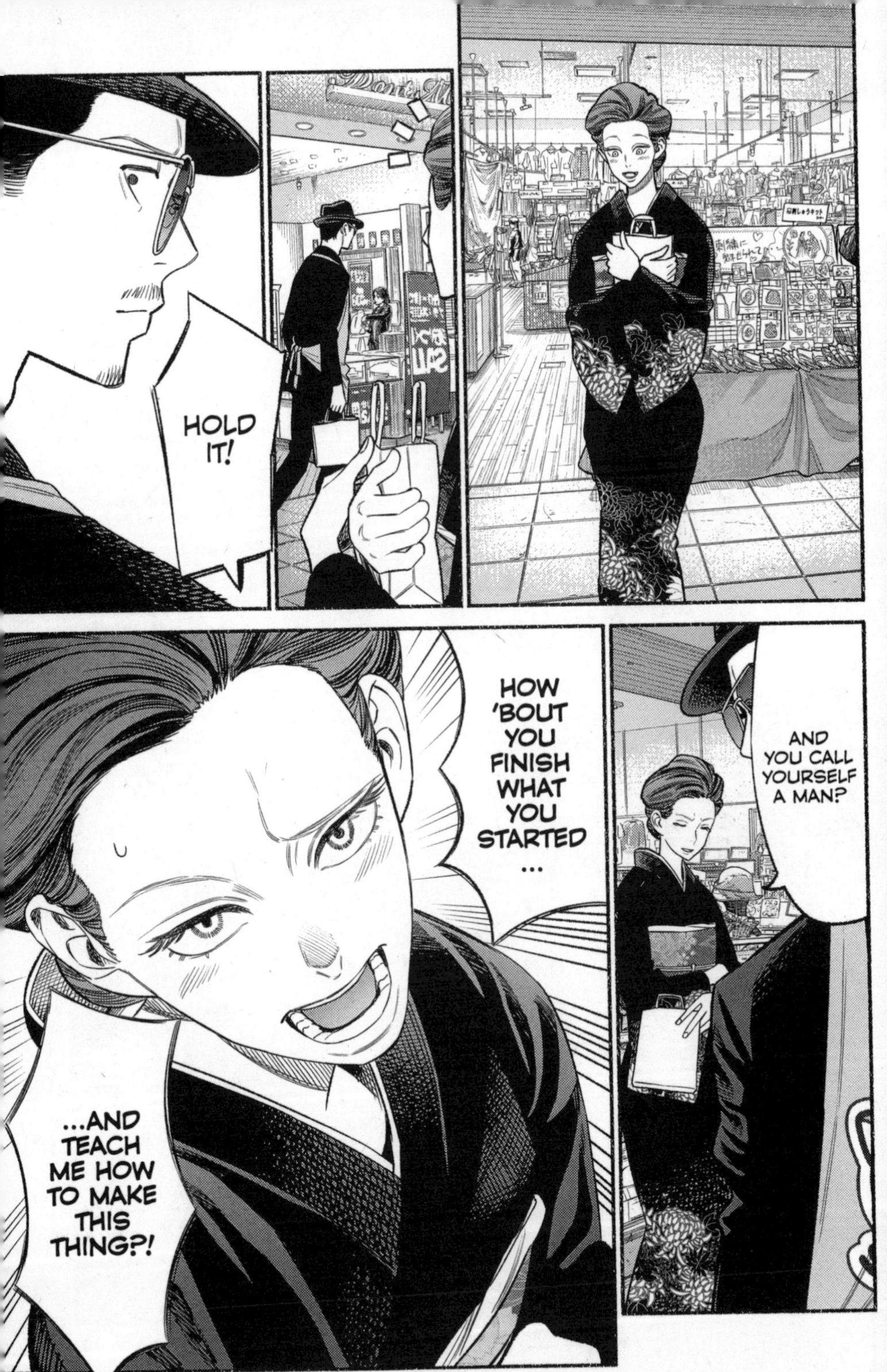
HOLD IT!
AND YOU CALL YOURSELF A MAN?
HOW 'BOUT YOU FINISH WHAT YOU STARTED...
...AND TEACH ME HOW TO MAKE THIS THING?!

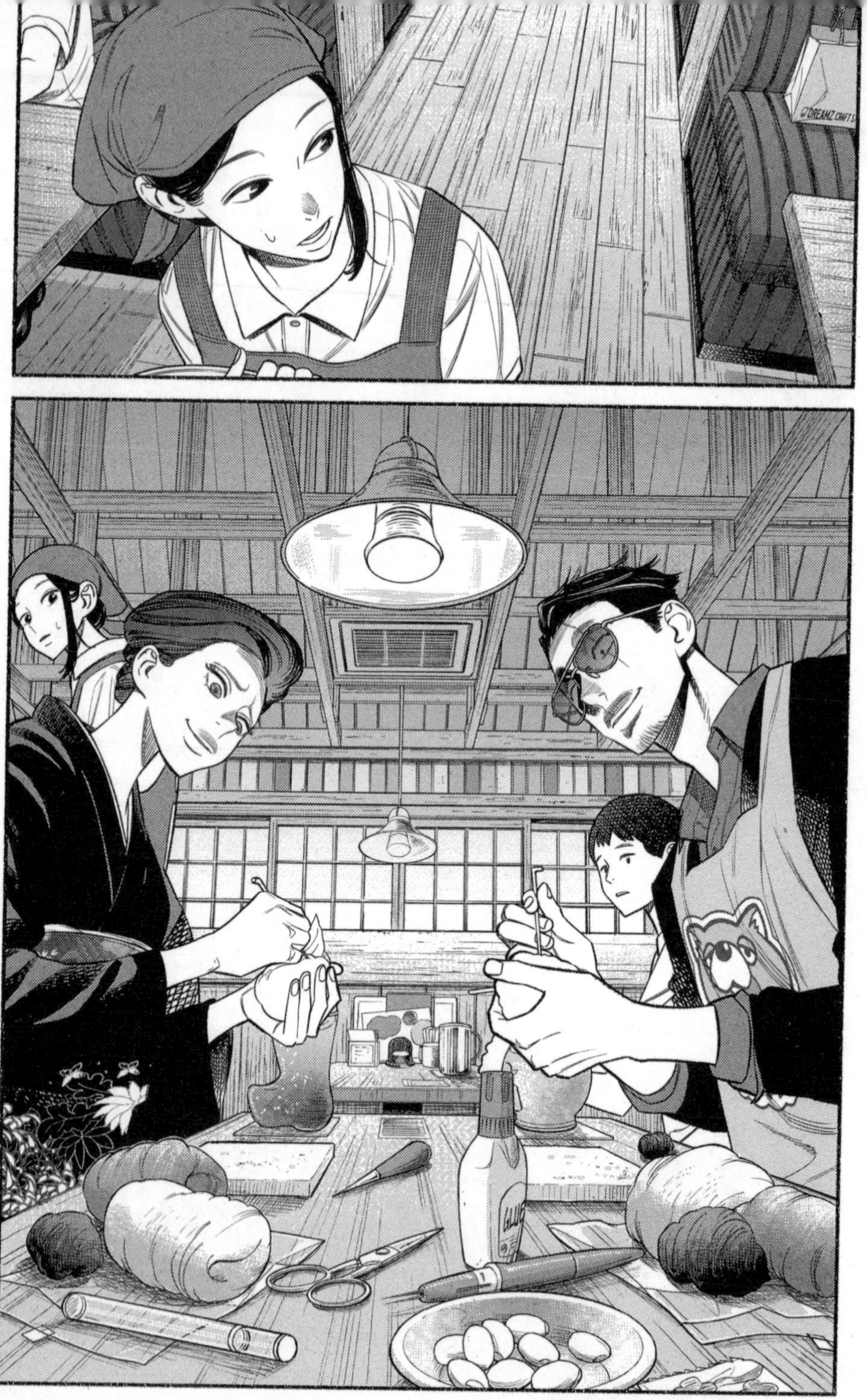

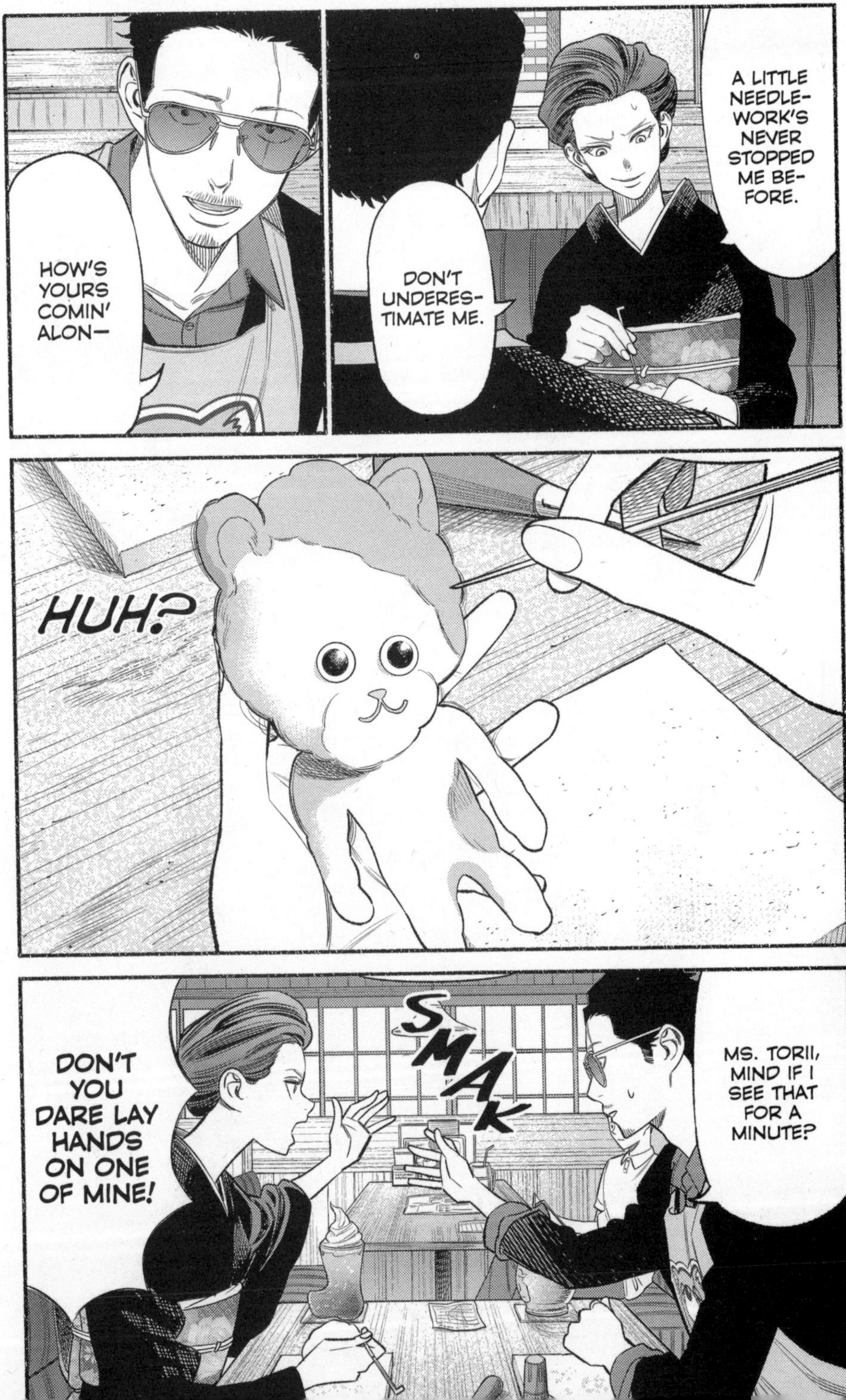
A LITTLE NEEDLE-WORK'S NEVER STOPPED ME BE-FORE.
DON'T UNDERES-TIMATE ME.
HOW'S YOURS COMIN' ALON—
HUH?
MS. TORII, MIND IF I SEE THAT FOR A MINUTE?
SMAK
DON'T YOU DARE LAY HANDS ON ONE OF MINE!

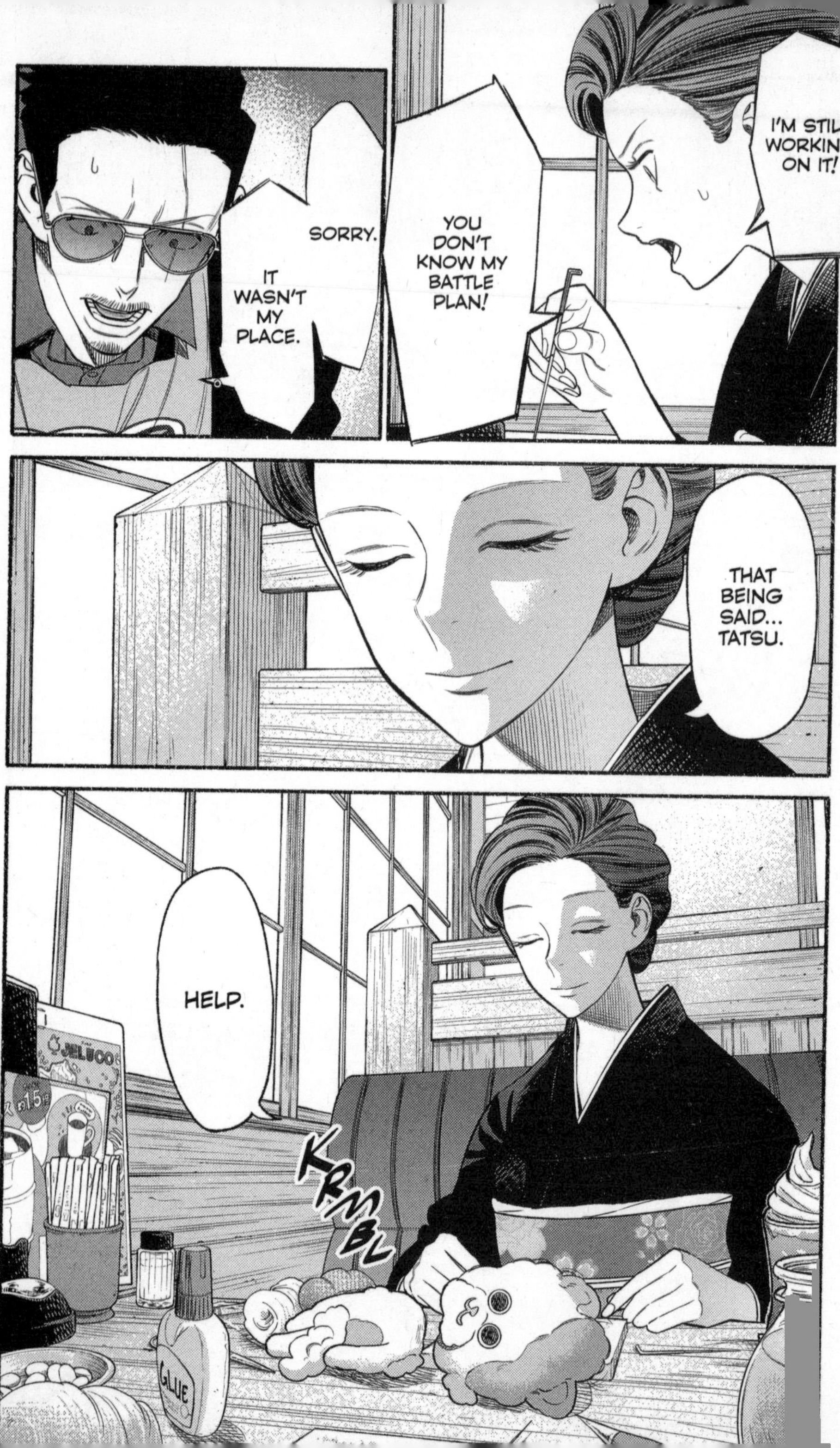
I'M STILL WORKING ON IT!
YOU DON'T KNOW MY BATTLE PLAN!
SORRY.
IT WASN'T MY PLACE.
THAT BEING SAID... TATSU.
HELP.
KRMBL
GLUE

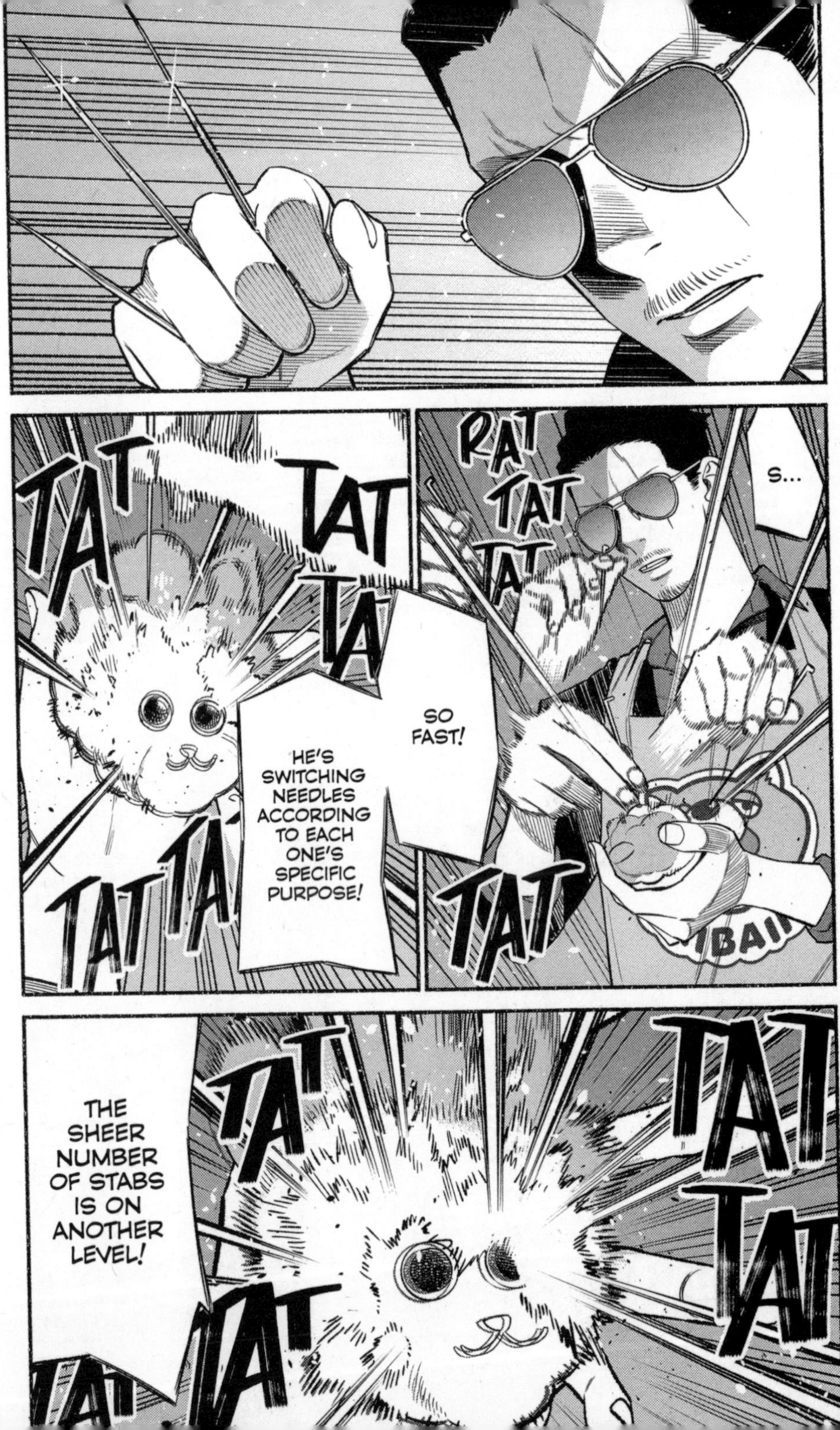
S...
RAT TAT TAT
TAT
SO FAST!
HE'S SWITCHING NEEDLES ACCORDING TO EACH ONE'S SPECIFIC PURPOSE!
TAT TAT TAT
TAT TAT TAT
TAT TAT
THE SHEER NUMBER OF STABS IS ON ANOTHER LEVEL!
TAT TAT

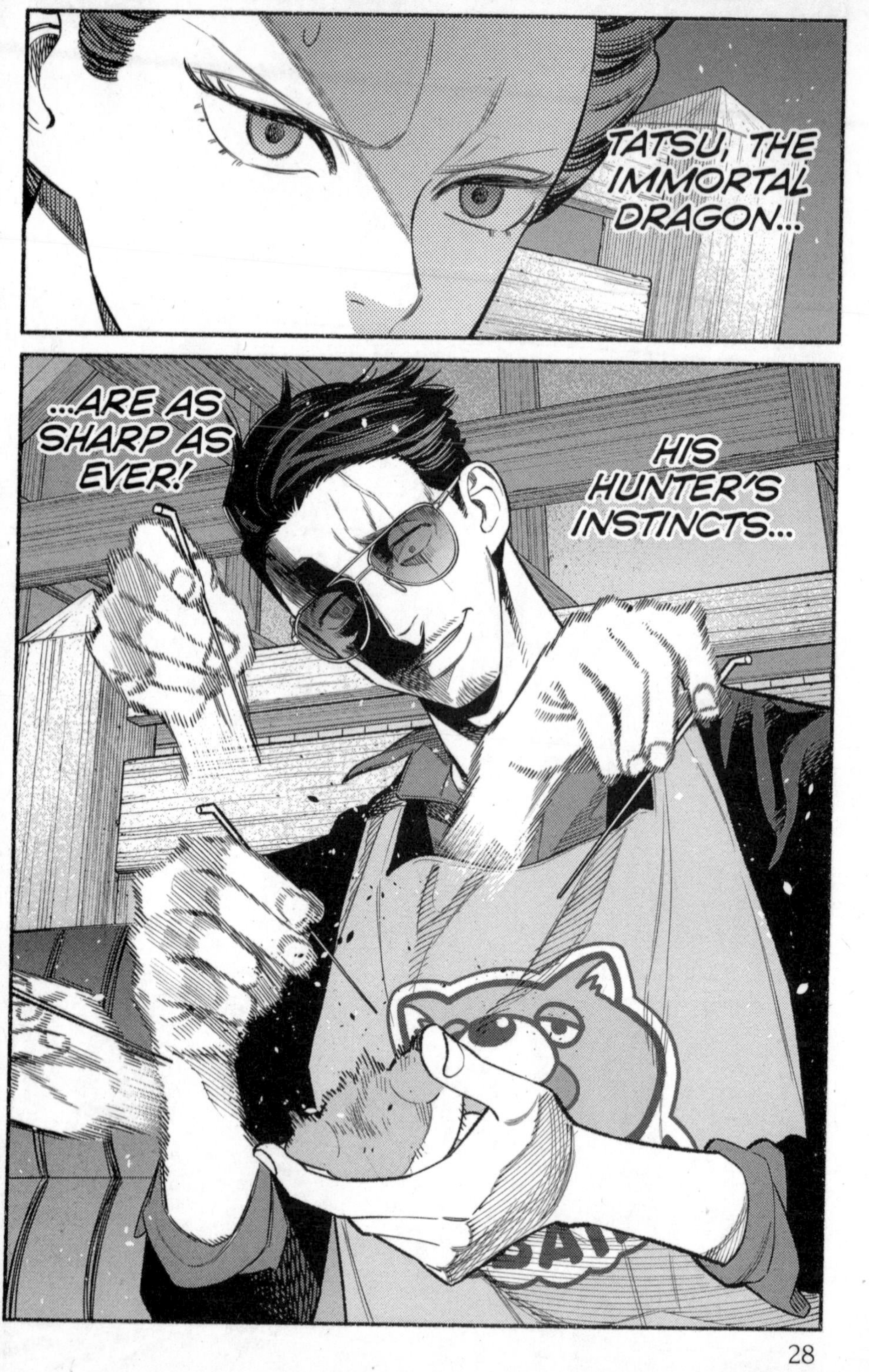
TATSU, THE IMMORTAL DRAGON...
HIS HUNTER'S INSTINCTS...
...ARE AS SHARP AS EVER!

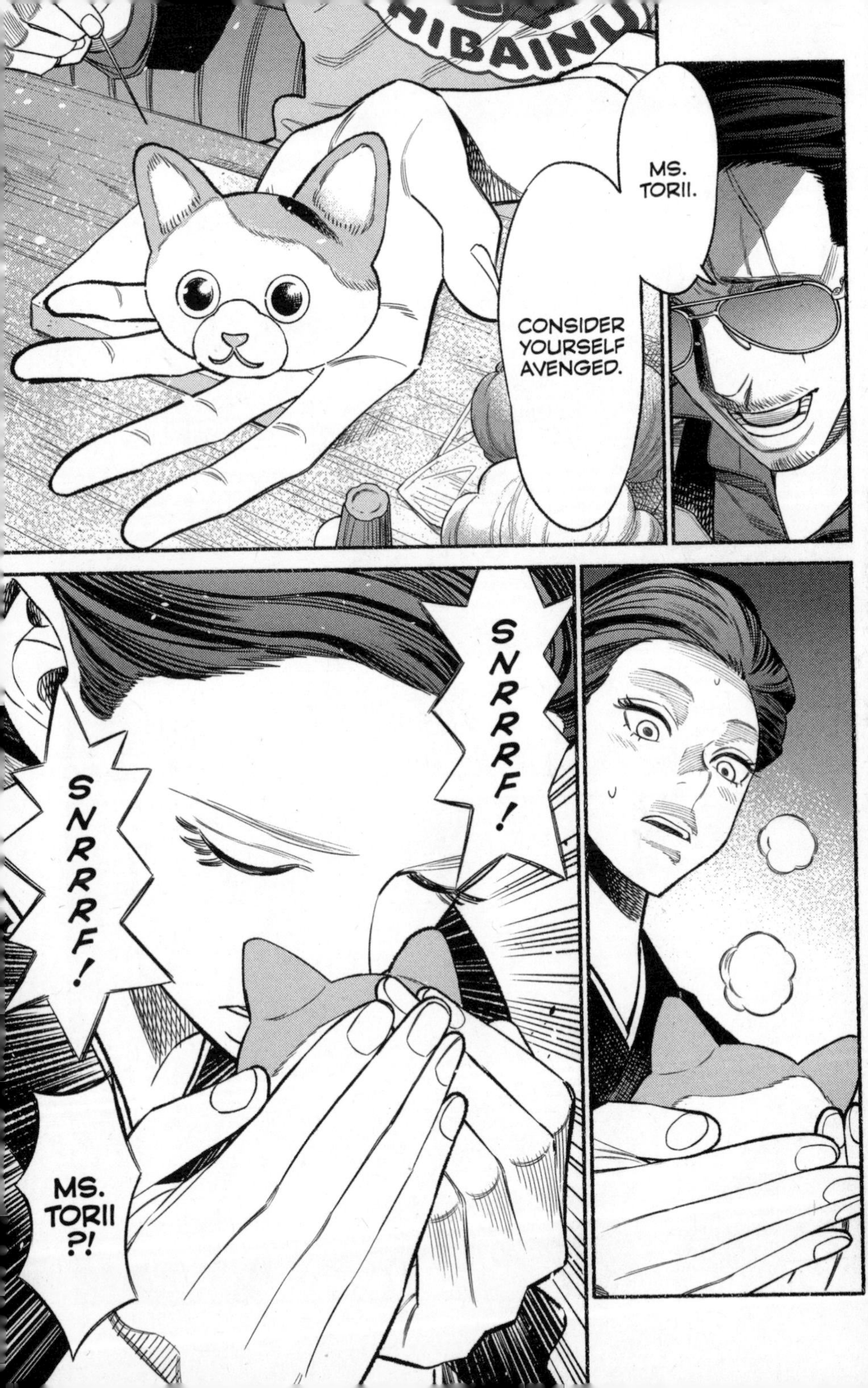
MS. TORII.
CONSIDER YOURSELF AVENGED.
SNRRRF!
SNRRRF!
MS. TORII ?!

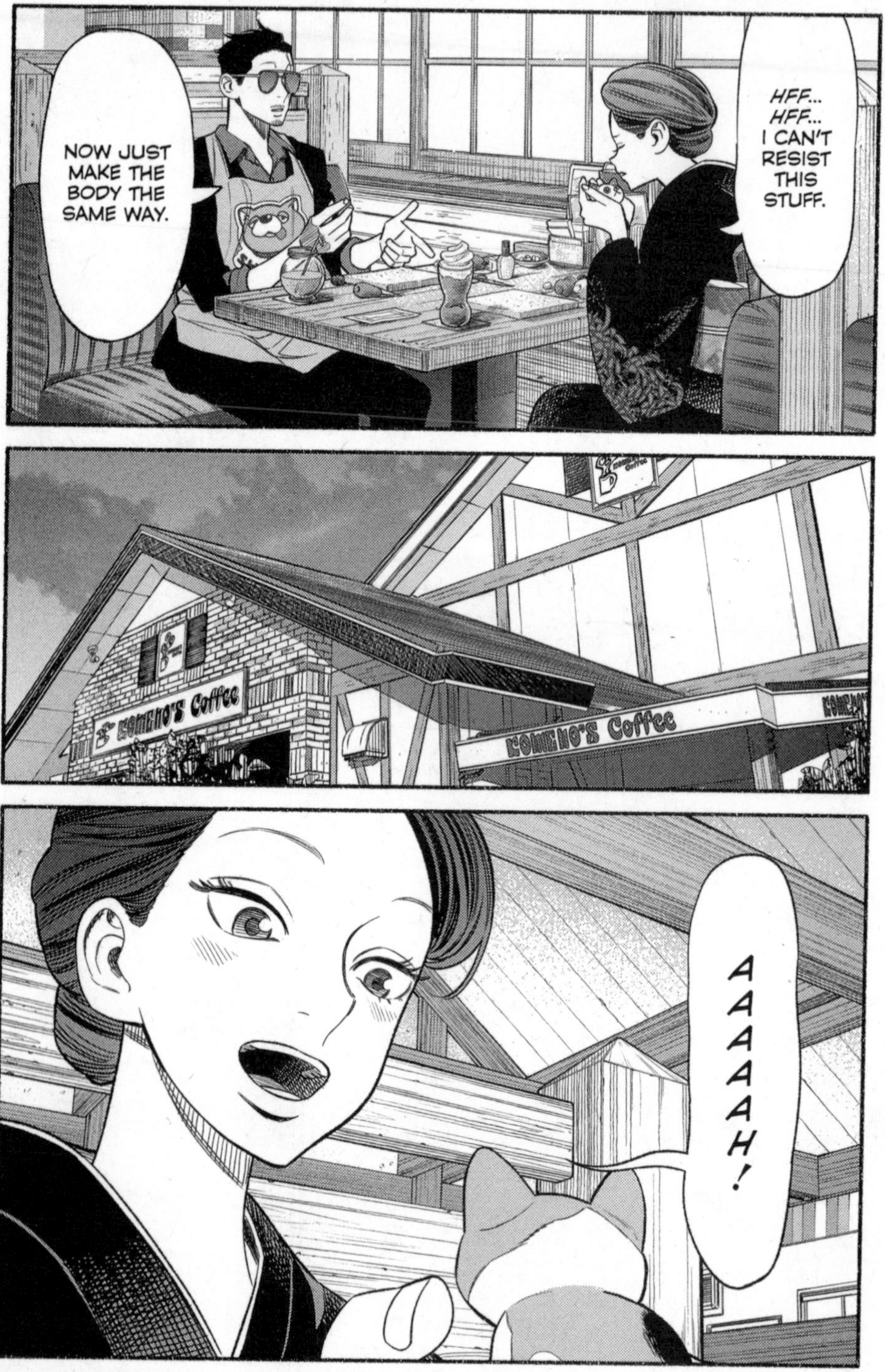
HFF... HFF... I CAN'T RESIST THIS STUFF.
NOW JUST MAKE THE BODY THE SAME WAY.
AAAAAH!

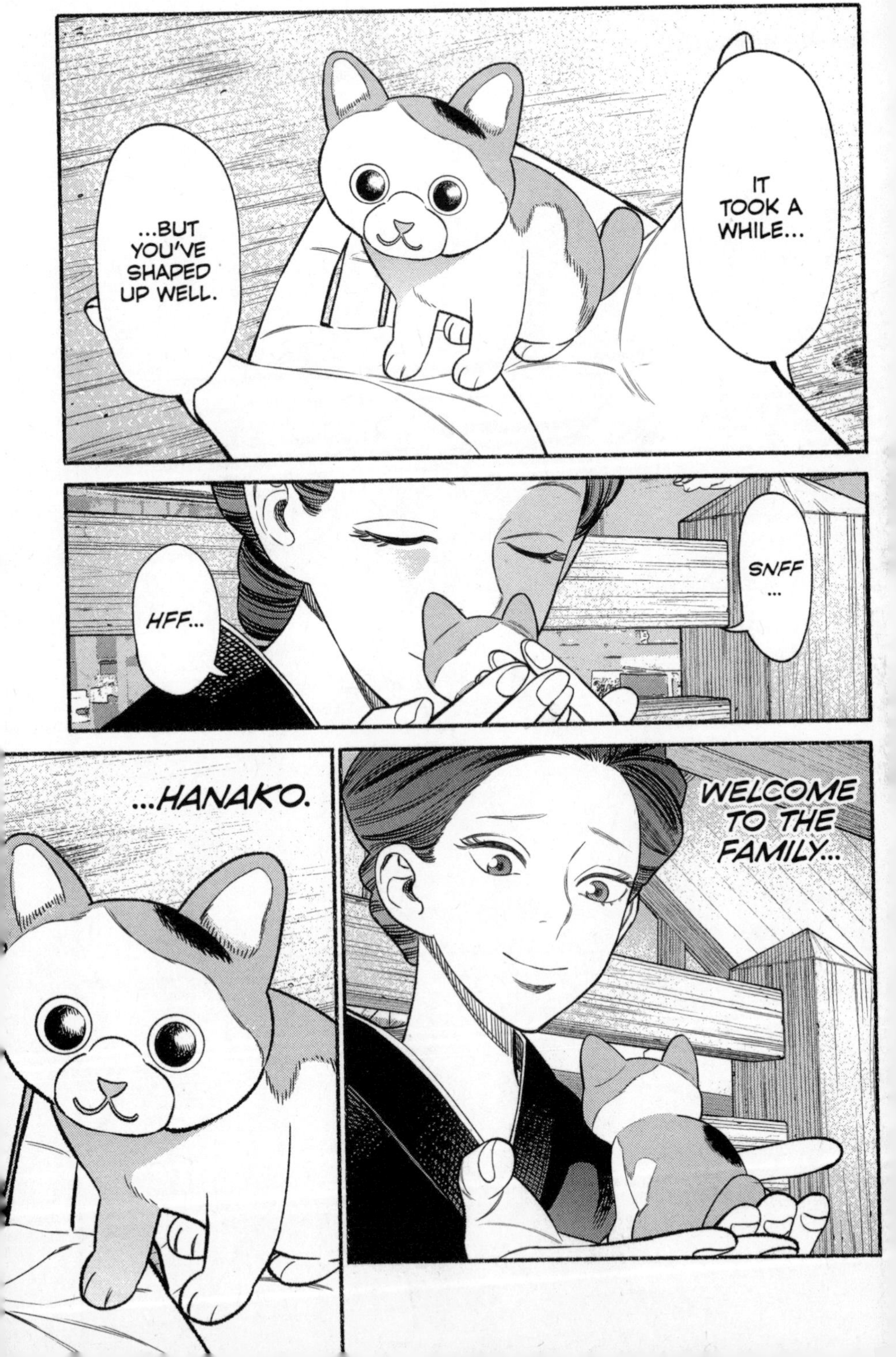
IT TOOK A WHILE...
...BUT YOU'VE SHAPED UP WELL.
SNFF ...
HFF...
WELCOME TO THE FAMILY...
...HANAKO.

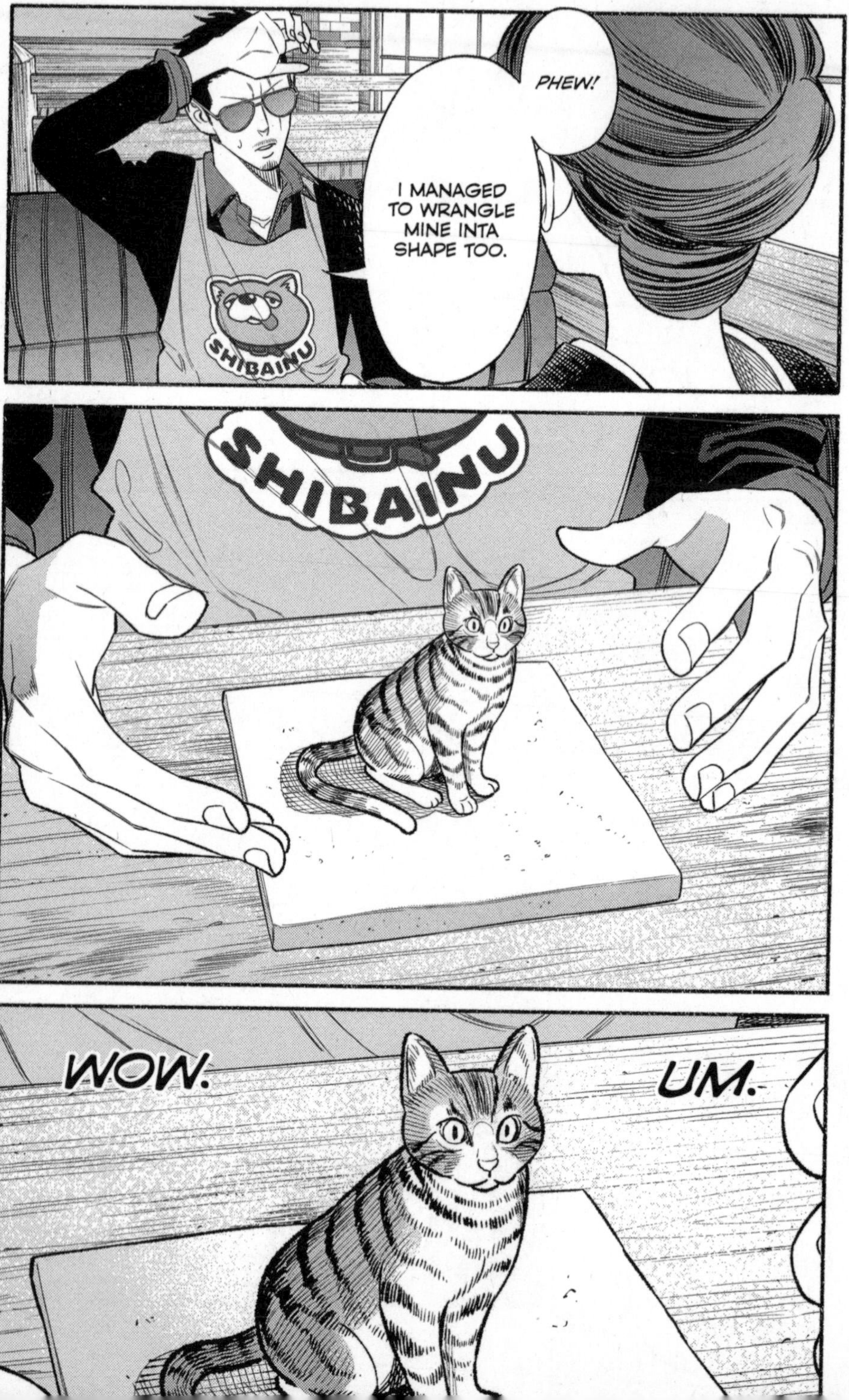
PHEW!
I MANAGED TO WRANGLE MINE INTA SHAPE TOO.
SHIBAINU
SHIBAINU
UM.
WOW.

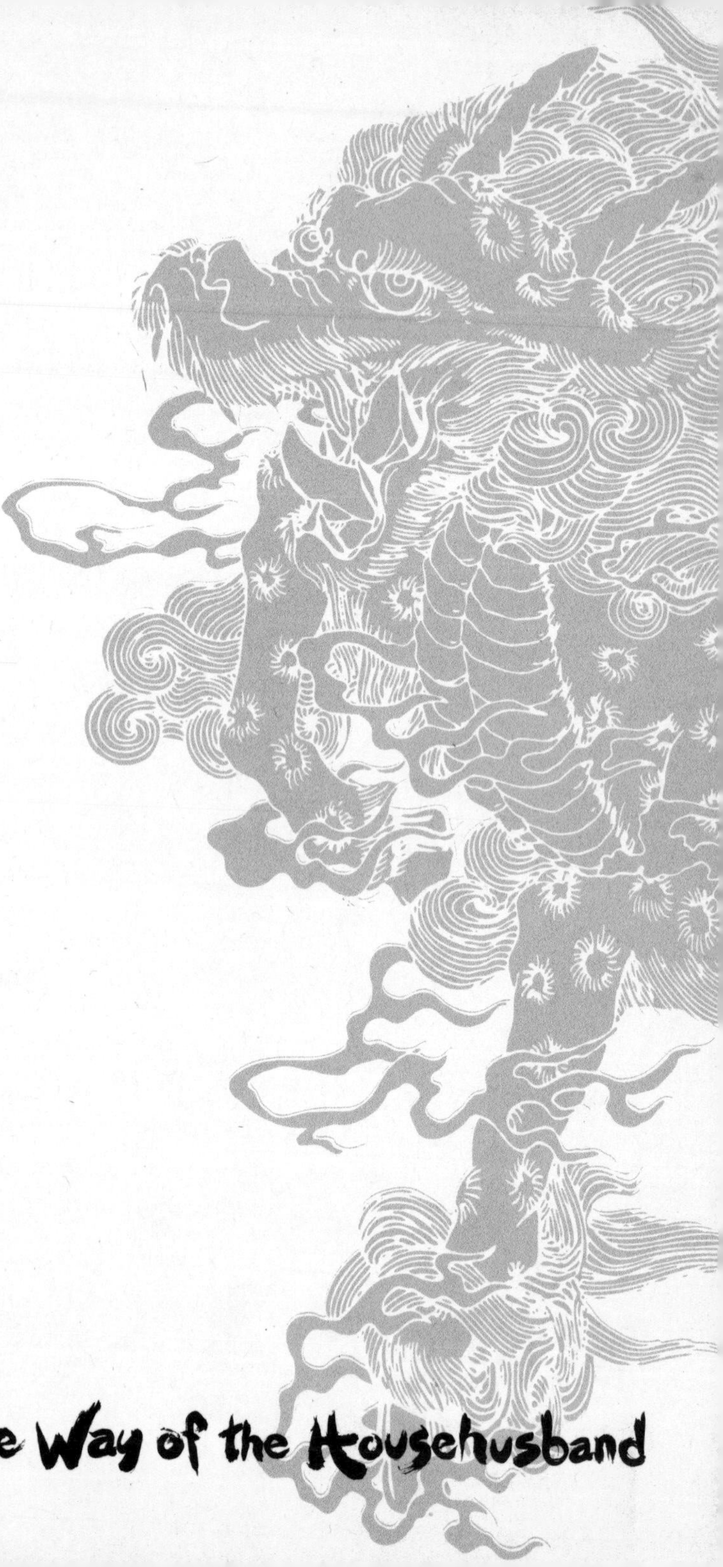

The Way of the Househusband

CHAPTER 75

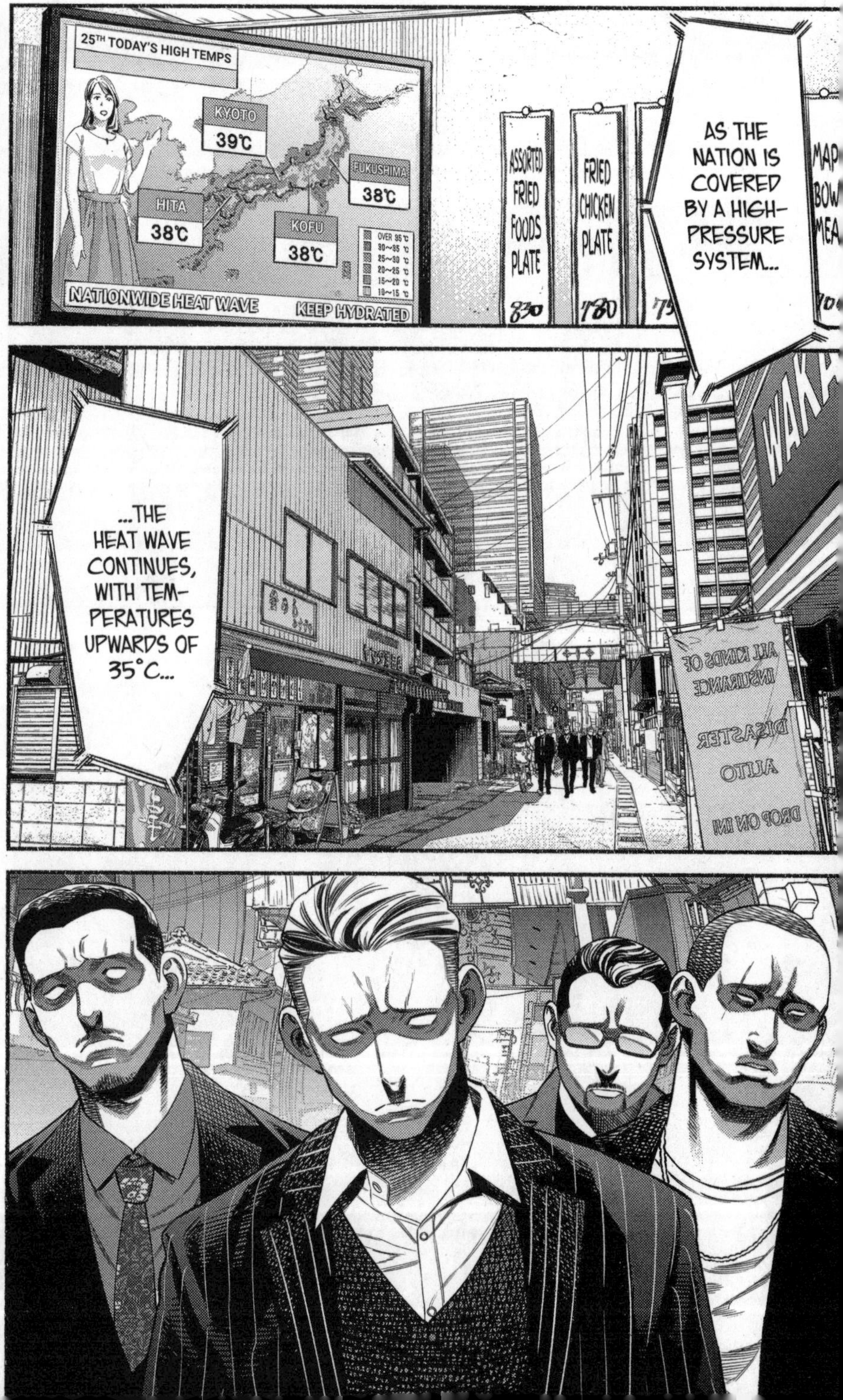
AS THE NATION IS COVERED BY A HIGH-PRESSURE SYSTEM...
FRIED CHICKEN PLATE
780
ASSORTED FRIED FOODS PLATE
830
25TH TODAY'S HIGH TEMPS
KYOTO
39℃
FUKUSHIMA
38℃
HITA
38℃
KOFU
38℃
OVER 95 ℃
90~95 ℃
25~30 ℃
20~25 ℃
15~20 ℃
10~15 ℃
NATIONWIDE HEAT WAVE
KEEP HYDRATED
...THE HEAT WAVE CONTINUES, WITH TEMPERATURES UPWARDS OF 35°C...
ALL KINDS OF INSURANCE
DISASTER
AUTO
DROP ON IN!

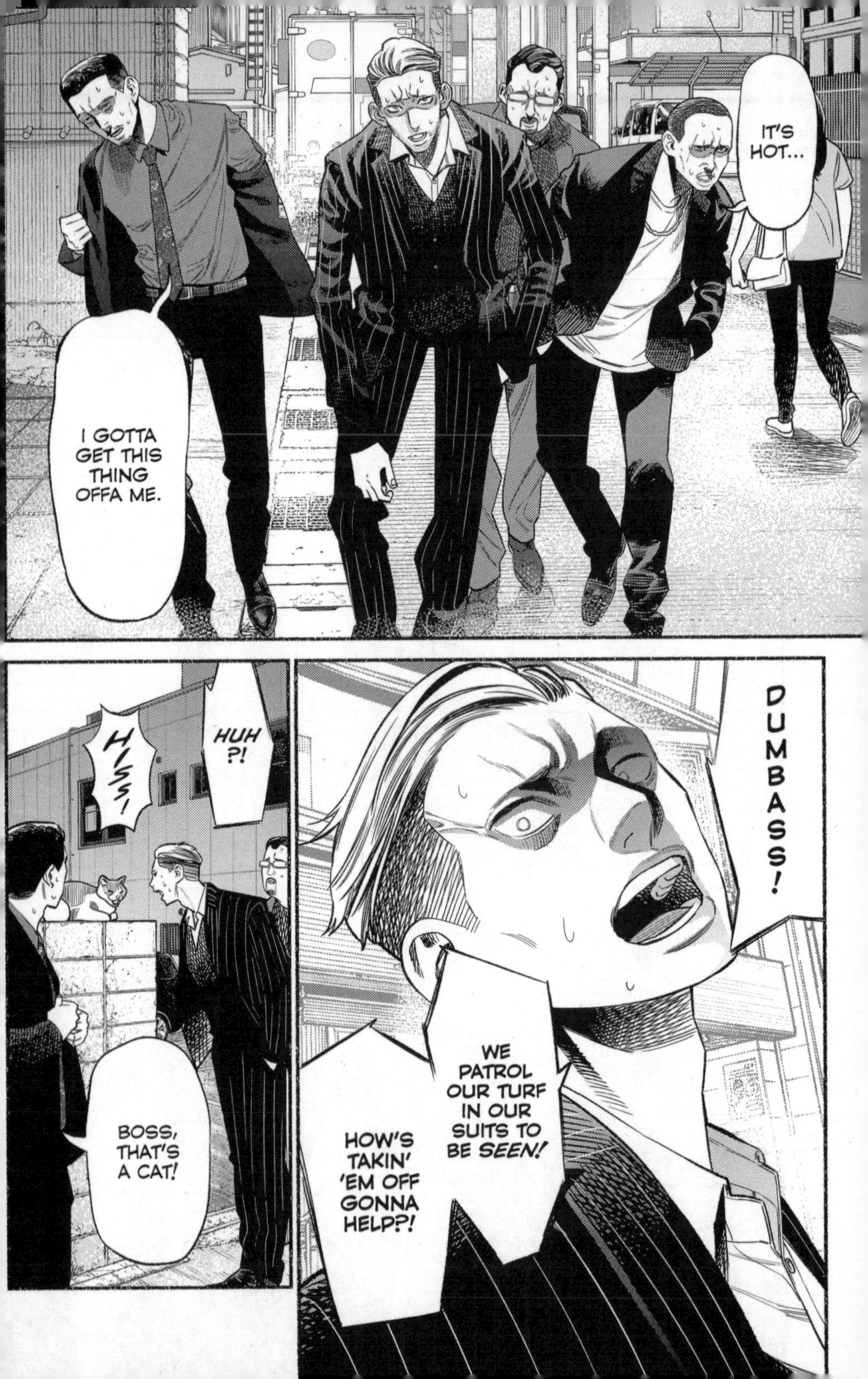
IT'S HOT...
I GOTTA GET THIS THING OFFA ME.
DUMBASS!
WE PATROL OUR TURF IN OUR SUITS TO BE SEEN!
HOW'S TAKIN' 'EM OFF GONNA HELP?!
HUH?!
HISS!
BOSS, THAT'S A CAT!

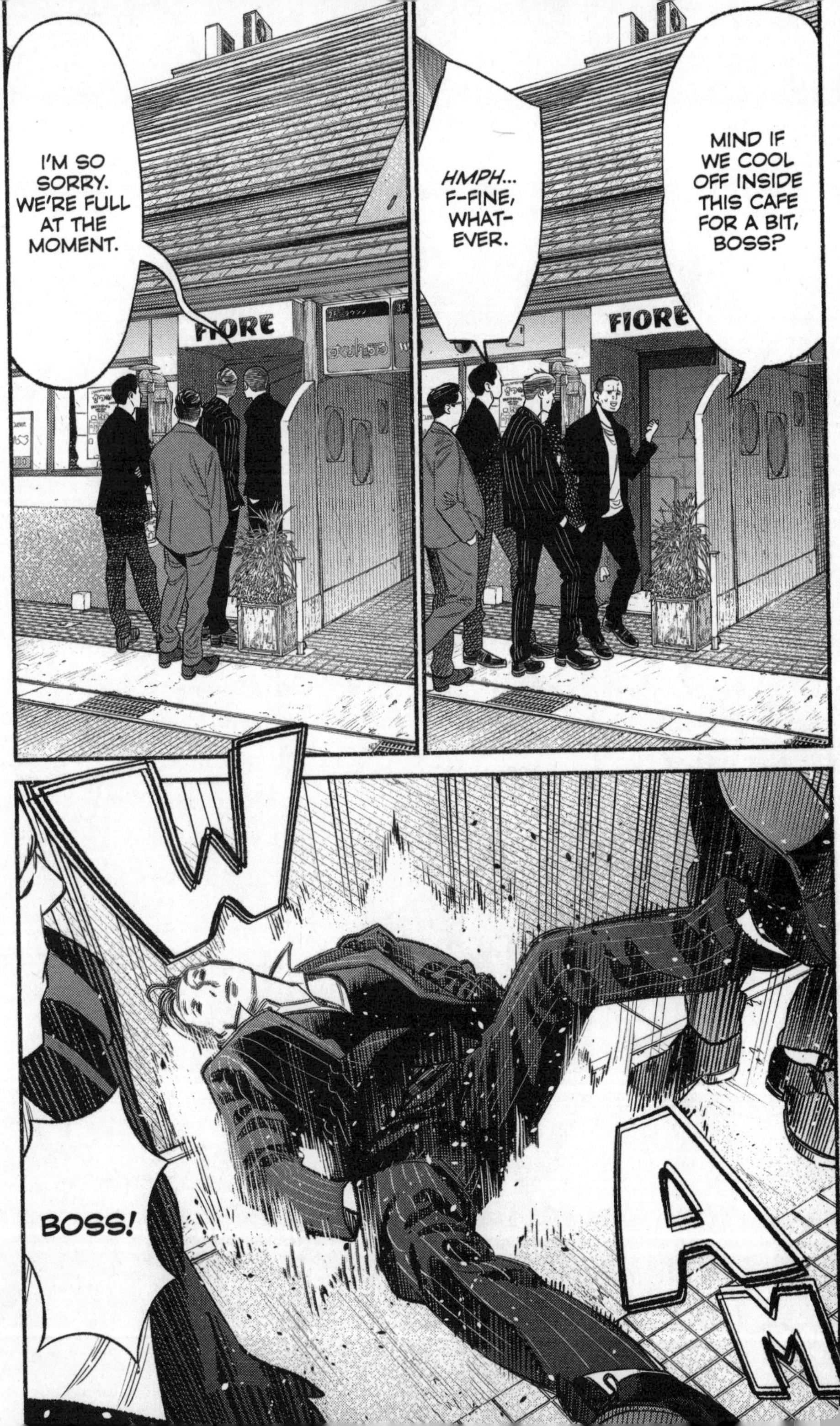
MIND IF WE COOL OFF INSIDE THIS CAFE FOR A BIT, BOSS?
FIORE
HMPH... F-FINE, WHAT-EVER.
I'M SO SORRY. WE'RE FULL AT THE MOMENT.
FIORE
BOSS!

WE'RE SAVED!

IT'S A VENDING MACHINE!

WATER!

BOSS!

38

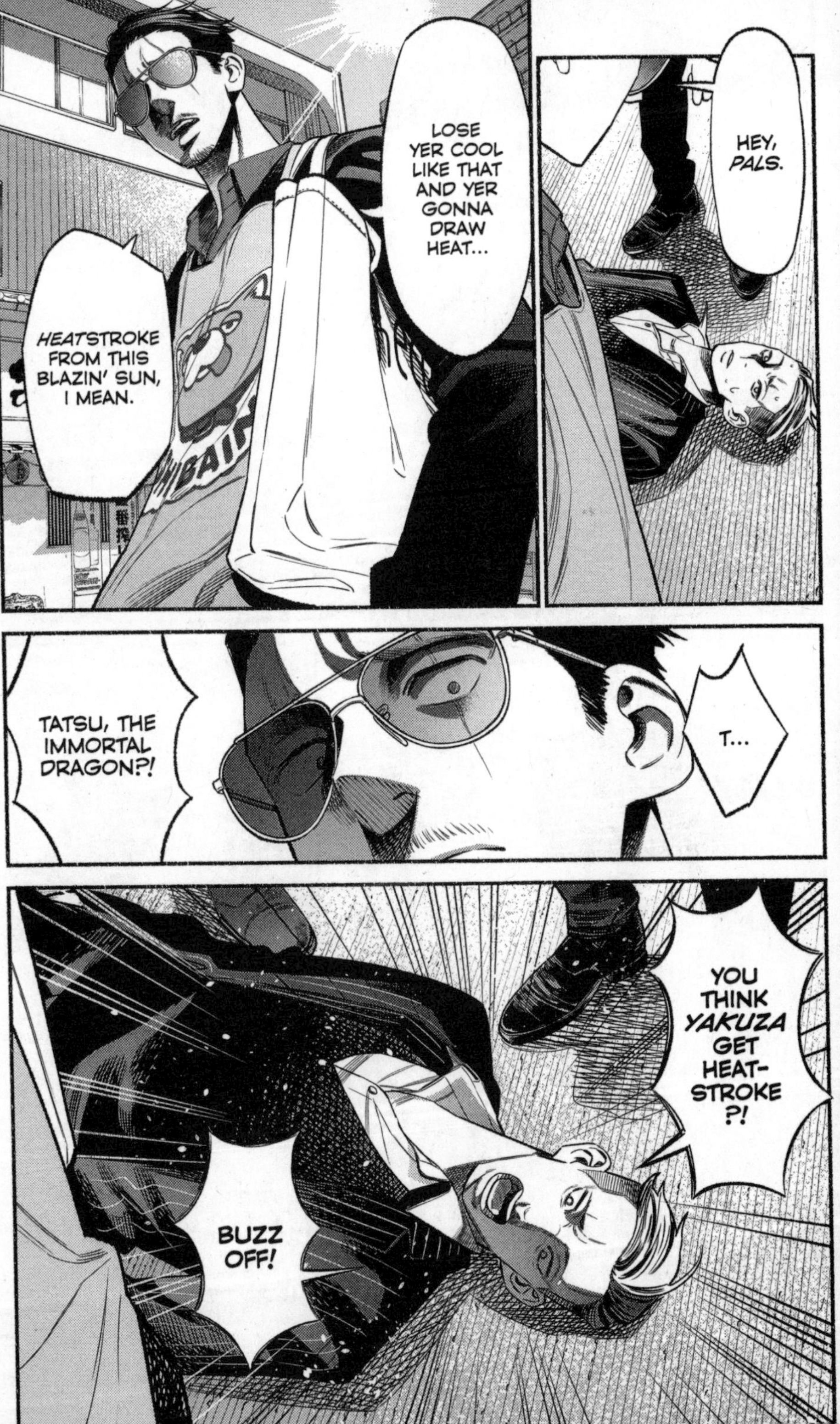
HEY, *PALS.*
LOSE YER COOL LIKE THAT AND YER GONNA DRAW HEAT...
*HEAT*STROKE FROM THIS BLAZIN' SUN, I MEAN.
T...
TATSU, THE IMMORTAL DRAGON?!
YOU THINK *YAKUZA* GET HEAT-STROKE?!
BUZZ OFF!

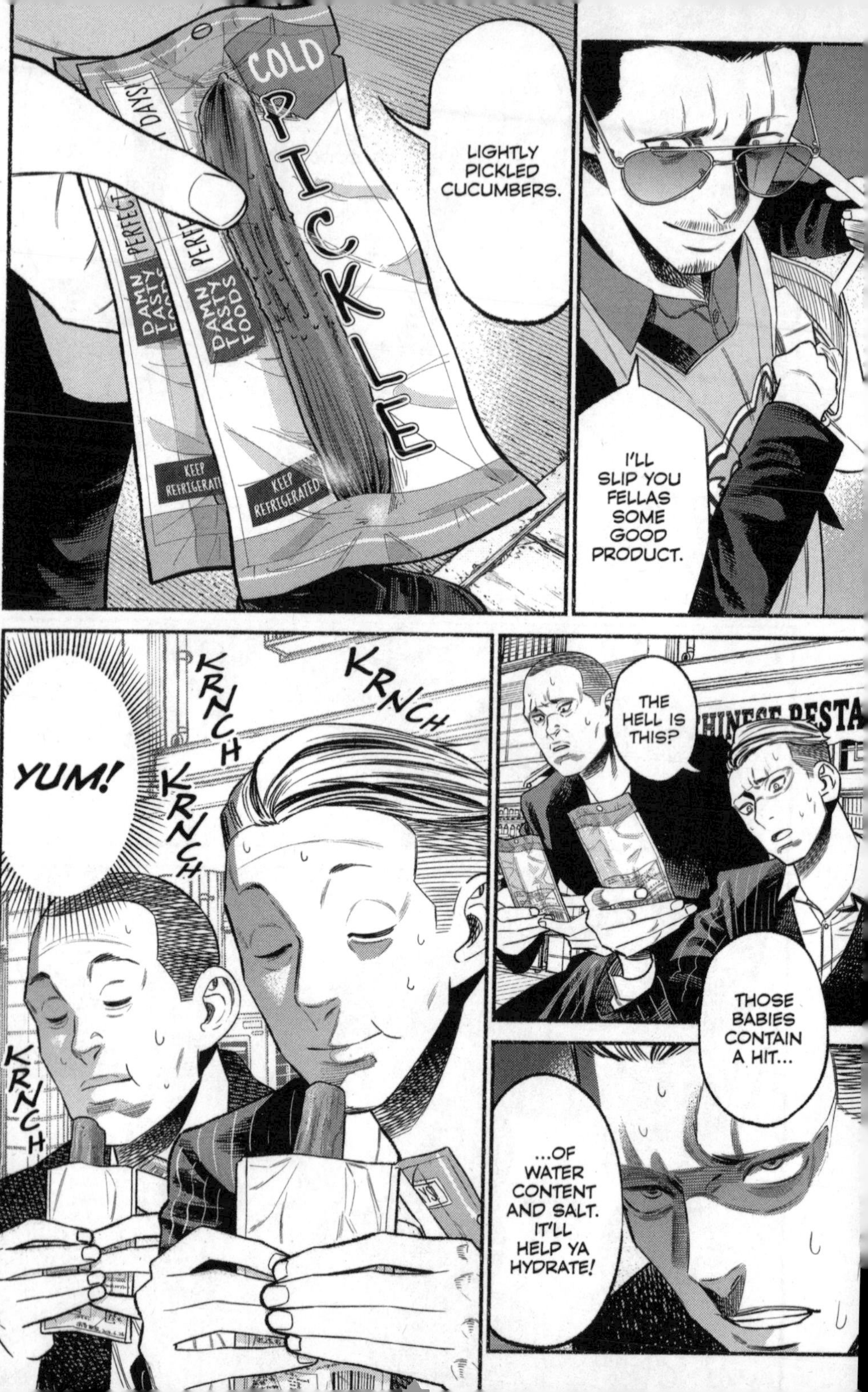
I'LL SLIP YOU FELLAS SOME GOOD PRODUCT.
LIGHTLY PICKLED CUCUMBERS.
COLD
PICKLE
PERFECT
DAMN TASTY FOODS
KEEP REFRIGERATED
THE HELL IS THIS?
THOSE BABIES CONTAIN A HIT...
...OF WATER CONTENT AND SALT. IT'LL HELP YA HYDRATE!
KRNCH
KRNCH
KRNCH
YUM!
KRNCH

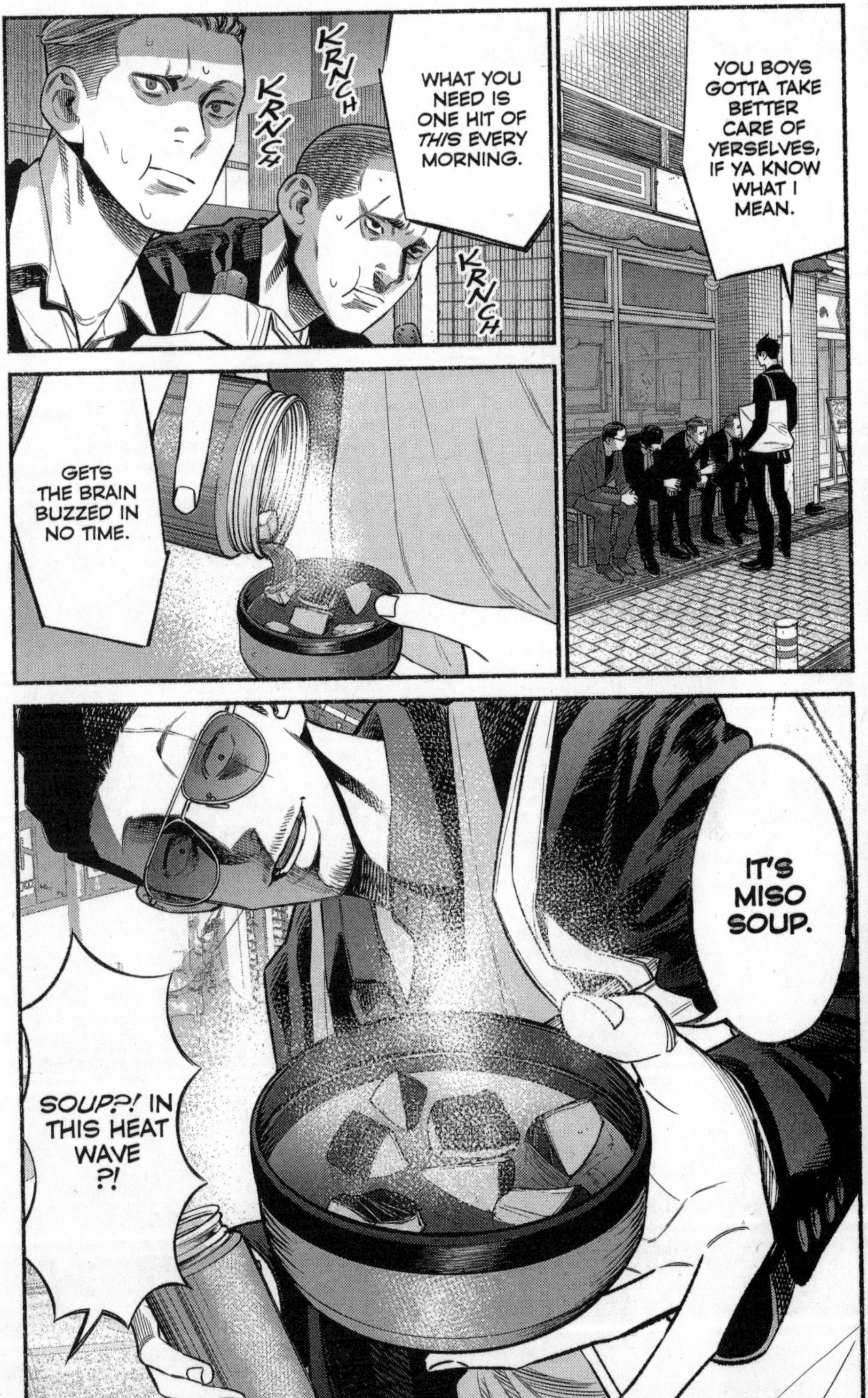
YOU BOYS GOTTA TAKE BETTER CARE OF YERSELVES, IF YA KNOW WHAT I MEAN.
WHAT YOU NEED IS ONE HIT OF *THIS* EVERY MORNING.
KRNCH
KRNCH
KRNCH
GETS THE BRAIN BUZZED IN NO TIME.
IT'S MISO SOUP.
SOUP?! IN THIS HEAT WAVE ?!

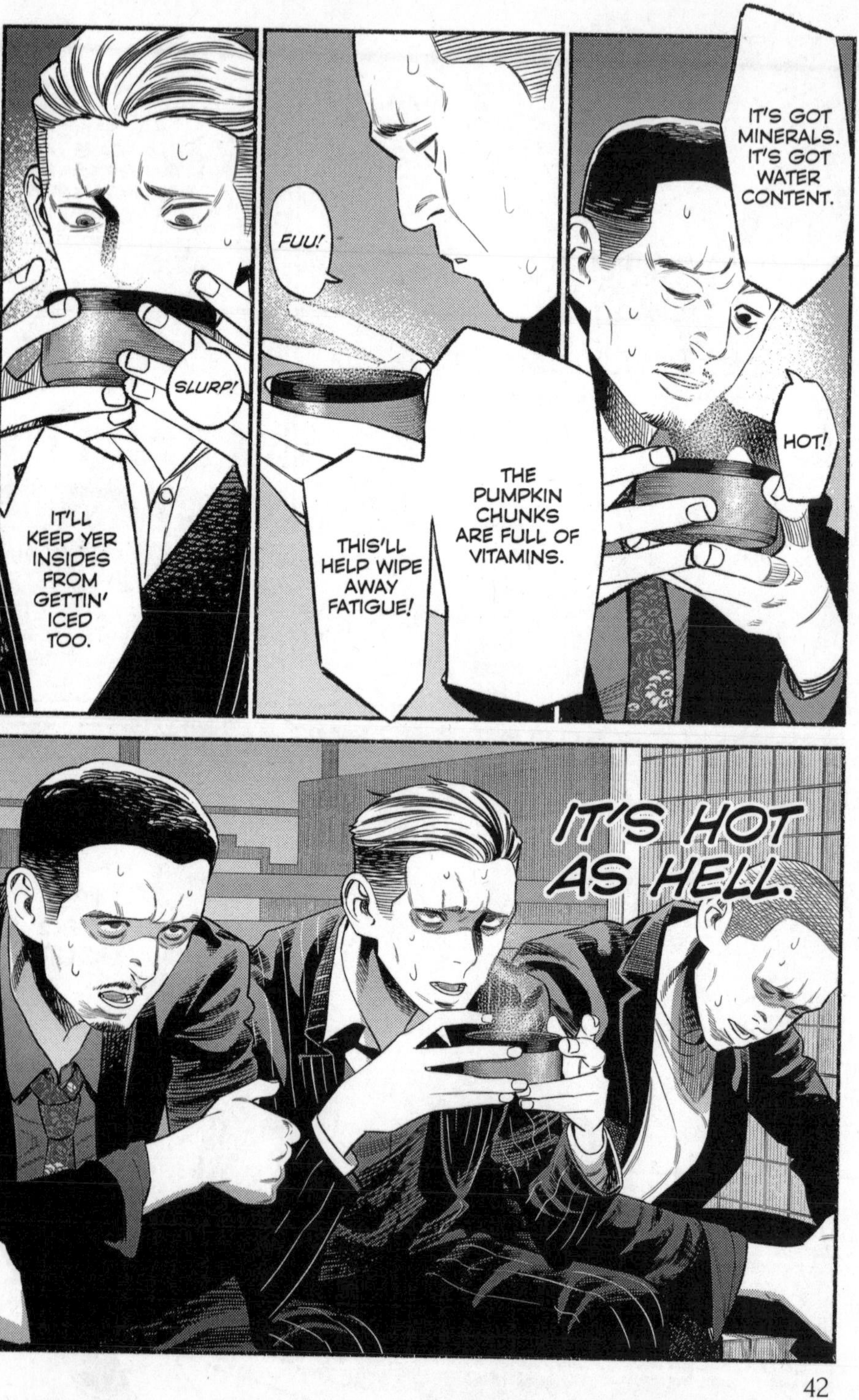
IT'S GOT MINERALS. IT'S GOT WATER CONTENT.
HOT!
THE PUMPKIN CHUNKS ARE FULL OF VITAMINS.
FUU!
THIS'LL HELP WIPE AWAY FATIGUE!
SLURP!
IT'LL KEEP YER INSIDES FROM GETTIN' ICED TOO.
IT'S HOT AS HELL.

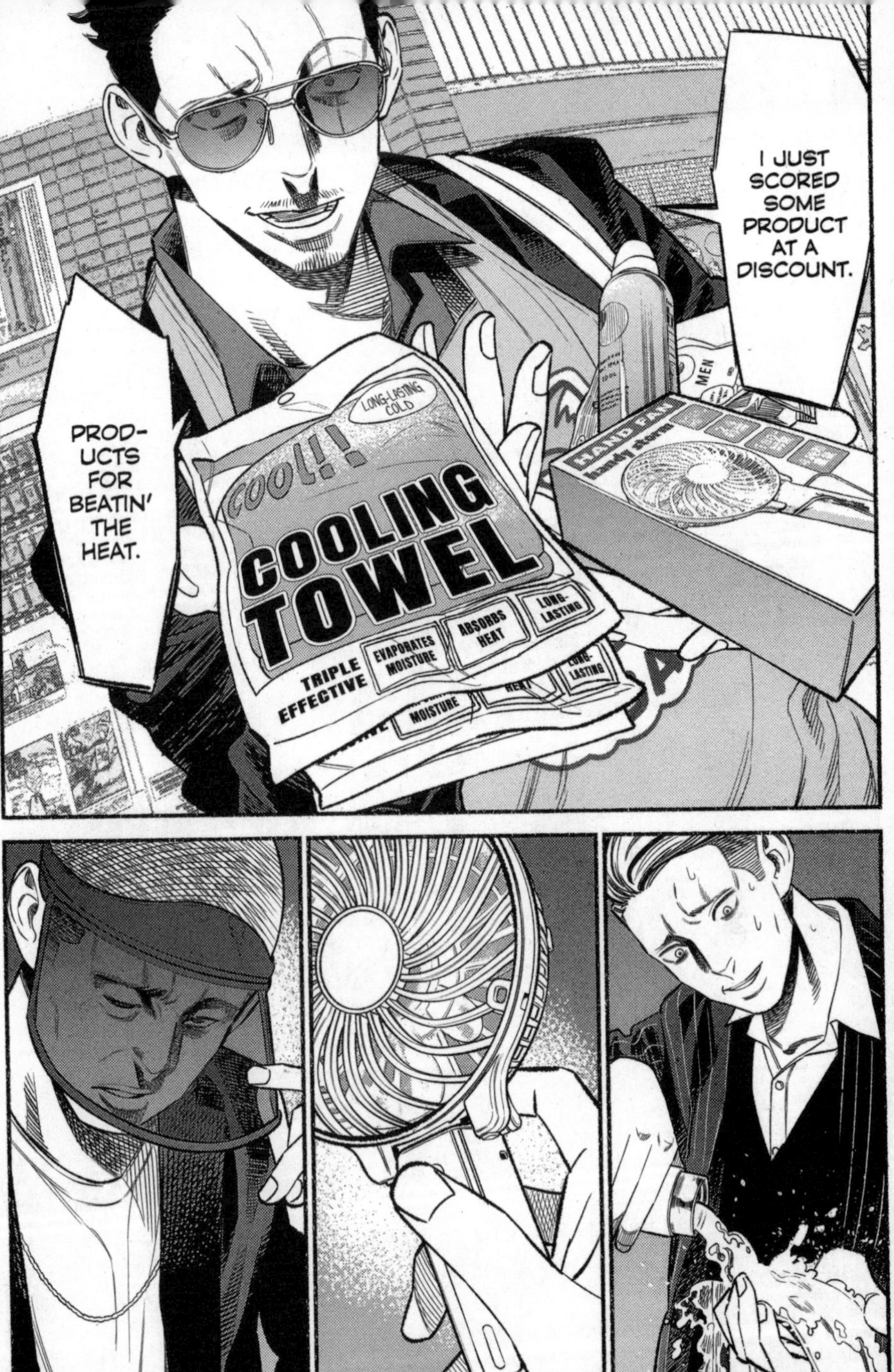
I JUST SCORED SOME PRODUCT AT A DISCOUNT.
PROD-UCTS FOR BEATIN' THE HEAT.
LONG-LASTING COLD
COOL!!
COOLING TOWEL
TRIPLE EFFECTIVE
EVAPORATES MOISTURE
ABSORBS HEAT
LONG-LASTING

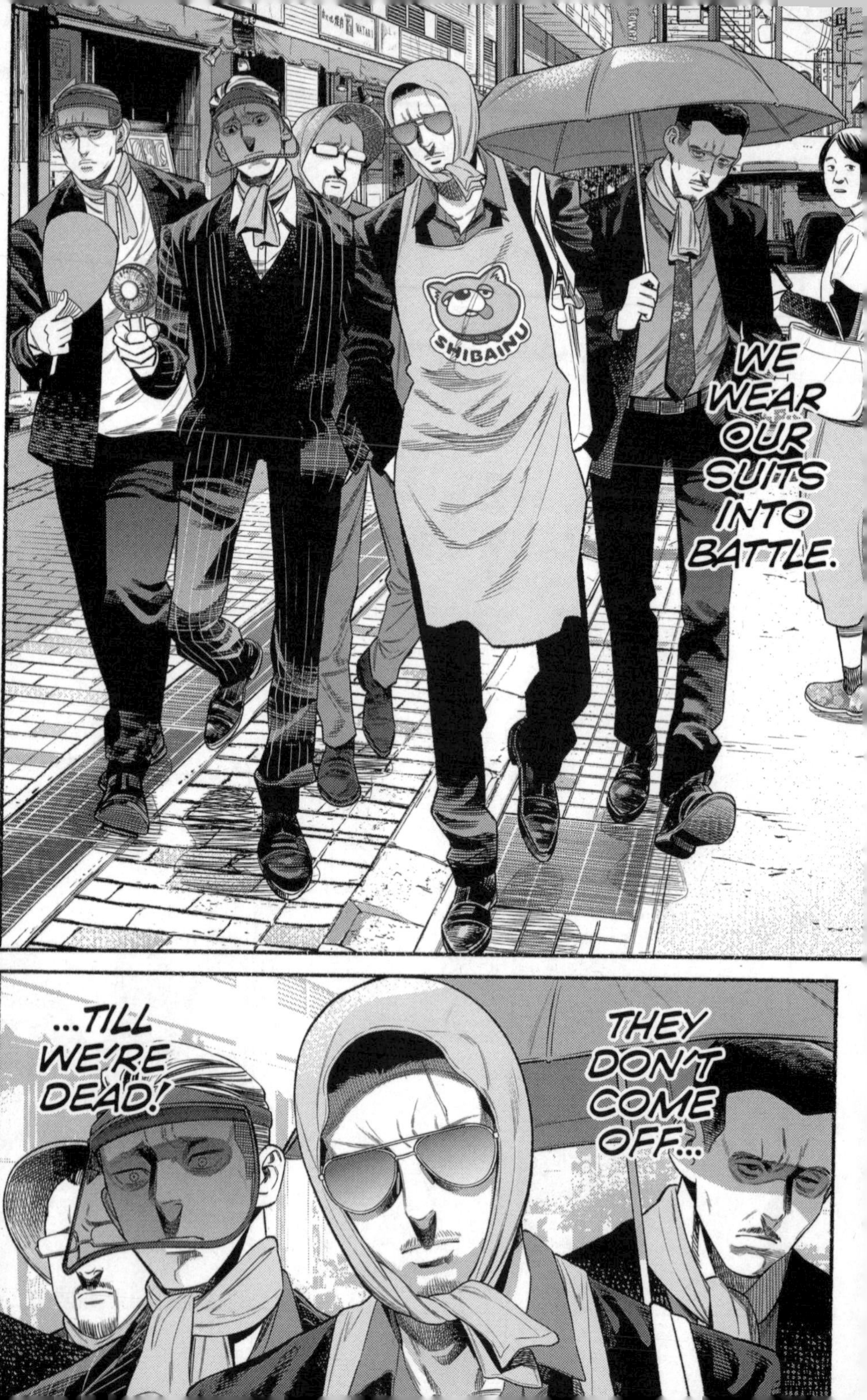
SHIBAINU
WE WEAR OUR SUITS INTO BATTLE.
THEY DON'T COME OFF...
...TILL WE'RE DEAD!

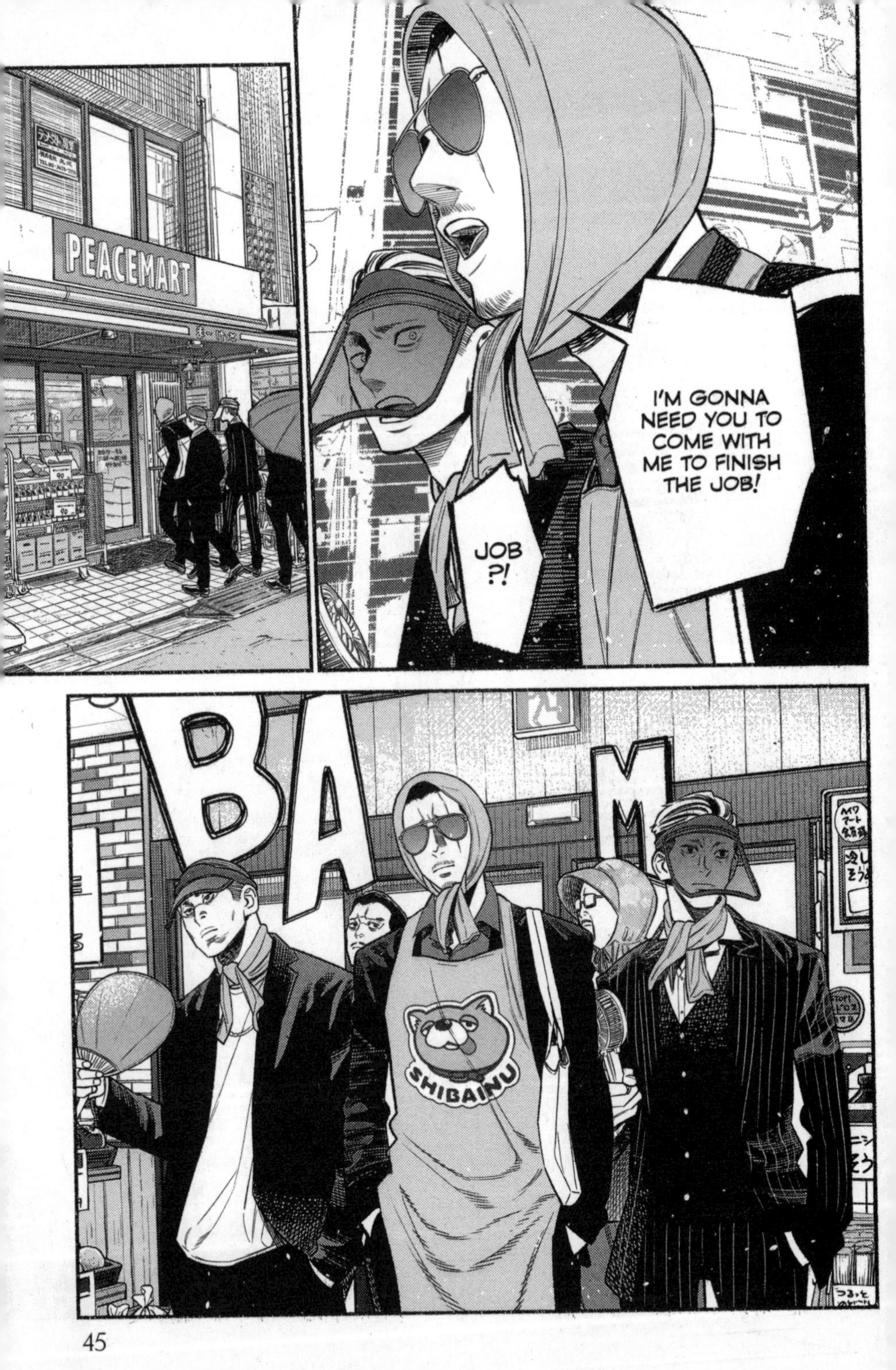
I'M GONNA NEED YOU TO COME WITH ME TO FINISH THE JOB!
JOB ?!
PEACEMART
BAM
SHIBAINU

GROCERY STORES SLINGIN' FRESH FOODS...

...ALWAYS KEEP THE AIR CONDITIONING ON!

LET'S BUY SOME, BOSS!

EGGPLANT'S IN SEASON. IT'S A STEAL!

LOOKS LIKE WE'RE HAVIN' EGGPLANT STEW FOR DINNER TONIGHT, BOYS!

PLUS, YOU CAN SHOP FOR DINNER.

IT'S KILLIN' TWO BIRDS WITH ONE STONE.

CHILLIN'

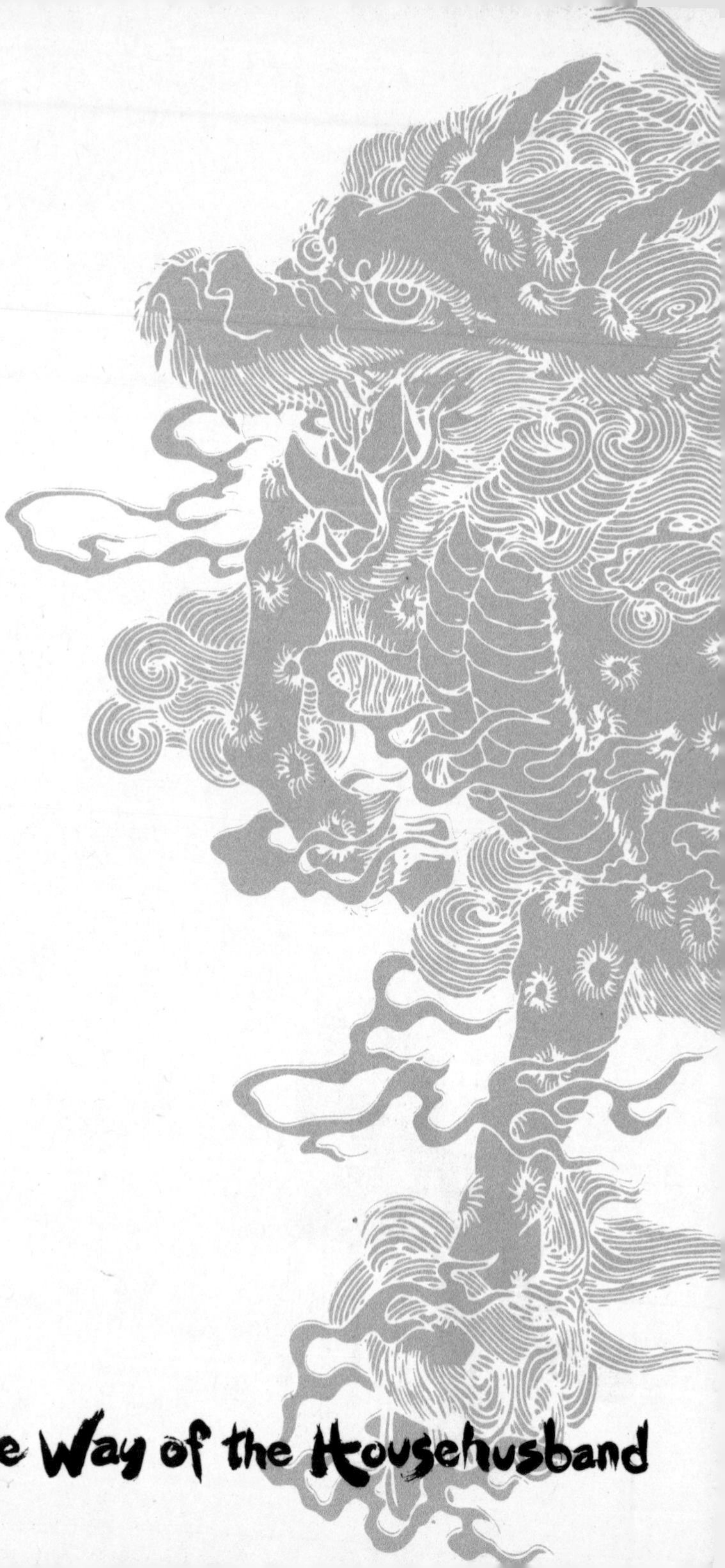

The Way of the Househusband

CHAPTER 76

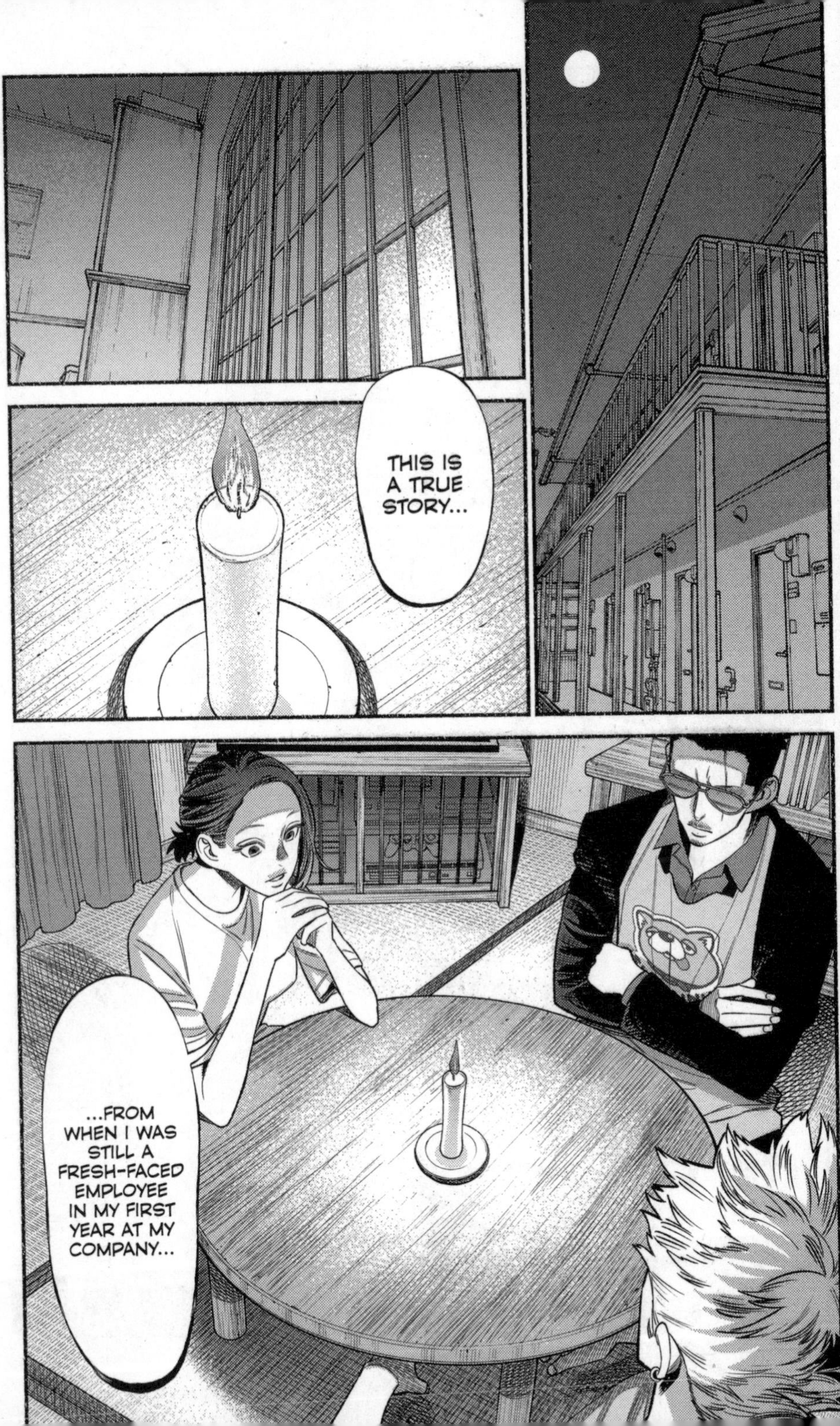
THIS IS A TRUE STORY...
...FROM WHEN I WAS STILL A FRESH-FACED EMPLOYEE IN MY FIRST YEAR AT MY COMPANY...

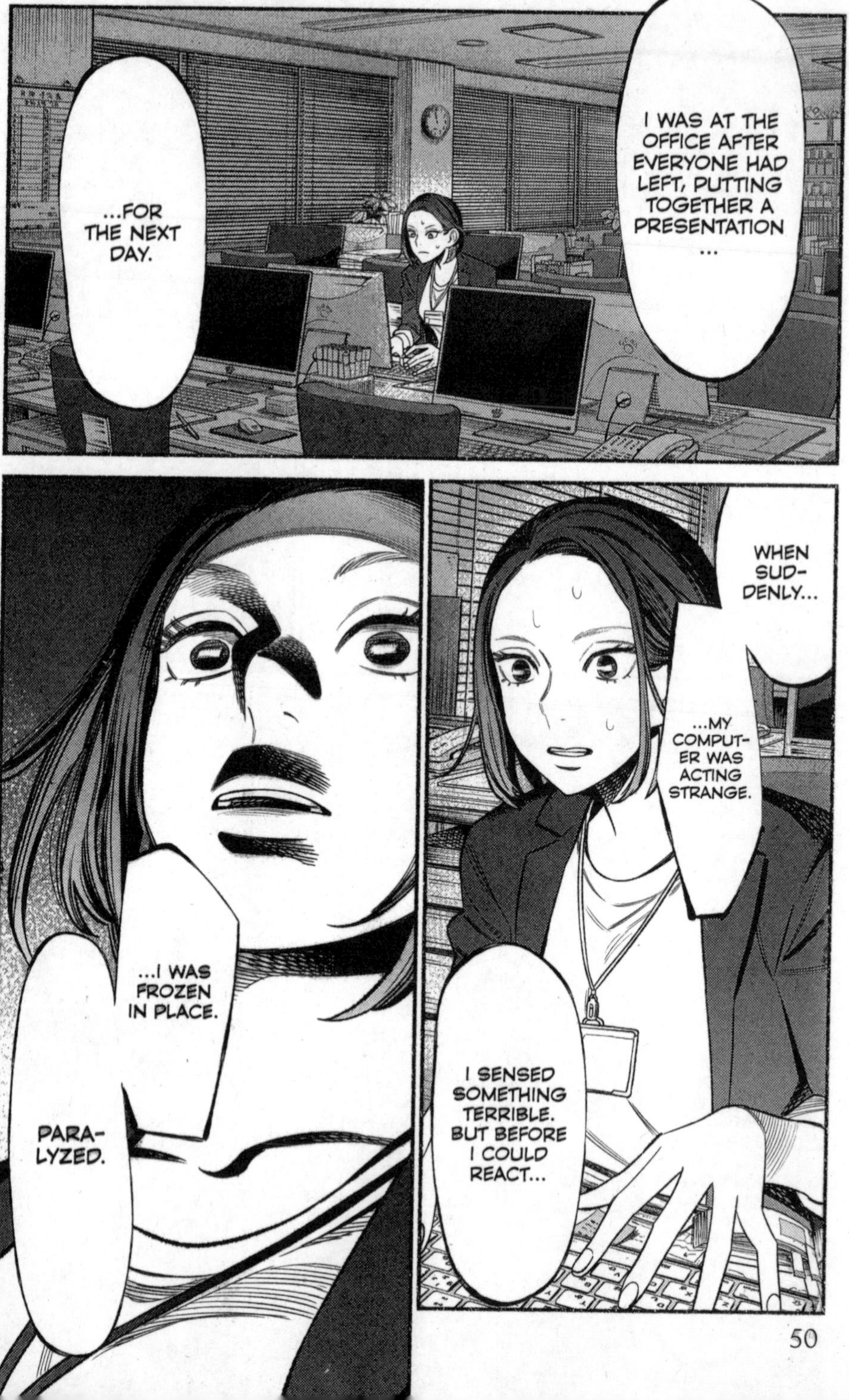
I WAS AT THE OFFICE AFTER EVERYONE HAD LEFT, PUTTING TOGETHER A PRESENTATION ...
...FOR THE NEXT DAY.
WHEN SUD-DENLY...
...MY COMPUT-ER WAS ACTING STRANGE.
I SENSED SOMETHING TERRIBLE. BUT BEFORE I COULD REACT...
...I WAS FROZEN IN PLACE.
PARA-LYZED.

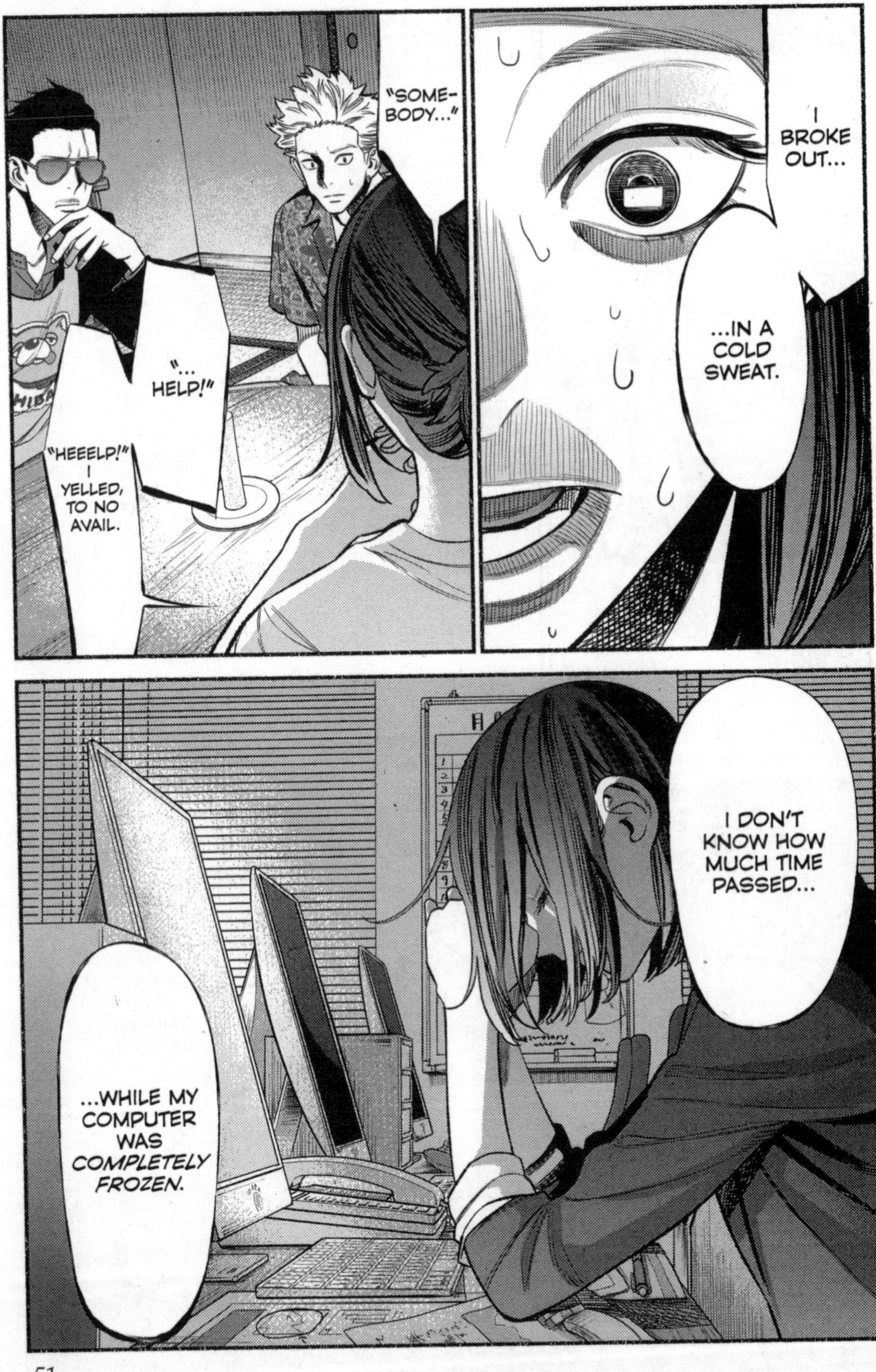
I BROKE OUT...
...IN A COLD SWEAT.
"SOMEBODY..."
"...HELP!"
"HEEELP!" I YELLED, TO NO AVAIL.
I DON'T KNOW HOW MUCH TIME PASSED...
...WHILE MY COMPUTER WAS *COMPLETELY FROZEN*.

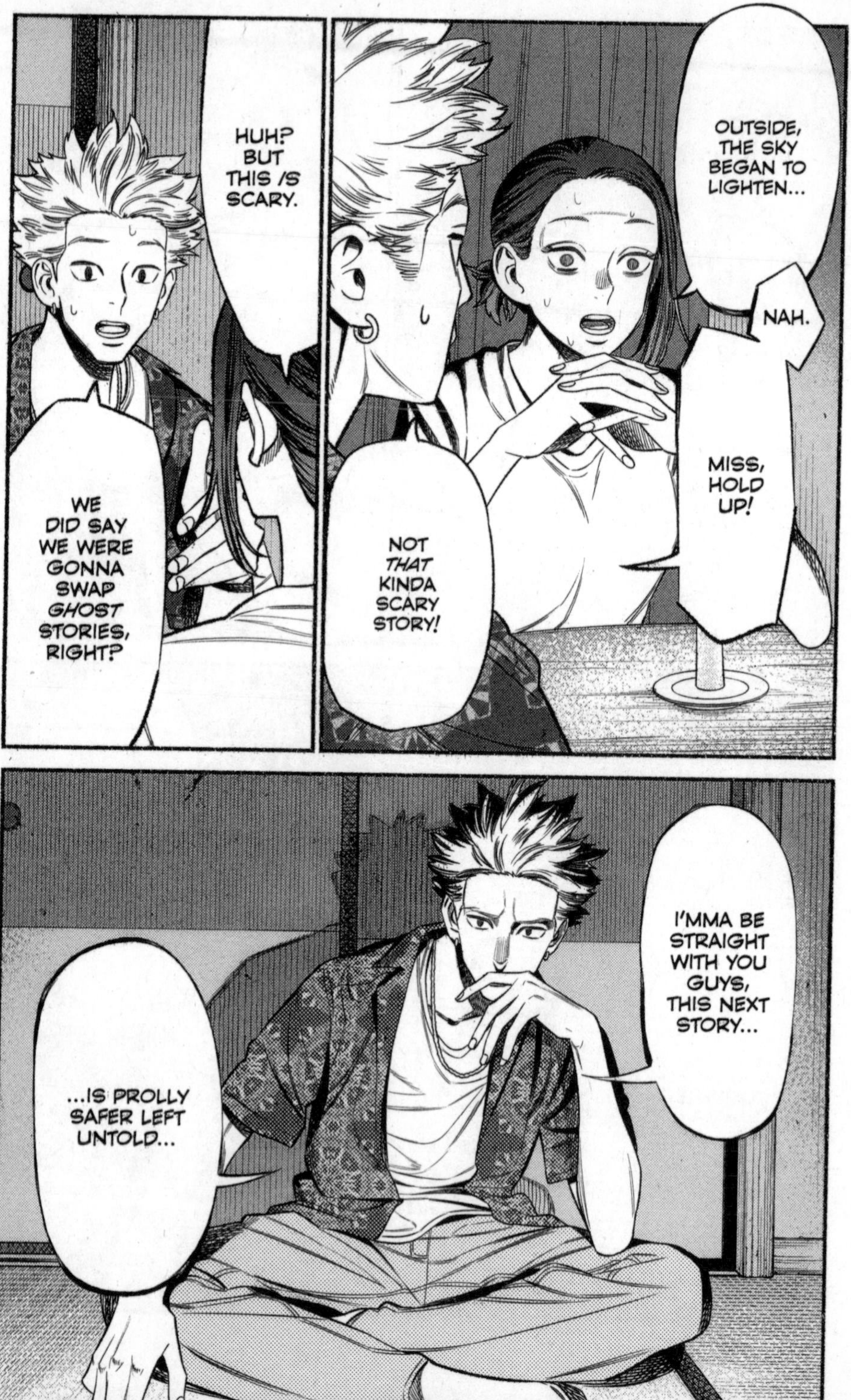
OUTSIDE, THE SKY BEGAN TO LIGHTEN...
NAH.
MISS, HOLD UP!
NOT *THAT* KINDA SCARY STORY!
HUH? BUT THIS *IS* SCARY.
WE DID SAY WE WERE GONNA SWAP *GHOST* STORIES, RIGHT?
I'MMA BE STRAIGHT WITH YOU GUYS, THIS NEXT STORY...
...IS PROLLY SAFER LEFT UNTOLD...

THERE WAS THIS PLACE THAT WAS INFAMOUS IN THE AREA FOR BEING HAUNTED.

THIS GUY AND SOME OF HIS PALS HAD DECIDED TO CHECK IT OUT. YOLO AND ALL THAT.

I HEARD THIS STORY BACK HOME...

...SEVERAL YEARS AGO FROM THIS OLDER GUY I KNEW.

SO OFF THEY WENT TO...

YOU KNOW, LIKE A BUILDING THAT AIN'T USED ANYMORE... STARTS WITH AN "A"?

WHAT'S IT CALLED?

ABAN-DONED. THAT'S IT. AN ABAN-DONED BUILDING.

...EVEN THOUGH IT'S THE DEAD OF SUMMER...

...ONE OF 'EM STARTS SHAKIN'...

...AND GOIN' ON ABOUT HOW HE'S FREEZIN' HIS ASS OFF.

ANYWAY, SO THEY HEAD IN, AND AS THEY'RE WALKIN' DOWN THIS NARROW HALLWAY...

SO THEY FLASH HIM WITH THE, UH... YOU KNOW... ONE OF THOSE THINGS.

YOU PRESS A BUTTON AND BING, THE LIGHT GOES ON?

THEY FLASH MR. FREEZE WITH THAT THING.

THE OTHERS ARE LIKE, THAT'S RIDIC. WHAT'S HIS DEAL?

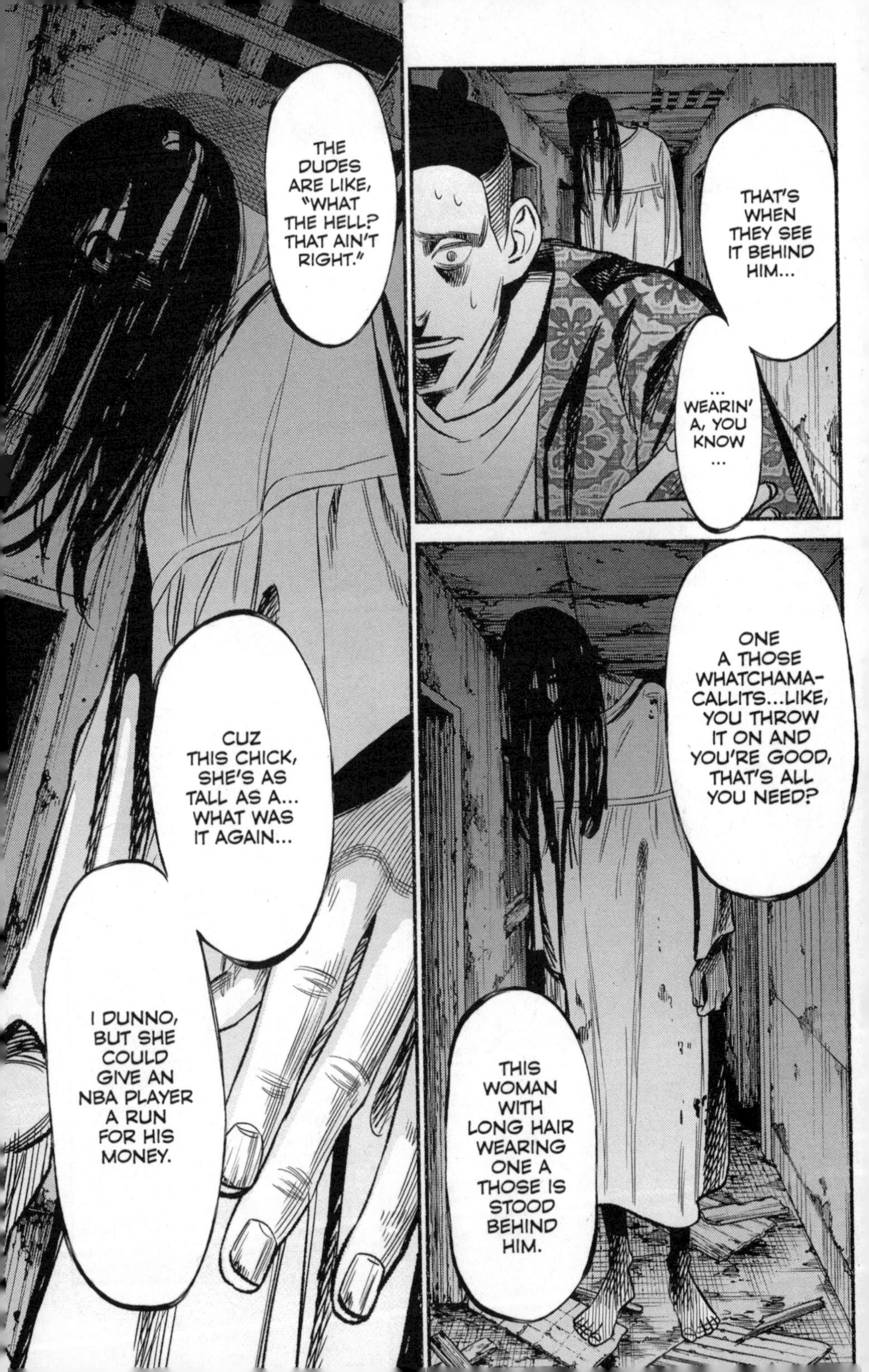
THAT'S WHEN THEY SEE IT BEHIND HIM...
... WEARIN' A, YOU KNOW ...
ONE A THOSE WHATCHAMA-CALLITS...LIKE, YOU THROW IT ON AND YOU'RE GOOD, THAT'S ALL YOU NEED?
THIS WOMAN WITH LONG HAIR WEARING ONE A THOSE IS STOOD BEHIND HIM.
THE DUDES ARE LIKE, "WHAT THE HELL? THAT AIN'T RIGHT."
CUZ THIS CHICK, SHE'S AS TALL AS A... WHAT WAS IT AGAIN...
I DUNNO, BUT SHE COULD GIVE AN NBA PLAYER A RUN FOR HIS MONEY.

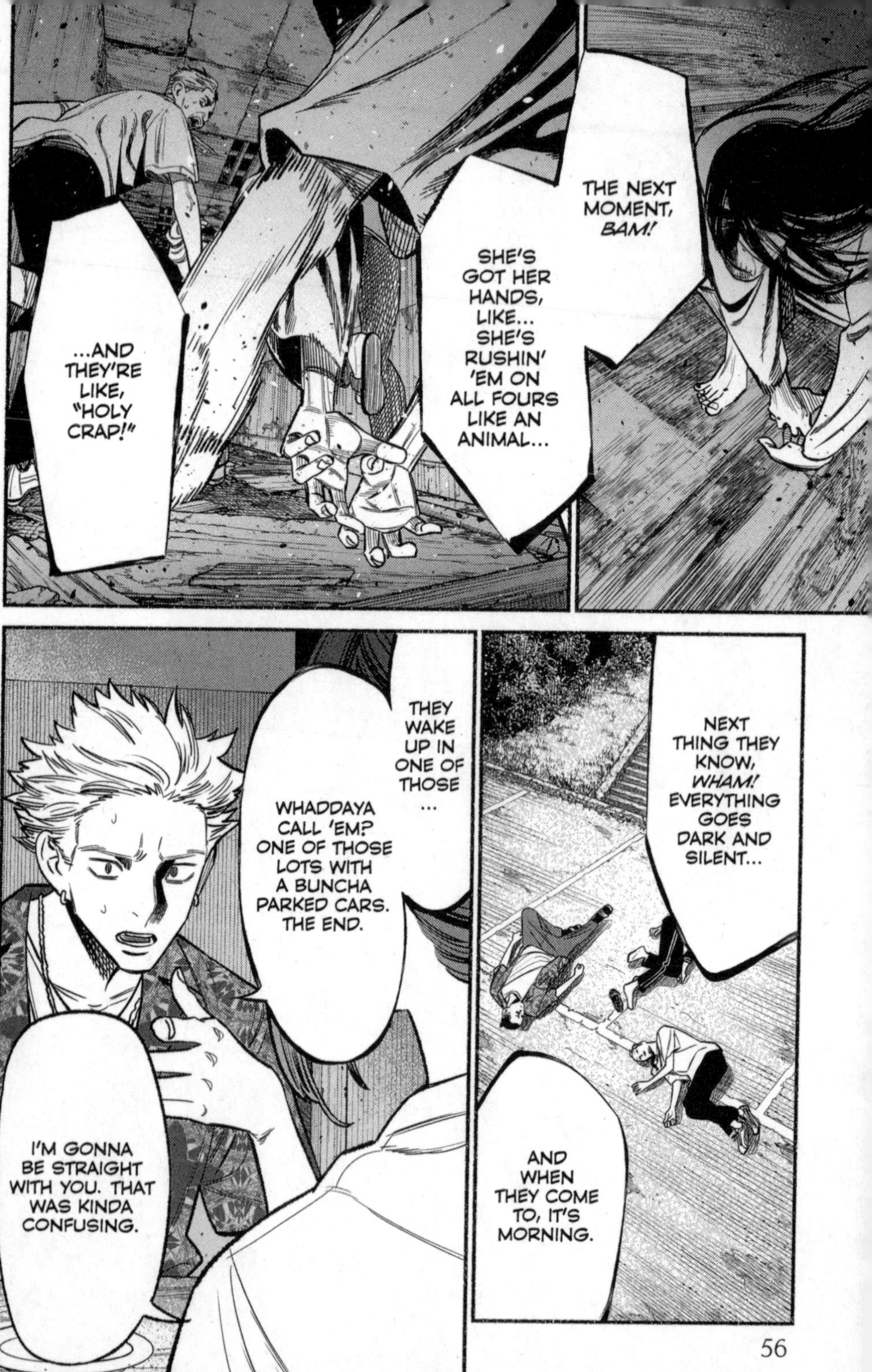
THE NEXT MOMENT, *BAM!*
SHE'S GOT HER HANDS, LIKE... SHE'S RUSHIN' 'EM ON ALL FOURS LIKE AN ANIMAL...
...AND THEY'RE LIKE, "HOLY CRAP!"
NEXT THING THEY KNOW, *WHAM!* EVERYTHING GOES DARK AND SILENT...
AND WHEN THEY COME TO, IT'S MORNING.
THEY WAKE UP IN ONE OF THOSE ...
WHADDAYA CALL 'EM? ONE OF THOSE LOTS WITH A BUNCHA PARKED CARS. THE END.
I'M GONNA BE STRAIGHT WITH YOU. THAT WAS KINDA CONFUSING.

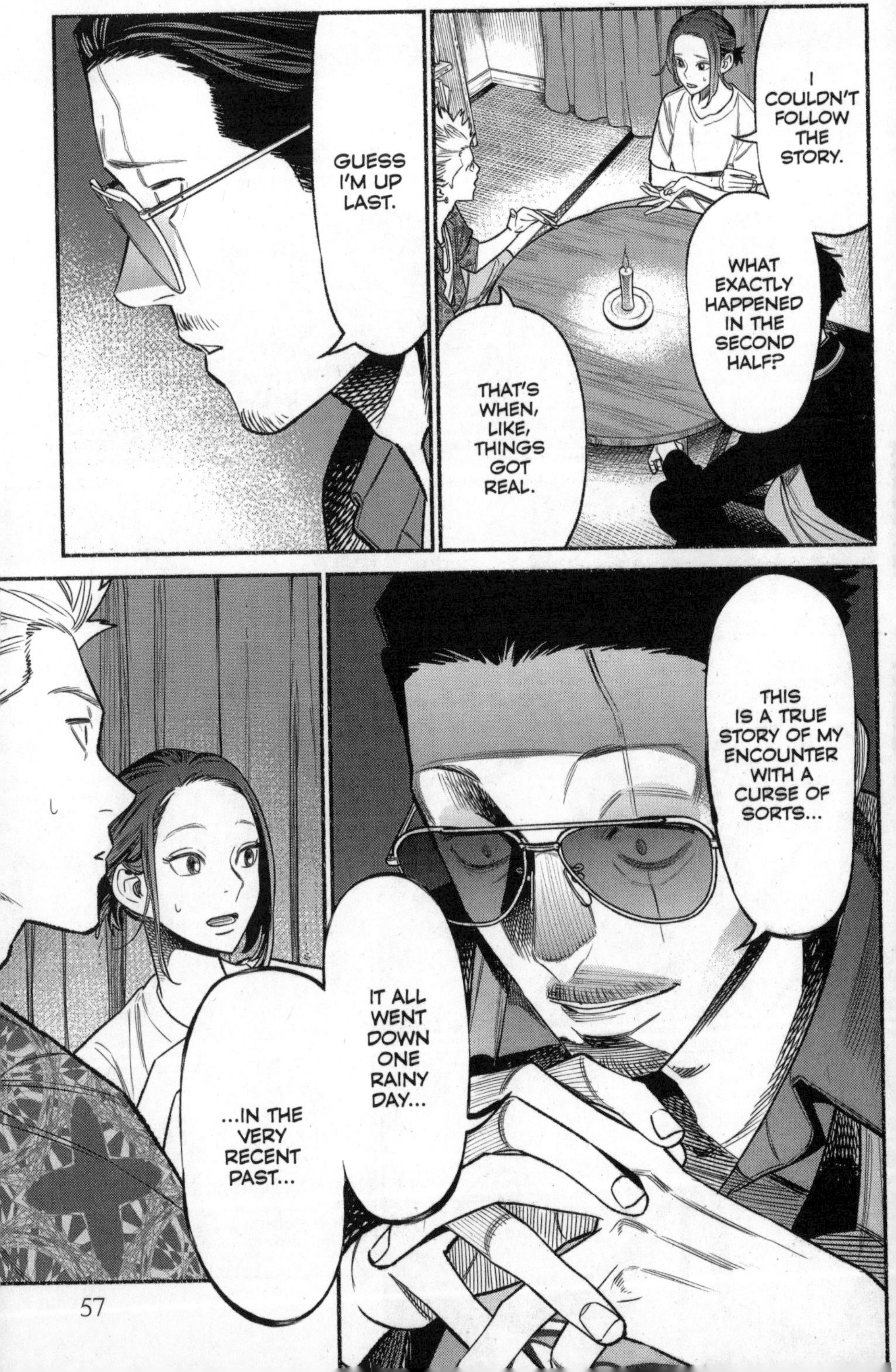
I COULDN'T FOLLOW THE STORY.
WHAT EXACTLY HAPPENED IN THE SECOND HALF?
THAT'S WHEN, LIKE, THINGS GOT REAL.
GUESS I'M UP LAST.
THIS IS A TRUE STORY OF MY ENCOUNTER WITH A CURSE OF SORTS...
IT ALL WENT DOWN ONE RAINY DAY...
...IN THE VERY RECENT PAST...

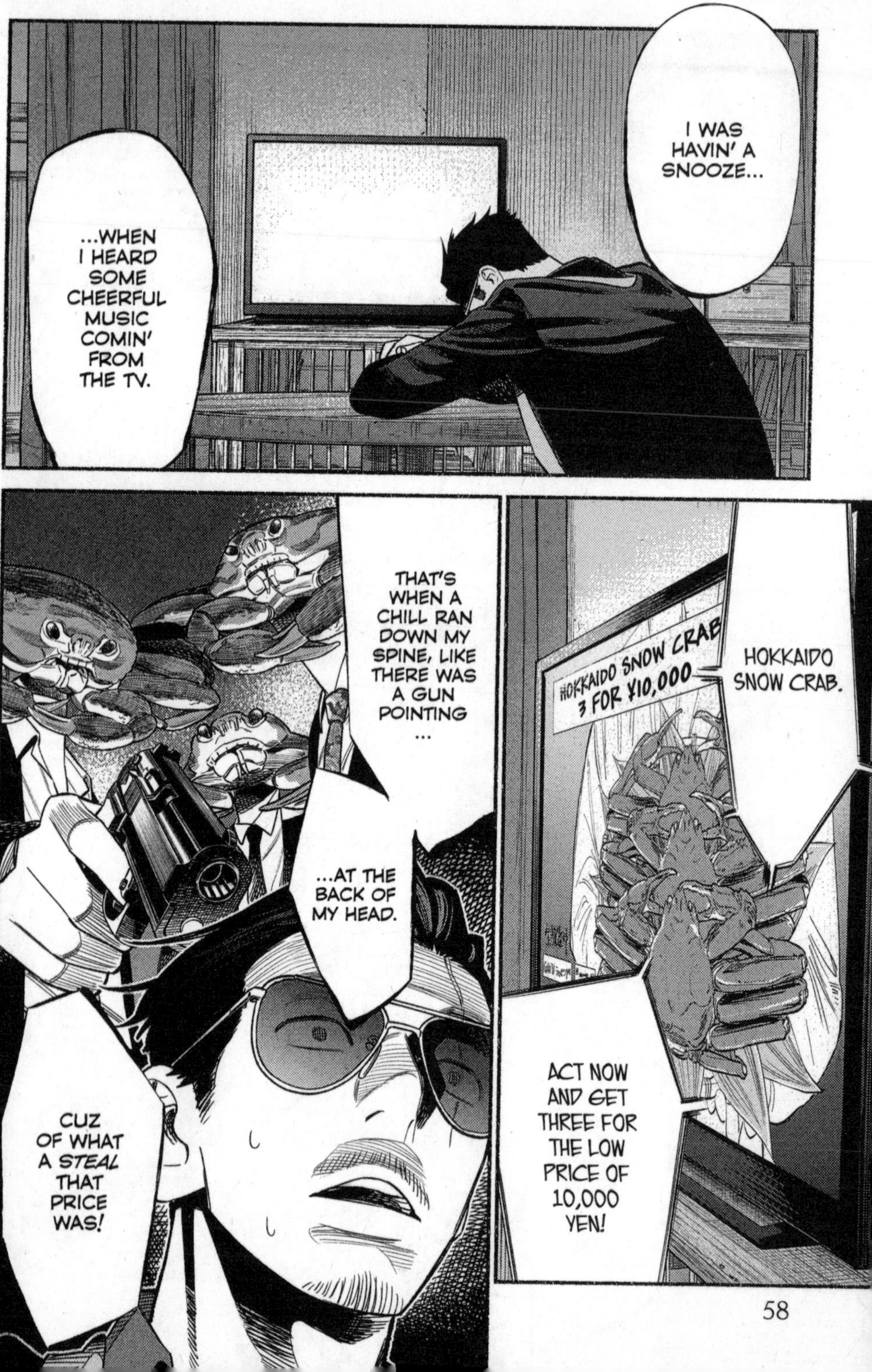
I WAS HAVIN' A SNOOZE...
...WHEN I HEARD SOME CHEERFUL MUSIC COMIN' FROM THE TV.
HOKKAIDO SNOW CRAB.
HOKKAIDO SNOW CRAB 3 FOR ¥10,000
ACT NOW AND GET THREE FOR THE LOW PRICE OF 10,000 YEN!
THAT'S WHEN A CHILL RAN DOWN MY SPINE, LIKE THERE WAS A GUN POINTING ...
...AT THE BACK OF MY HEAD.
CUZ OF WHAT A *STEAL* THAT PRICE WAS!

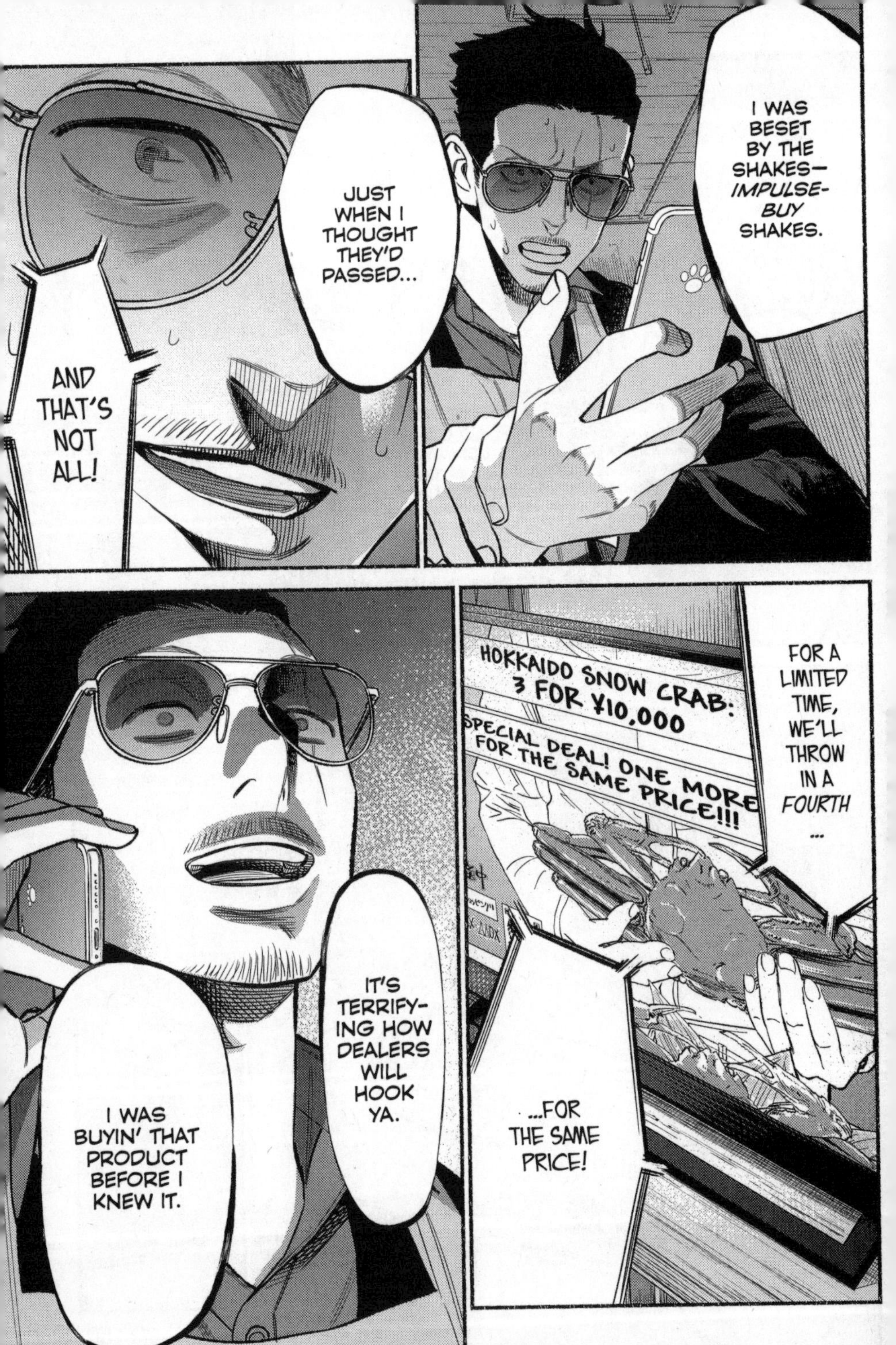
I WAS BESET BY THE SHAKES—*IMPULSE-BUY* SHAKES.
JUST WHEN I THOUGHT THEY'D PASSED...
AND THAT'S NOT ALL!
HOKKAIDO SNOW CRAB: 3 FOR ¥10,000
SPECIAL DEAL! ONE MORE FOR THE SAME PRICE!!!
FOR A LIMITED TIME, WE'LL THROW IN A *FOURTH* ...
...FOR THE SAME PRICE!
IT'S TERRIFYING HOW DEALERS WILL HOOK YA.
I WAS BUYIN' THAT PRODUCT BEFORE I KNEW IT.

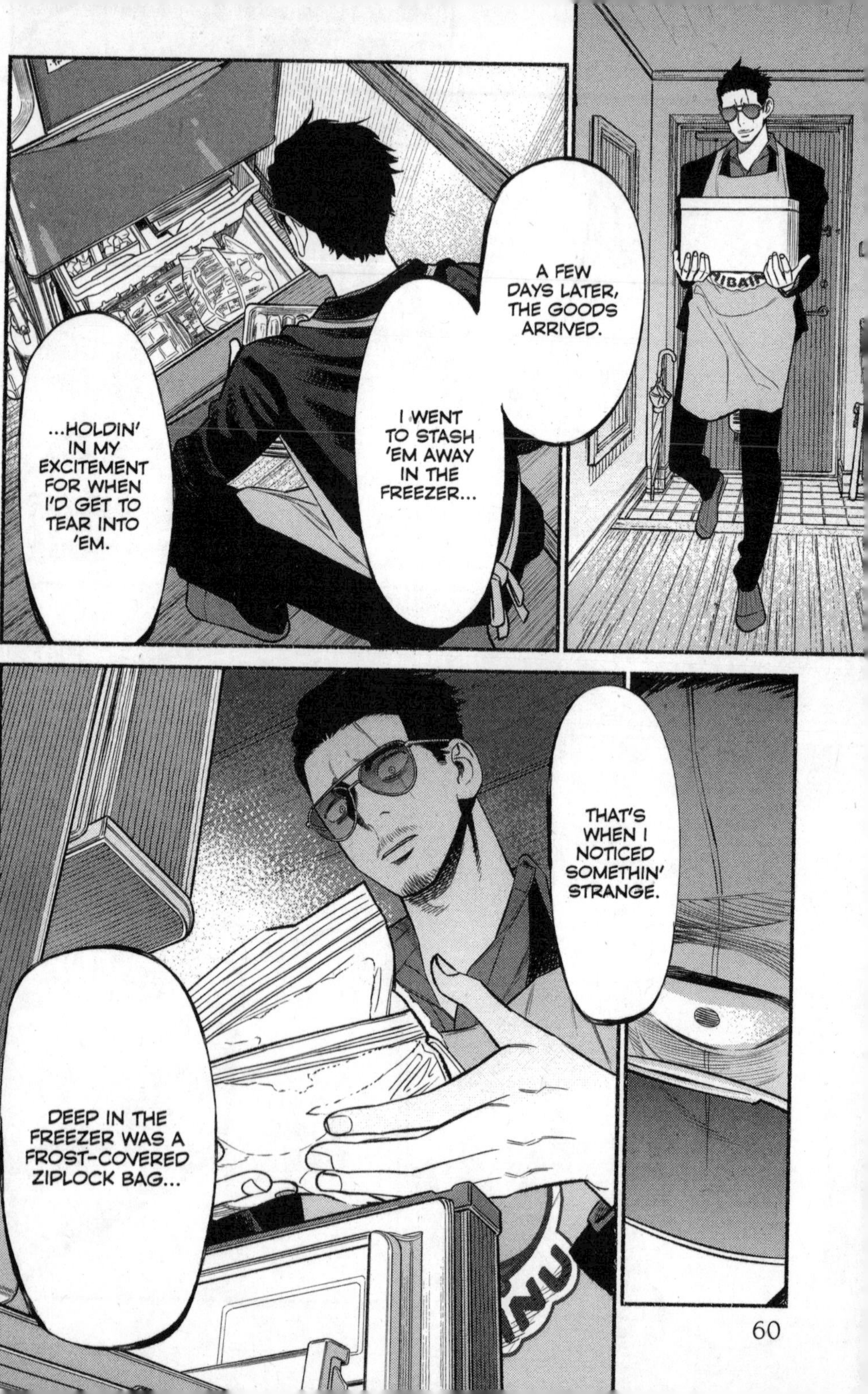
A FEW DAYS LATER, THE GOODS ARRIVED.
I WENT TO STASH 'EM AWAY IN THE FREEZER...
...HOLDIN' IN MY EXCITEMENT FOR WHEN I'D GET TO TEAR INTO 'EM.
THAT'S WHEN I NOTICED SOMETHIN' STRANGE.
DEEP IN THE FREEZER WAS A FROST-COVERED ZIPLOCK BAG...

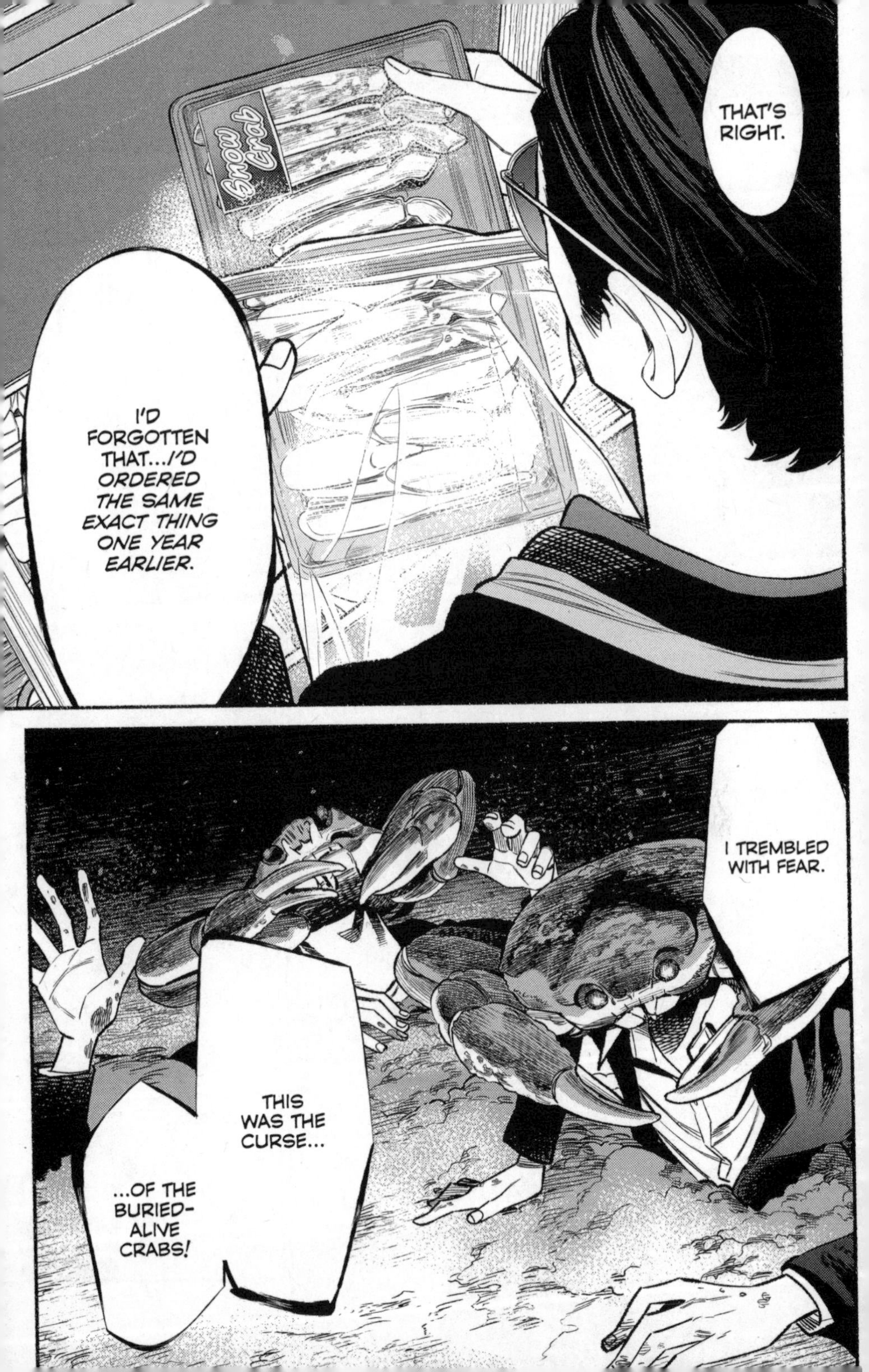
THAT'S RIGHT.
I'D FORGOTTEN THAT...*I'D* ORDERED THE SAME EXACT THING ONE YEAR EARLIER.
I TREMBLED WITH FEAR.
THIS WAS THE CURSE...
...OF THE BURIED-ALIVE CRABS!

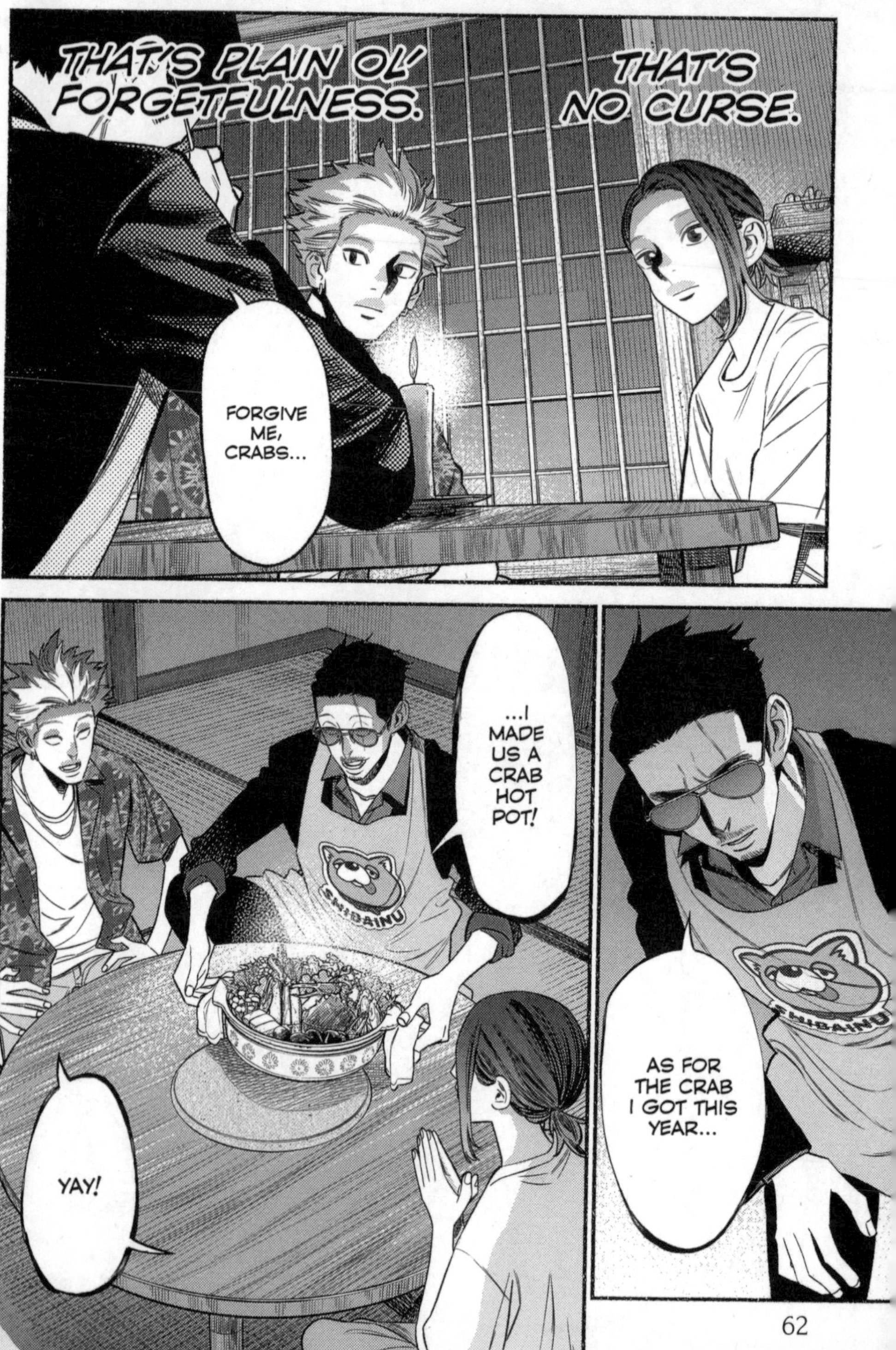
THAT'S NO CURSE.
THAT'S PLAIN OL' FORGETFULNESS.
FORGIVE ME, CRABS...
AS FOR THE CRAB I GOT THIS YEAR...
...I MADE US A CRAB HOT POT!
YAY!

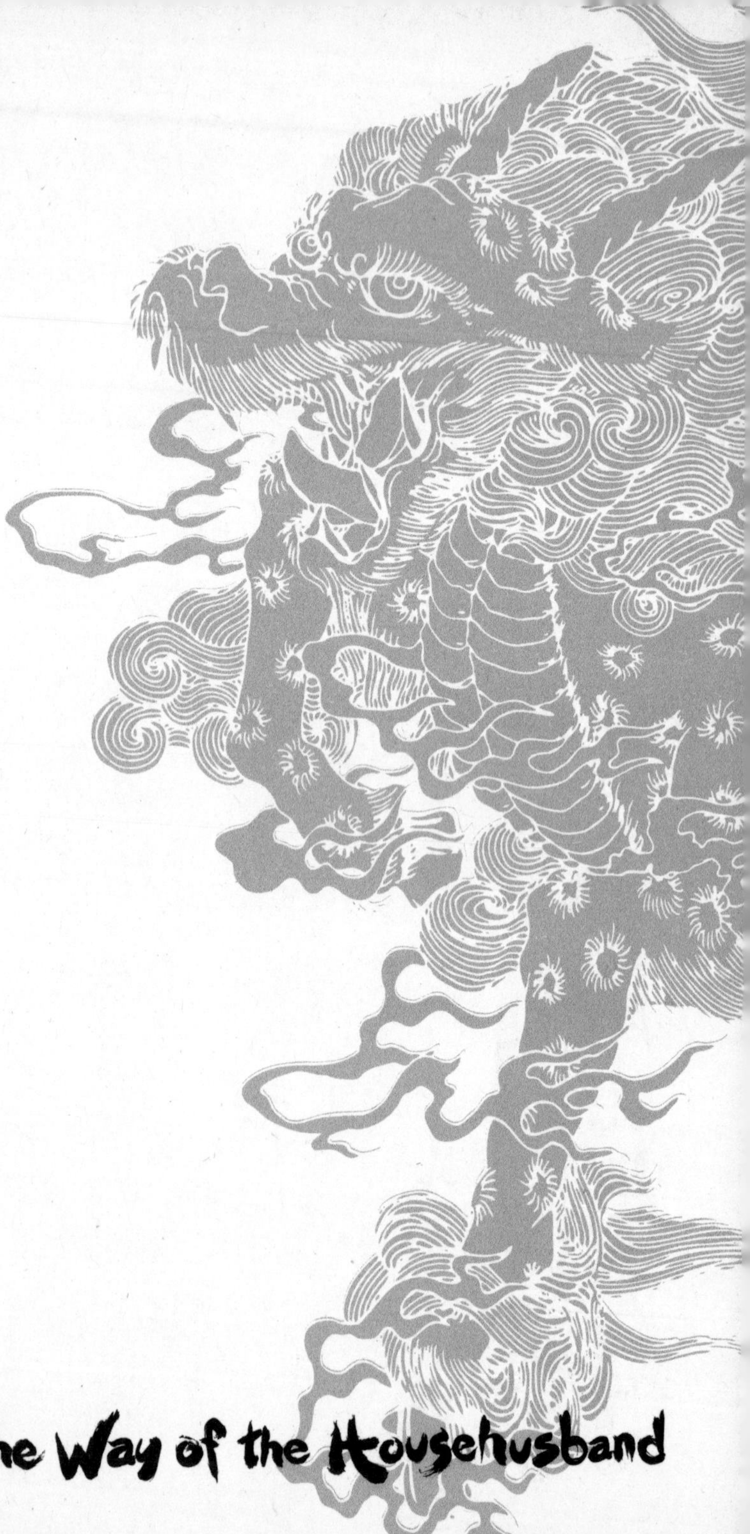

The Way of the Househusband

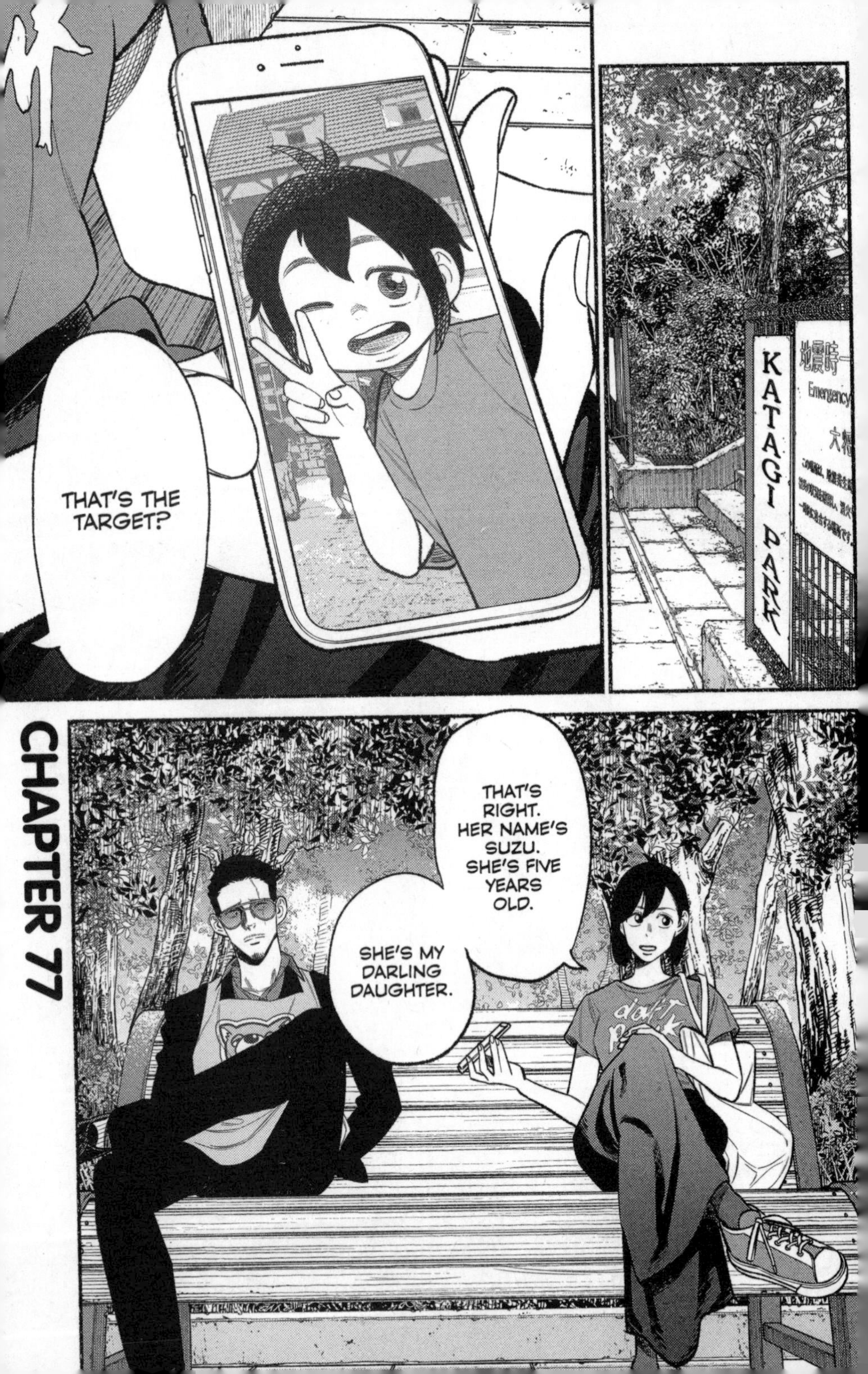
KATAGI PARK
Emergency
THAT'S THE TARGET?
THAT'S RIGHT. HER NAME'S SUZU. SHE'S FIVE YEARS OLD.
SHE'S MY DARLING DAUGHTER.
CHAPTER 77

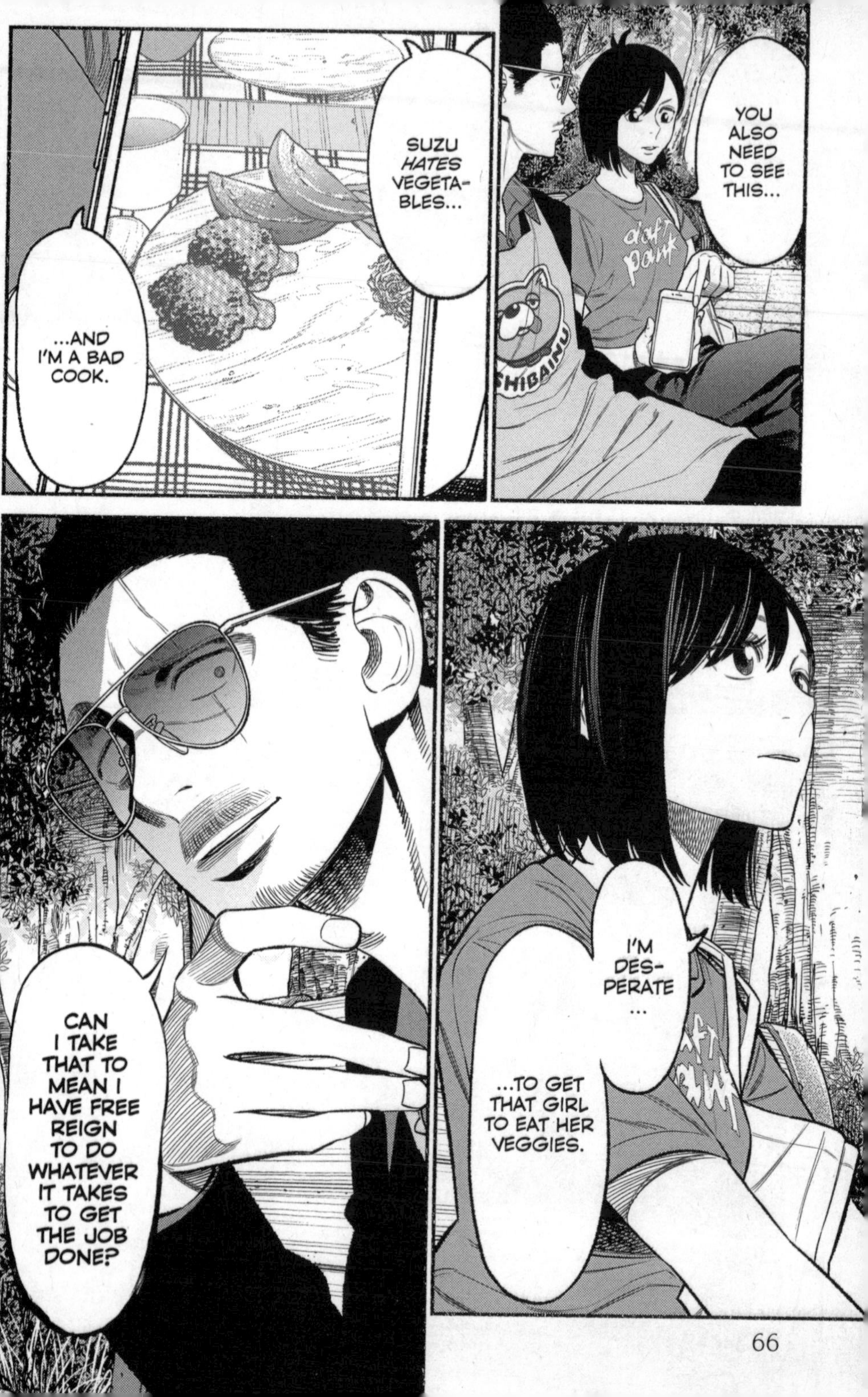
YOU ALSO NEED TO SEE THIS...
SUZU *HATES* VEGETA-BLES...
...AND I'M A BAD COOK.
I'M DES-PERATE...
...TO GET THAT GIRL TO EAT HER VEGGIES.
CAN I TAKE THAT TO MEAN I HAVE FREE REIGN TO DO WHATEVER IT TAKES TO GET THE JOB DONE?

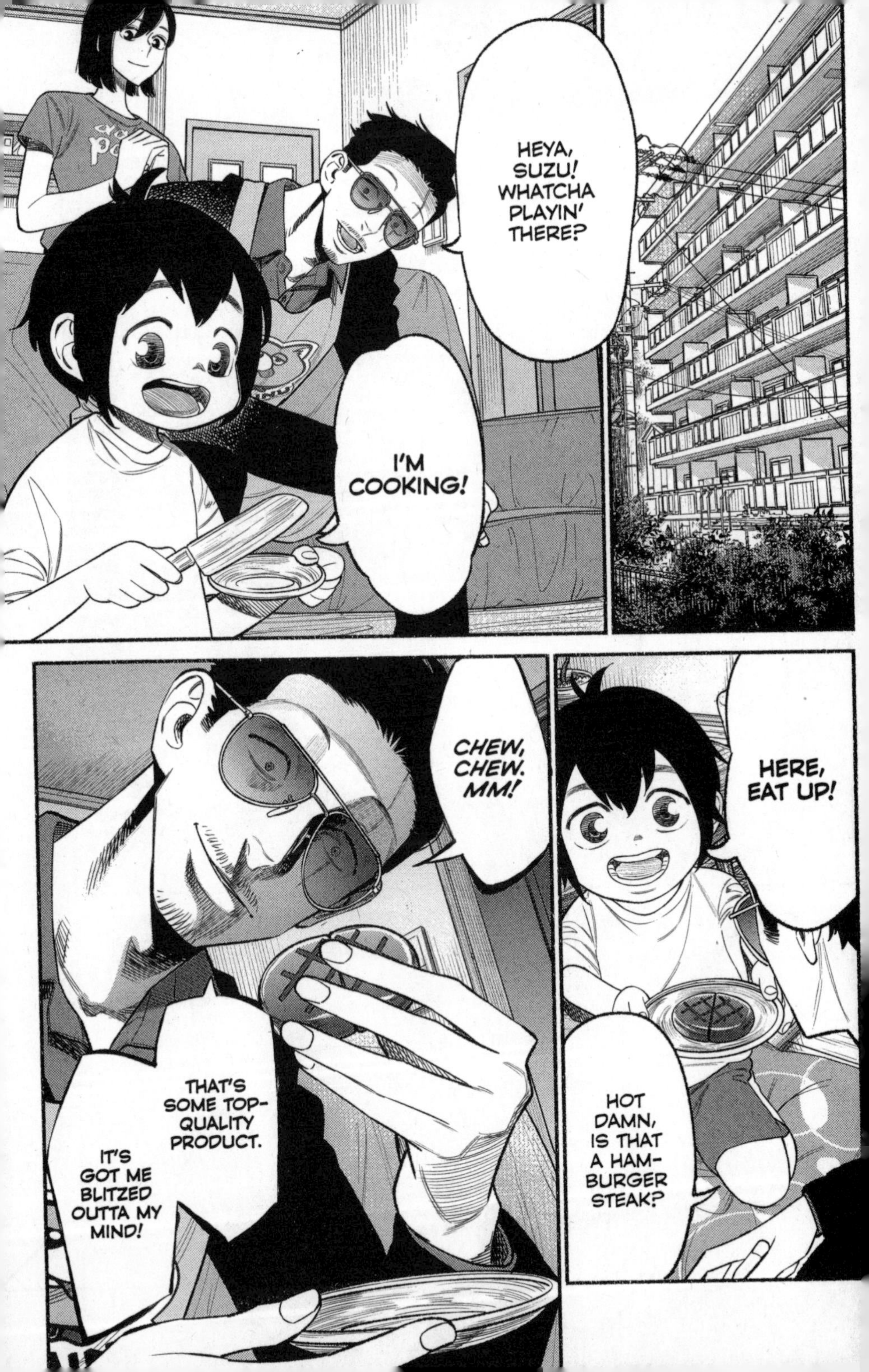
HEYA, SUZU! WHATCHA PLAYIN' THERE?
I'M COOKING!
HERE, EAT UP!
HOT DAMN, IS THAT A HAMBURGER STEAK?
CHEW, CHEW. MM!
THAT'S SOME TOP-QUALITY PRODUCT.
IT'S GOT ME BLITZED OUTTA MY MIND!

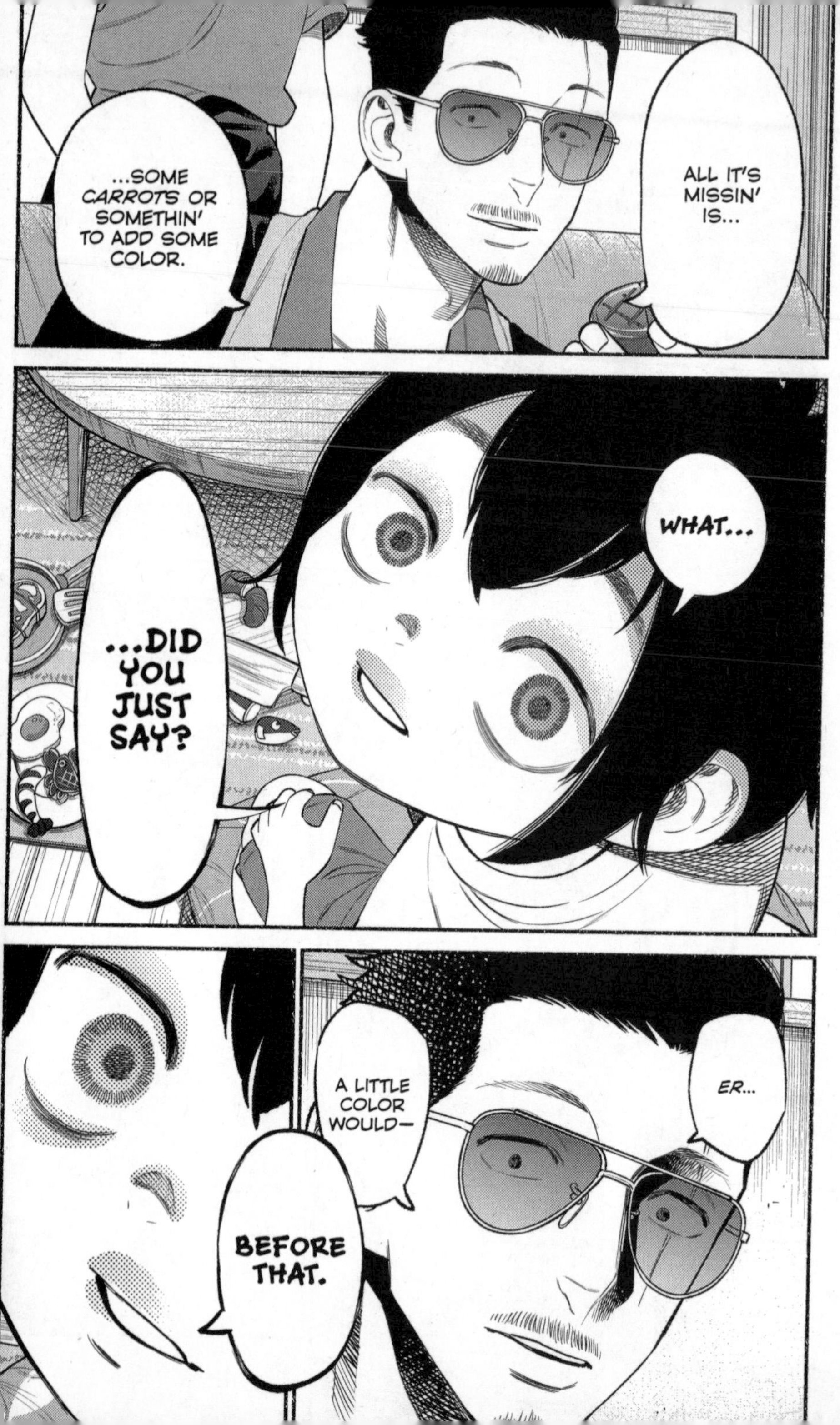
ALL IT'S MISSIN' IS...
...SOME *CARROTS* OR SOMETHIN' TO ADD SOME COLOR.
WHAT...
...DID YOU JUST SAY?
ER...
A LITTLE COLOR WOULD—
BEFORE THAT.

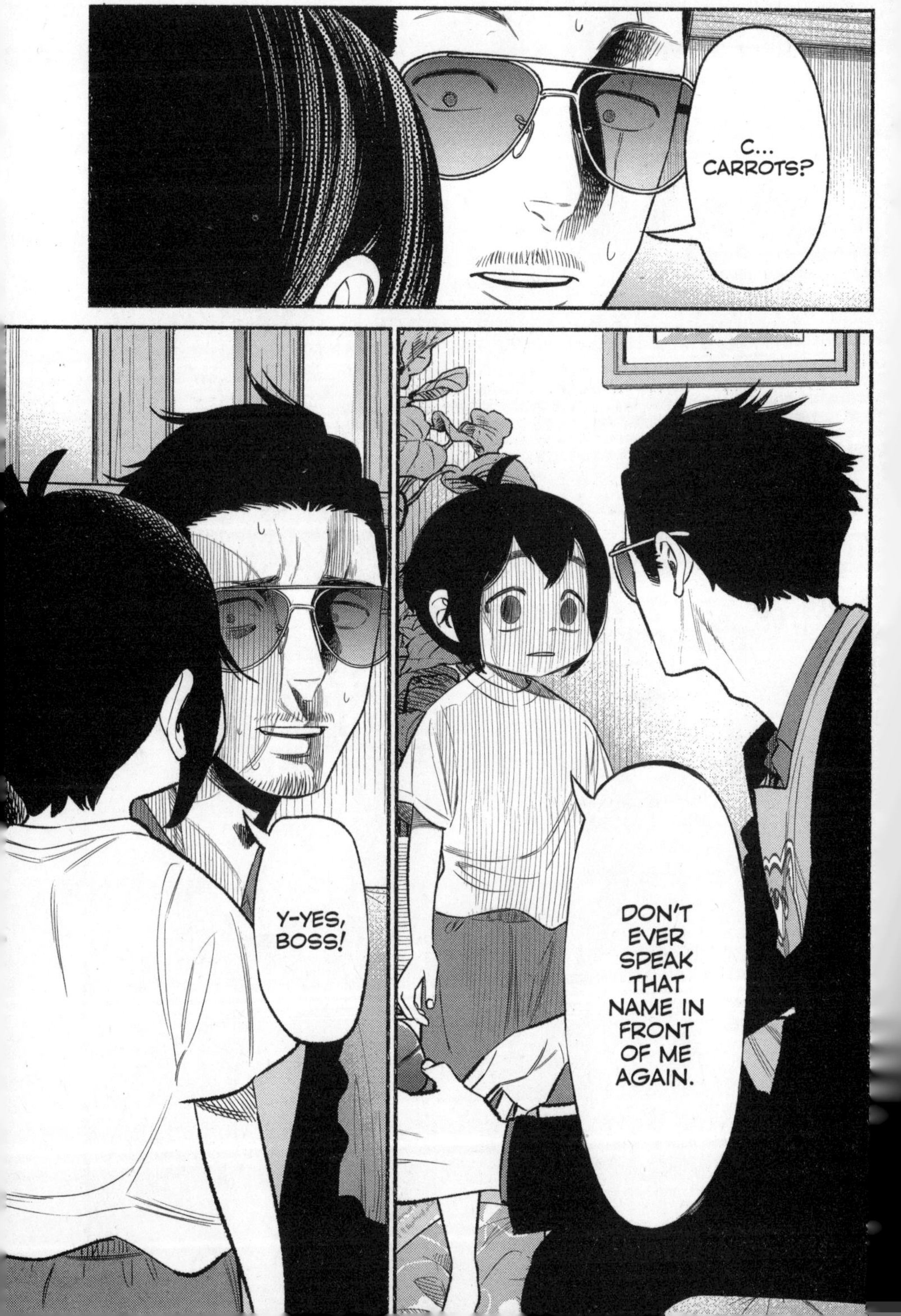
C... CARROTS?
DON'T EVER SPEAK THAT NAME IN FRONT OF ME AGAIN.
Y-YES, BOSS!

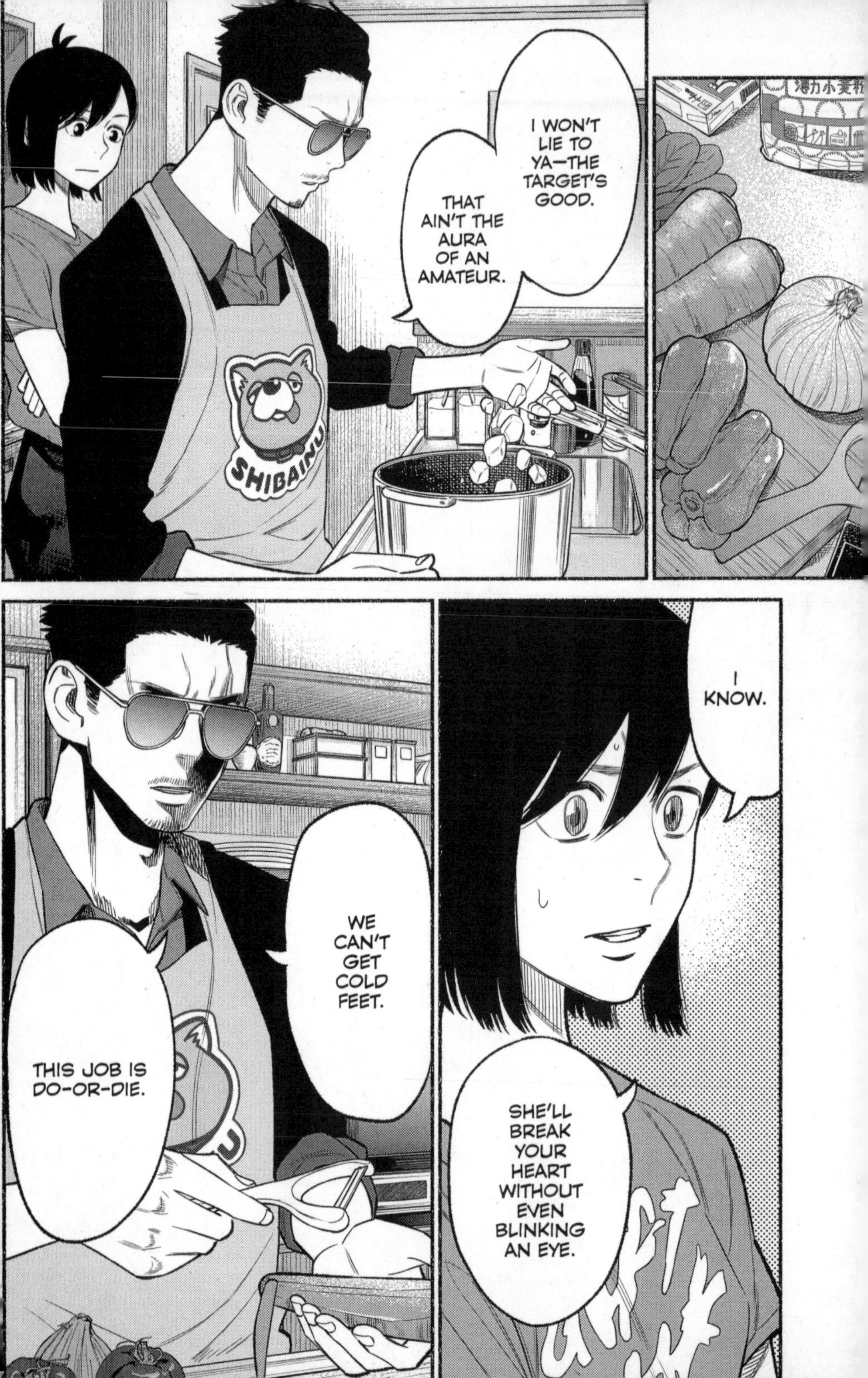
I WON'T LIE TO YA—THE TARGET'S GOOD.
THAT AIN'T THE AURA OF AN AMATEUR.
SHIBAINU
I KNOW.
SHE'LL BREAK YOUR HEART WITHOUT EVEN BLINKING AN EYE.
WE CAN'T GET COLD FEET.
THIS JOB IS DO-OR-DIE.

THAT PATTY IS NOTHIN' LESS THAN 100 PERCENT...

...UNCUT BEEF!

W...

WOULDN'T DREAM OF IT!

SHE CAUGHT ON...

...EVEN AFTER WE CHOPPED IT UP THAT SMALL?!

THEN WHAT DO YOU CALL THESE ONIONS? HMMM?

THIS CURRY IS...

I SMELL IT.

...SOME CURRY? I HEARD YA LOVE CURRY TOO!

H... HOW 'BOUT...

THIS KID'S GOT THE NOSE OF A DRUG-DETECTION DOG!

YOU MAY HAVE TURNED IT INTO A PASTE AND BOILED IT, BUT...

...THERE'S CARROT IN HERE, ISN'T THERE?

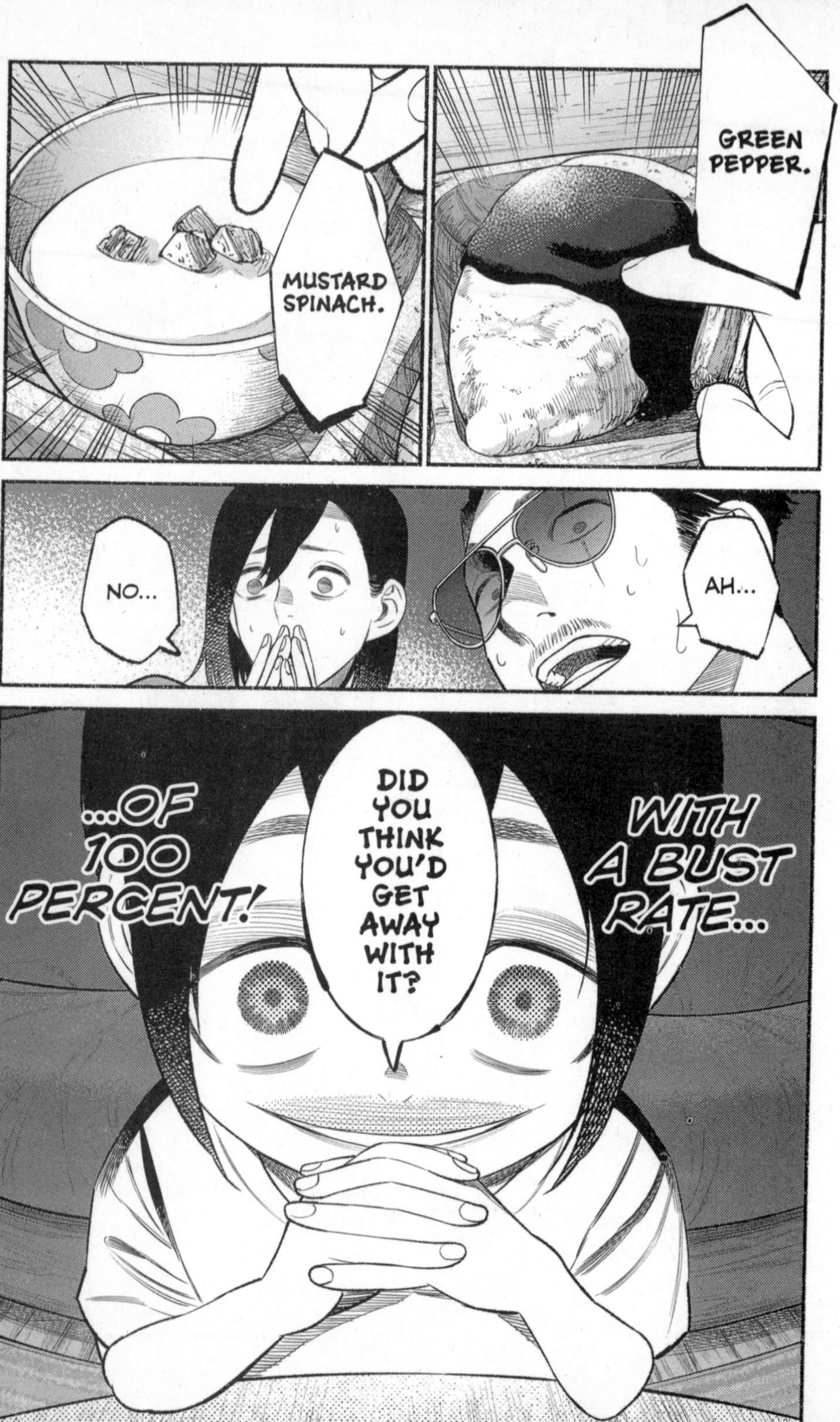
GREEN PEPPER.
MUSTARD SPINACH.
AH...
NO...
WITH A BUST RATE...
DID YOU THINK YOU'D GET AWAY WITH IT?
...OF 100 PERCENT!

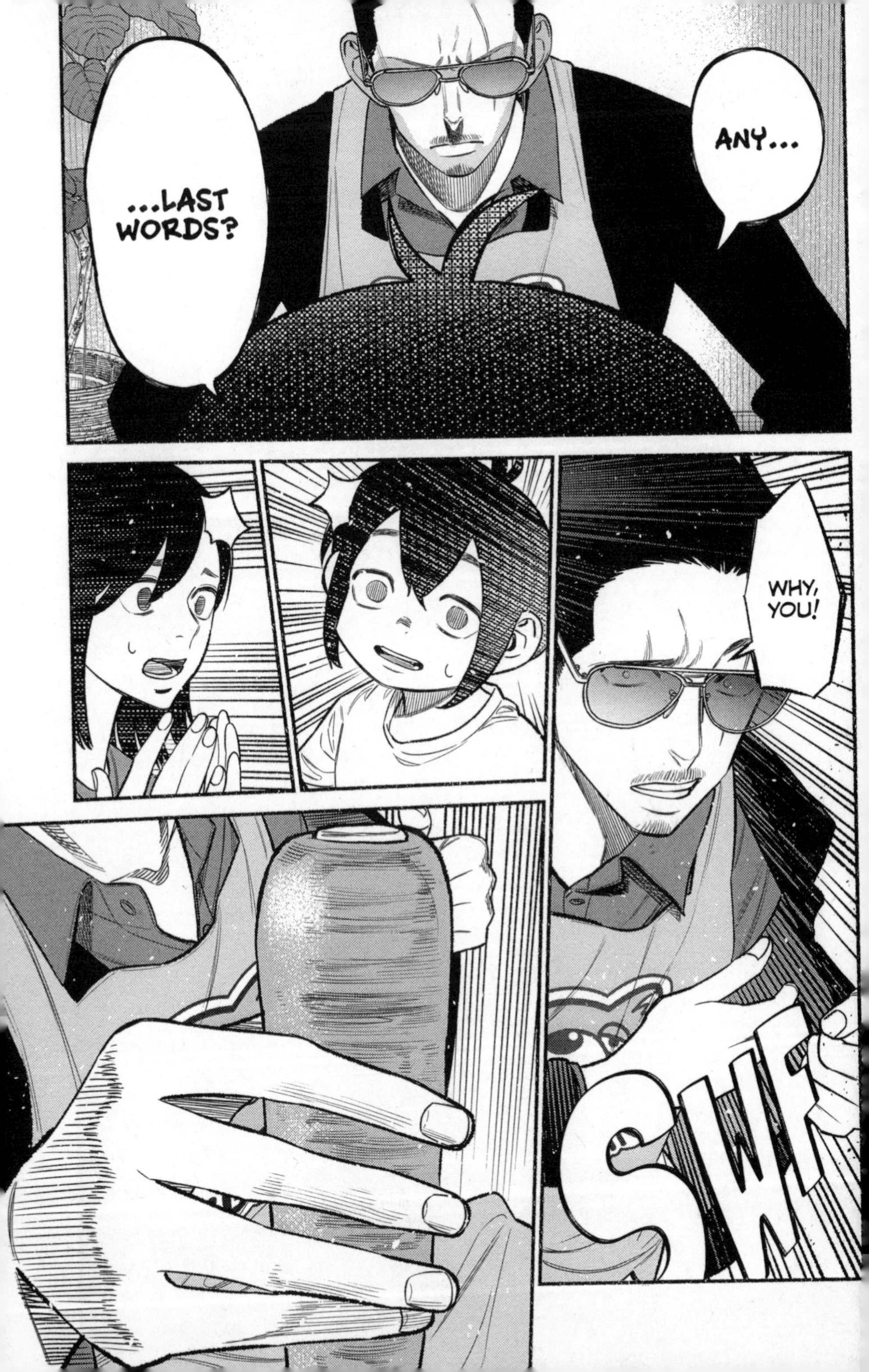
ANY...
...LAST WORDS?
WHY, YOU!

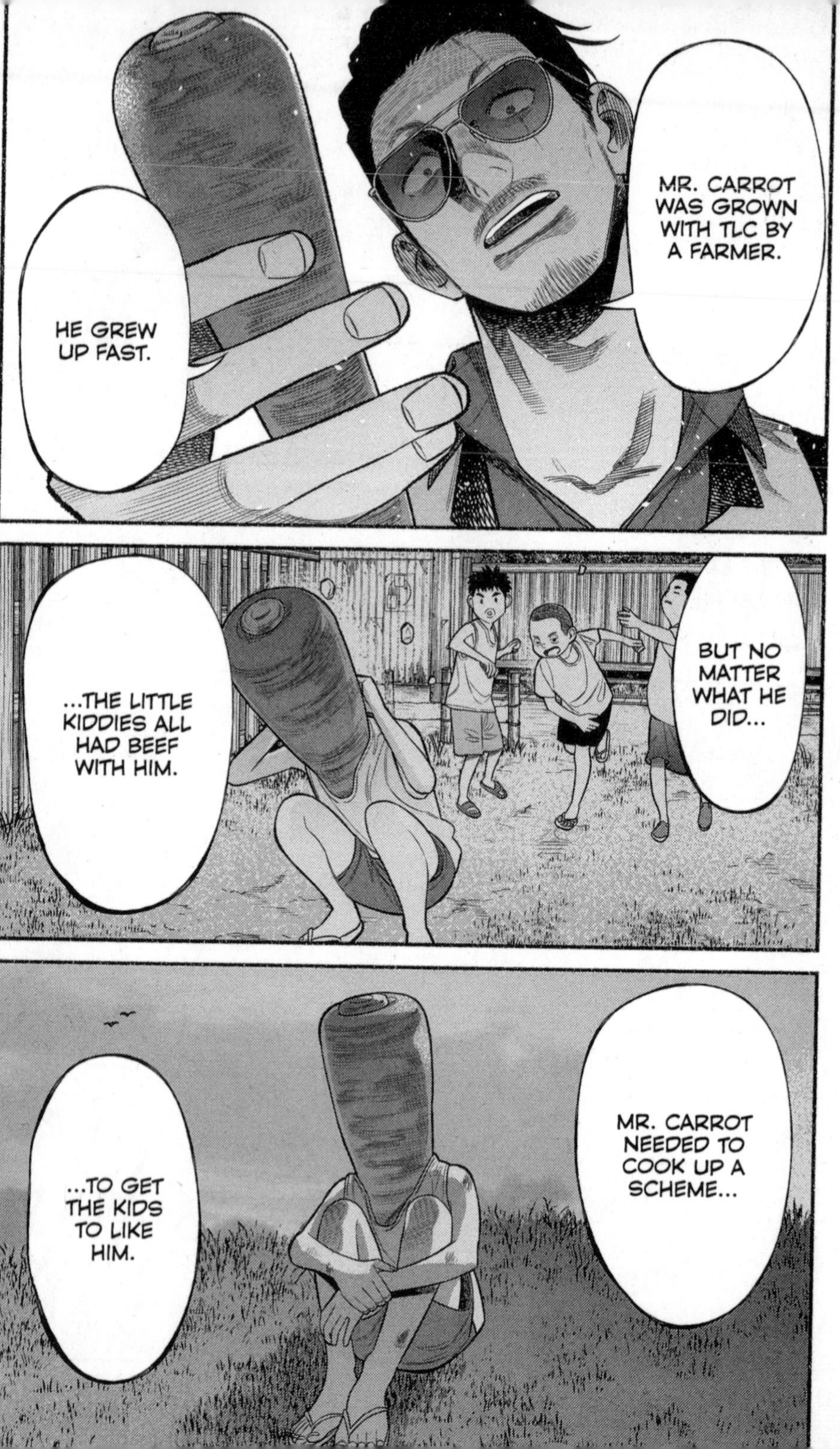
MR. CARROT WAS GROWN WITH TLC BY A FARMER.
HE GREW UP FAST.
BUT NO MATTER WHAT HE DID...
...THE LITTLE KIDDIES ALL HAD BEEF WITH HIM.
MR. CARROT NEEDED TO COOK UP A SCHEME...
...TO GET THE KIDS TO LIKE HIM.

"KIDS LOVE CURRY."

"PLEASE PUT ME IN CURRY."

SO HE CAME TO ME ASKIN' FOR A FAVOR.

AFTER HE'D MADE HIS CASE...

...HE GAVE A SMALL, SAD SMILE.

"THAT WAY, THEY'LL EAT ME."

77

I GUESS I CAN EAT A LITTLE—

THEN, MR. CARROT...

...GOT EVISCERATED IN THE BLENDER...

MR. CARROT...

DIDN'T NEED THAT LAST PART.

NOPE, NOPE, NOPE.

...AND I DROWNED 'IM...

...IN A BOILING POT OF CURRY.

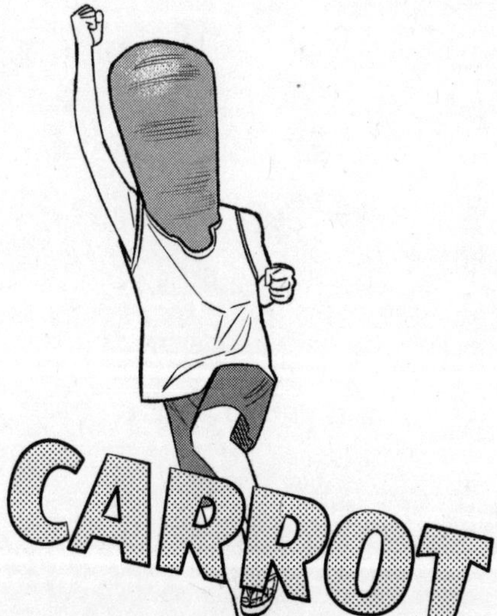
CARROT

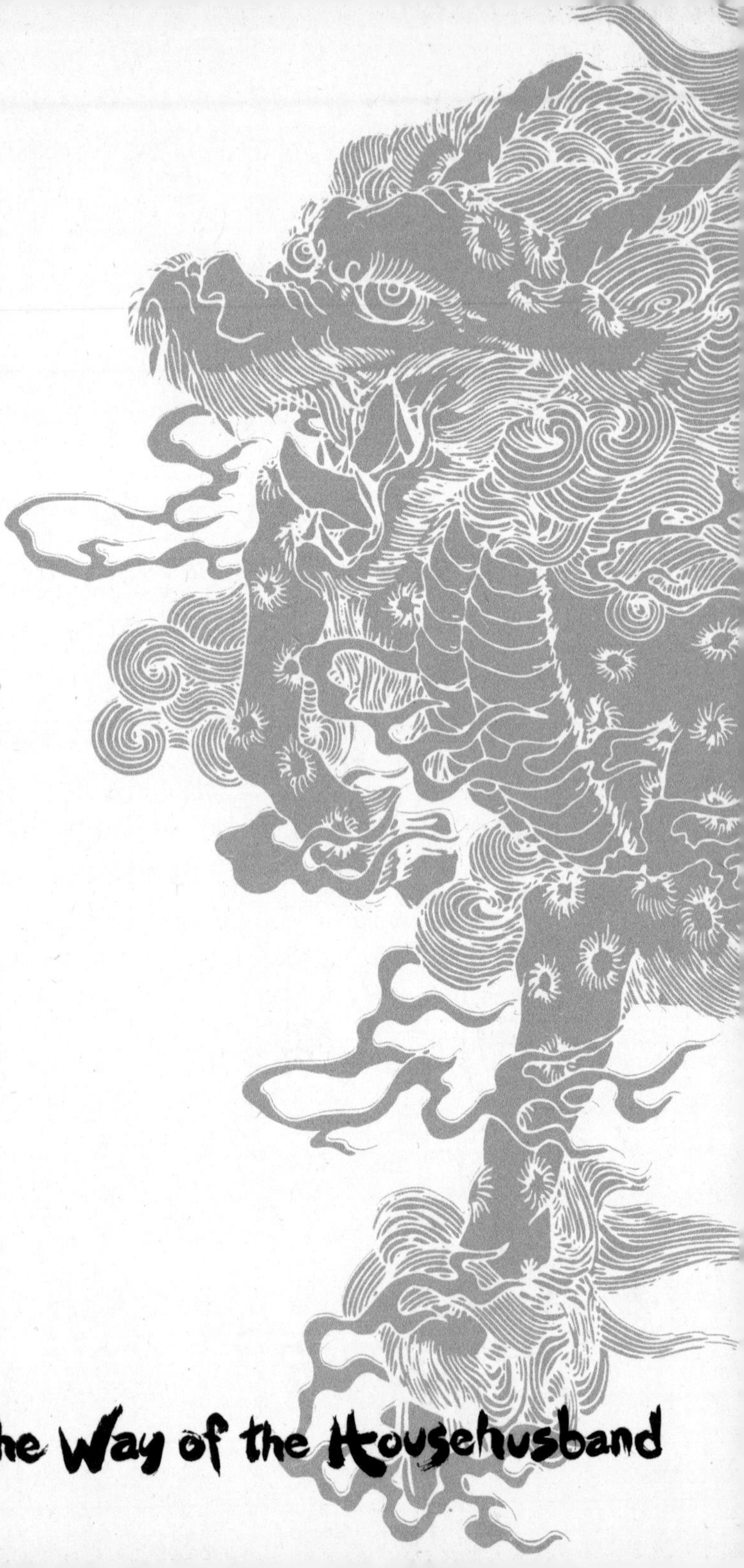

The Way of the Househusband

CHAPTER 78

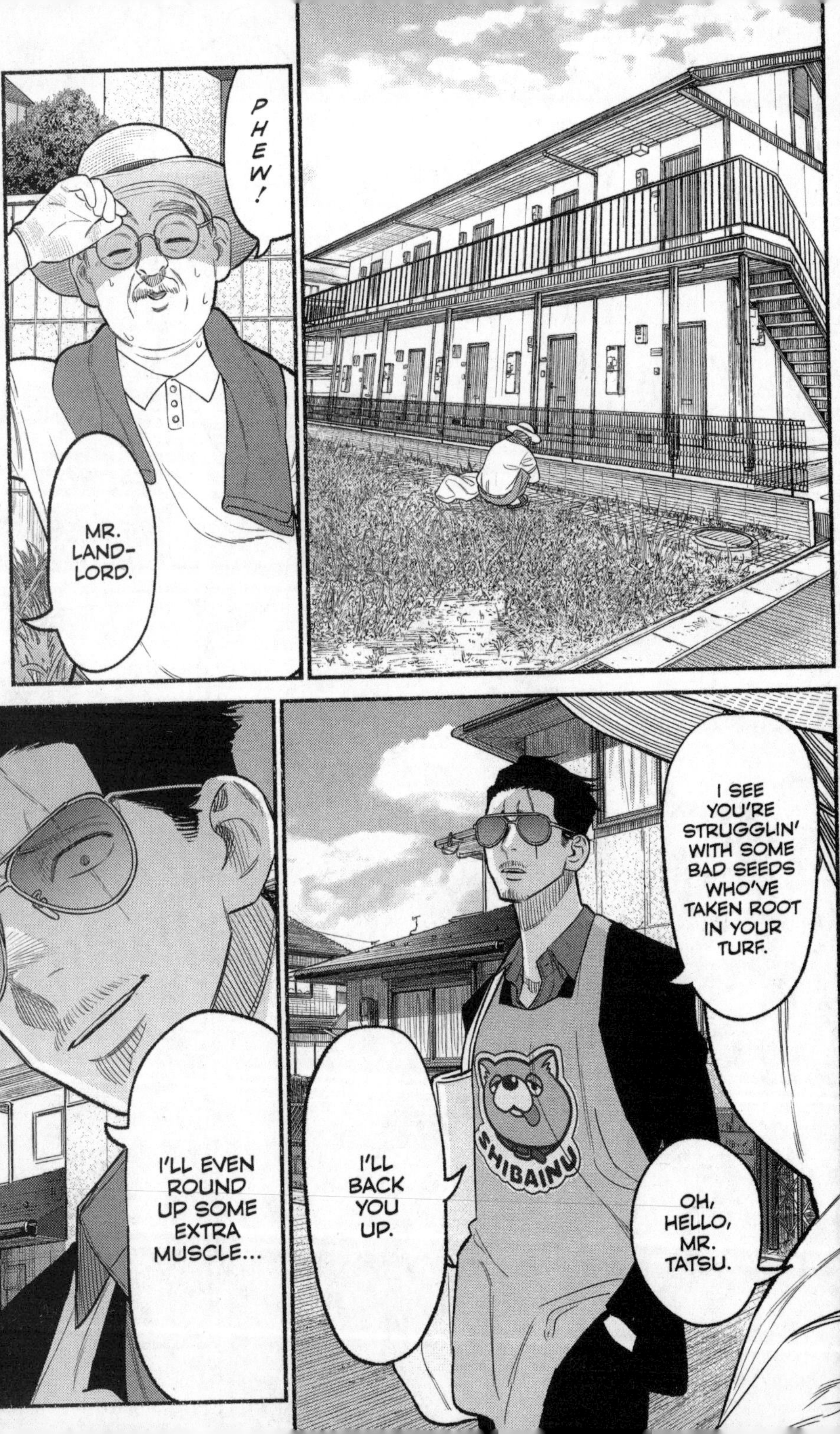
PHEW!
MR. LANDLORD.
OH, HELLO, MR. TATSU.
I SEE YOU'RE STRUGGLIN' WITH SOME BAD SEEDS WHO'VE TAKEN ROOT IN YOUR TURF.
SHIBAINU
I'LL BACK YOU UP.
I'LL EVEN ROUND UP SOME EXTRA MUSCLE...

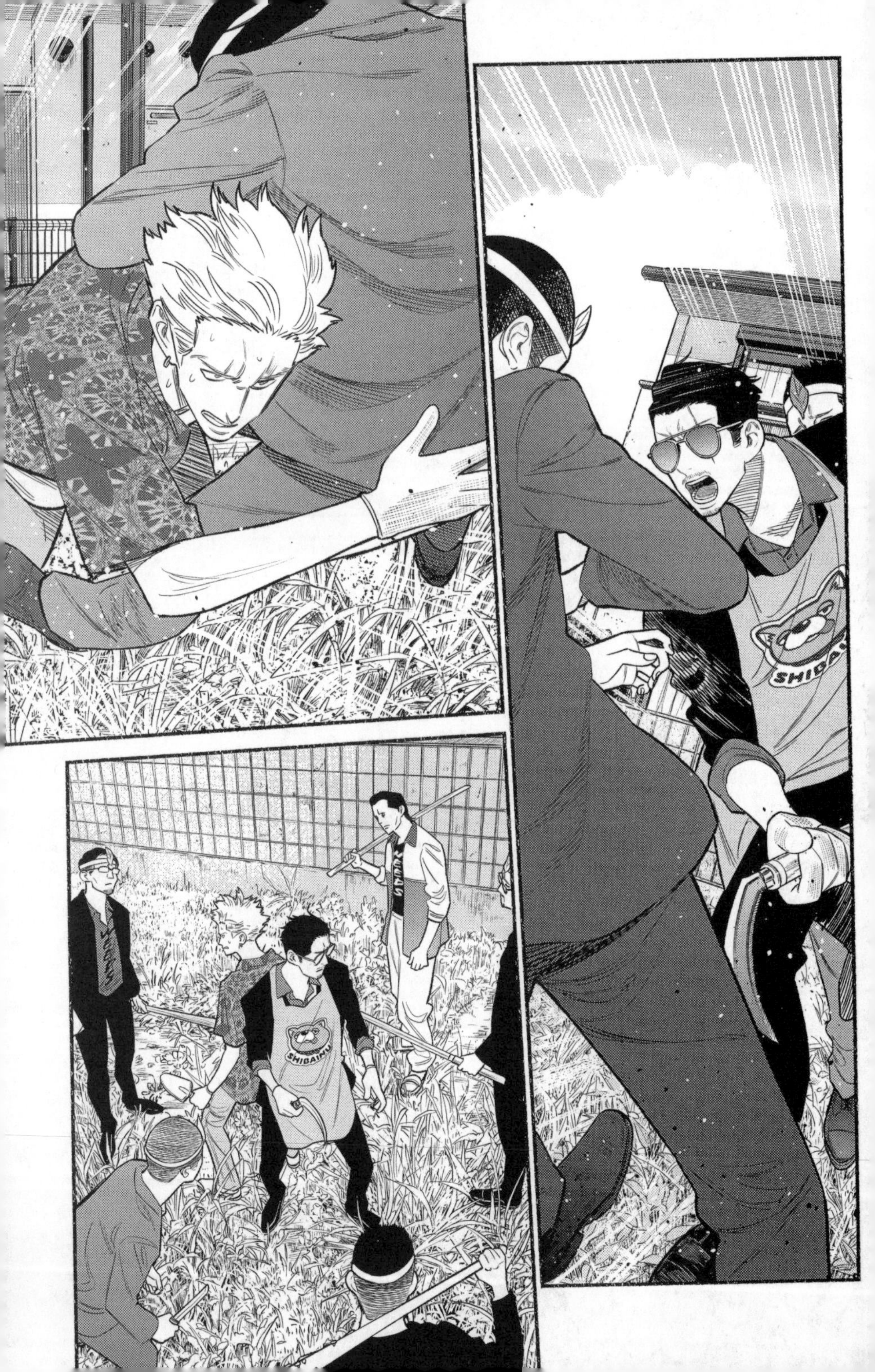
SHIBAINU

I DEALT WITH THE GUYS OVER HERE...

!

...BOSS!

HFF!

HFF!

THESE GUYS SPROUT BACK IN NO TIME...

DAMN IT, KID, YA DIDN'T PULL OUT THE ROOTS.

...UNLESS YA ROOT OUT EVERY LAST ONE.

I'LL FINISH 'EM OFF...

MIX SOME VIN-EGAR...

...WITH A SPRAY OF BULLETS FROM *THIS*!

SPECIAL HERBICIDE #1

...AND DETER-GENT.

THE ACIDITY OF VINEGAR MAKES IT AN EFFECTIVE WEED KILLER.

WHOA. YOU CAN USE VINEGAR LIKE THAT?

NOT ONLY IS IT EASY TO MAKE, IT'S SAFE TO USE AROUND KIDS AND PETS!

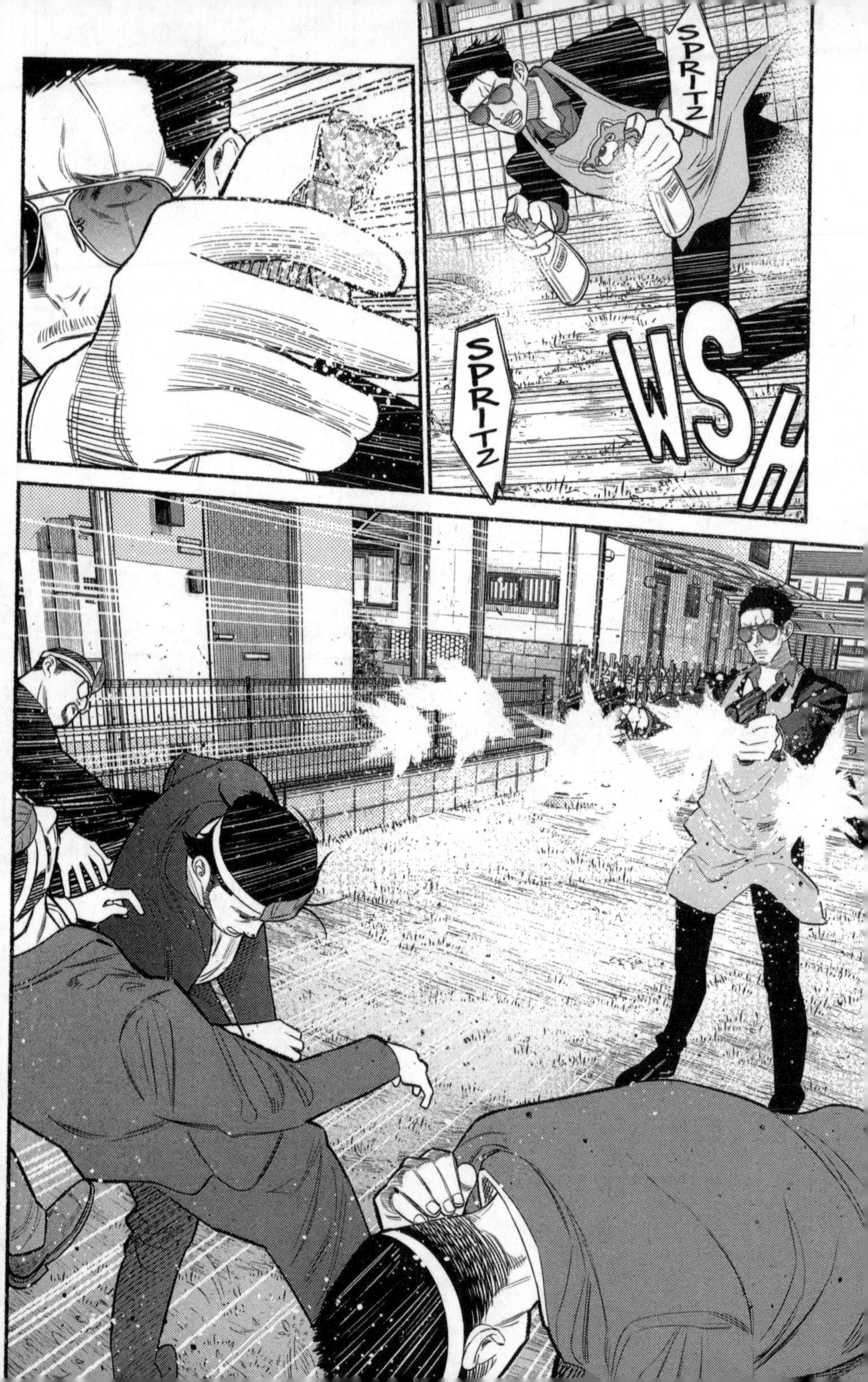
SPRITZ
WSH
SPRITZ

90

THAT'S A FUN LITTLE COCK-TAIL.

OHO!

IS THIS APPLE CIDER VINEGAR?

THE CITRIC ACID IN VINEGAR BOTH BOOSTS ENERGY AND HELPS CONTROL BLOOD SUGAR.

BUT IMBIBE WITH CAUTION. TOO MUCH OF THIS STUFF WILL MESS YOU UP...YOUR ESOPHAGUS AND STOMACH, TO BE EXACT.

IT'LL ERODE THE ENAMEL RIGHT OFF YOUR TEETH TOO, SO ORAL CARE IS INDIS-PENSABLE AFTER-WARD...

THE ANTIOXIDANTS ARE GOOD FOR THE SKIN AND PREVENT OSTEOPOROSIS.

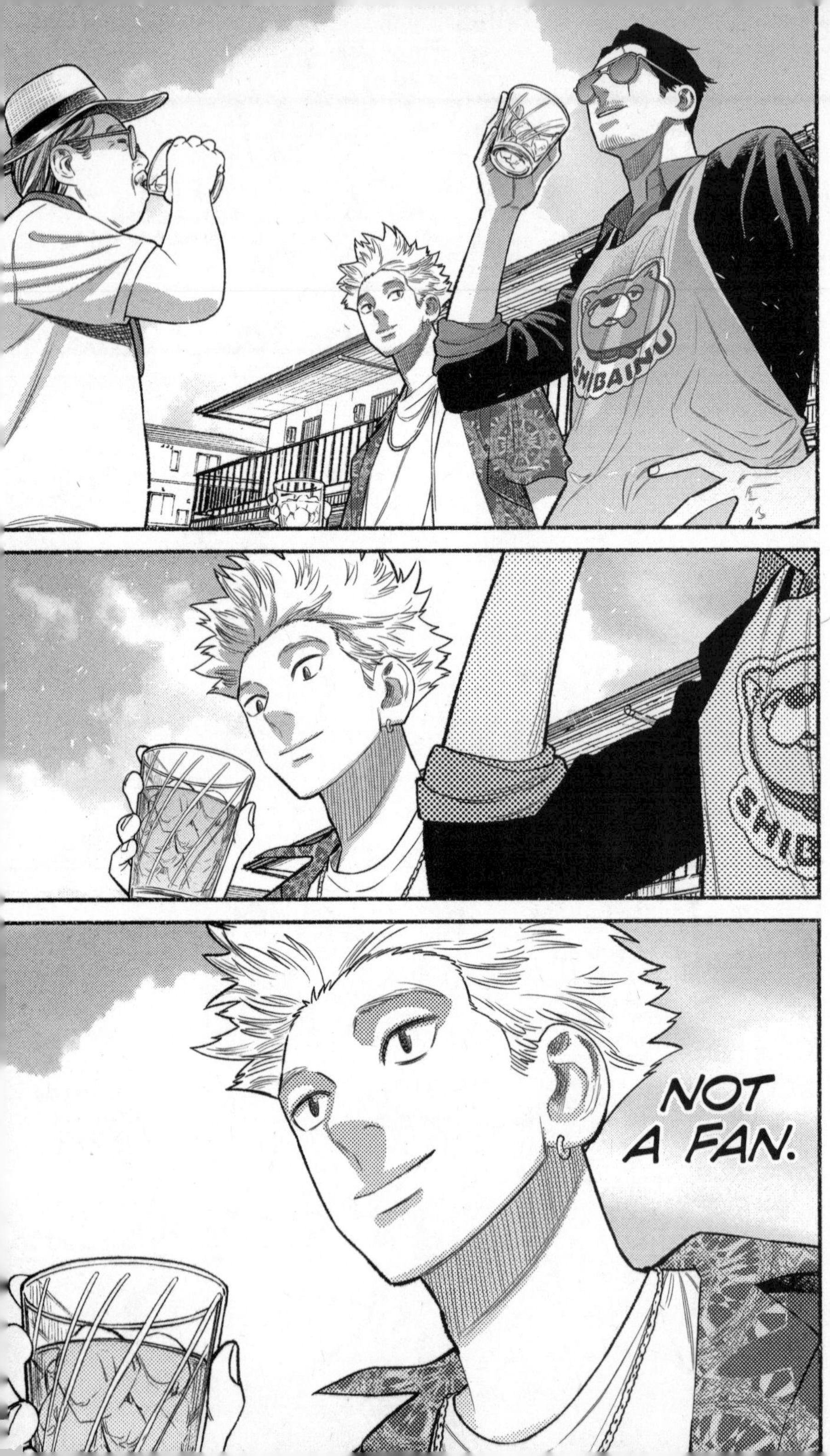
SHIBAINU
NOT A FAN.

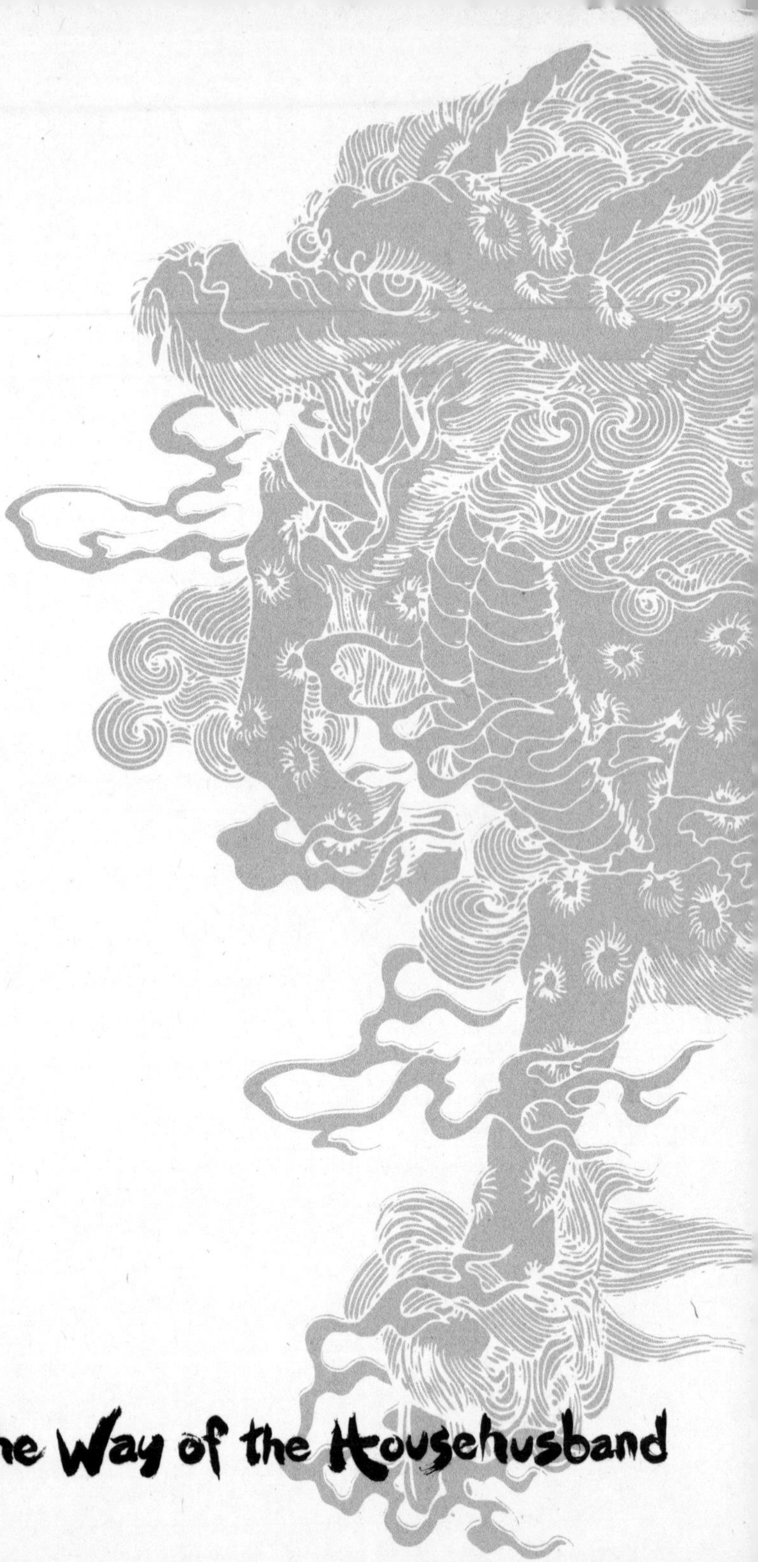

The Way of the Househusband

CHAPTER 79

DON'T MAKE LIGHT OF STAG BEETLES!

HA!

THE HEAD HONCHO OF BUGS ?!

EVER BEEN CAUGHT IN THEIR MANDIBLES?

NO LIE, THOSE THINGS WILL SEND YOUR PINKY FLYING!

NOW YER JUST EXAGGERATIN'.

OH NO. THERE'S NO BACKIN' DOWN AFTER ALL THE SHADE THIS PUNK THREW.

FORGET IT, MR. TATSU. I DON'T CARE *THAT* MUCH.

NO THANKS.

DON'T WORRY, SHORT STUFF—I'LL BRING YOU HIS HEAD!

LET THE BUG WARS BEGIN.

ARE THEY EVEN LISTEN-ING?

SO THIS IS THE FIGHTER? I LIKE THE CUT OF HIS JIB.

COOL, RIGHT?!

LET ME SHOW YA WHAT THE FAMILY'S BACKIN' CAN DO FOR YA.

WELL, MR. RHINO ...

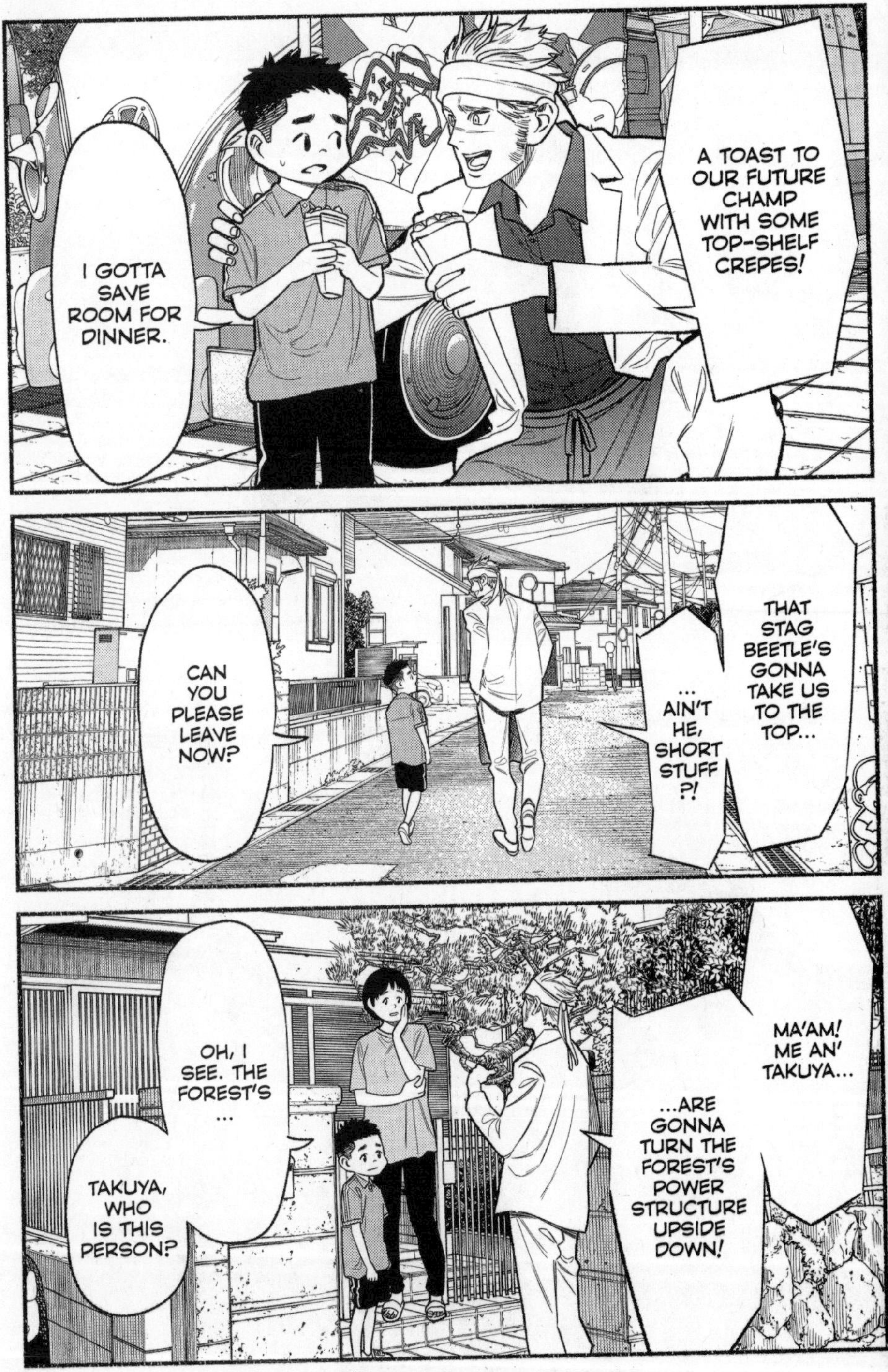
A TOAST TO OUR FUTURE CHAMP WITH SOME TOP-SHELF CREPES!
I GOTTA SAVE ROOM FOR DINNER.
THAT STAG BEETLE'S GONNA TAKE US TO THE TOP...
... AIN'T HE, SHORT STUFF?!
CAN YOU PLEASE LEAVE NOW?
MA'AM! ME AN' TAKUYA...
...ARE GONNA TURN THE FOREST'S POWER STRUCTURE UPSIDE DOWN!
OH, I SEE. THE FOREST'S ...
TAKUYA, WHO IS THIS PERSON?

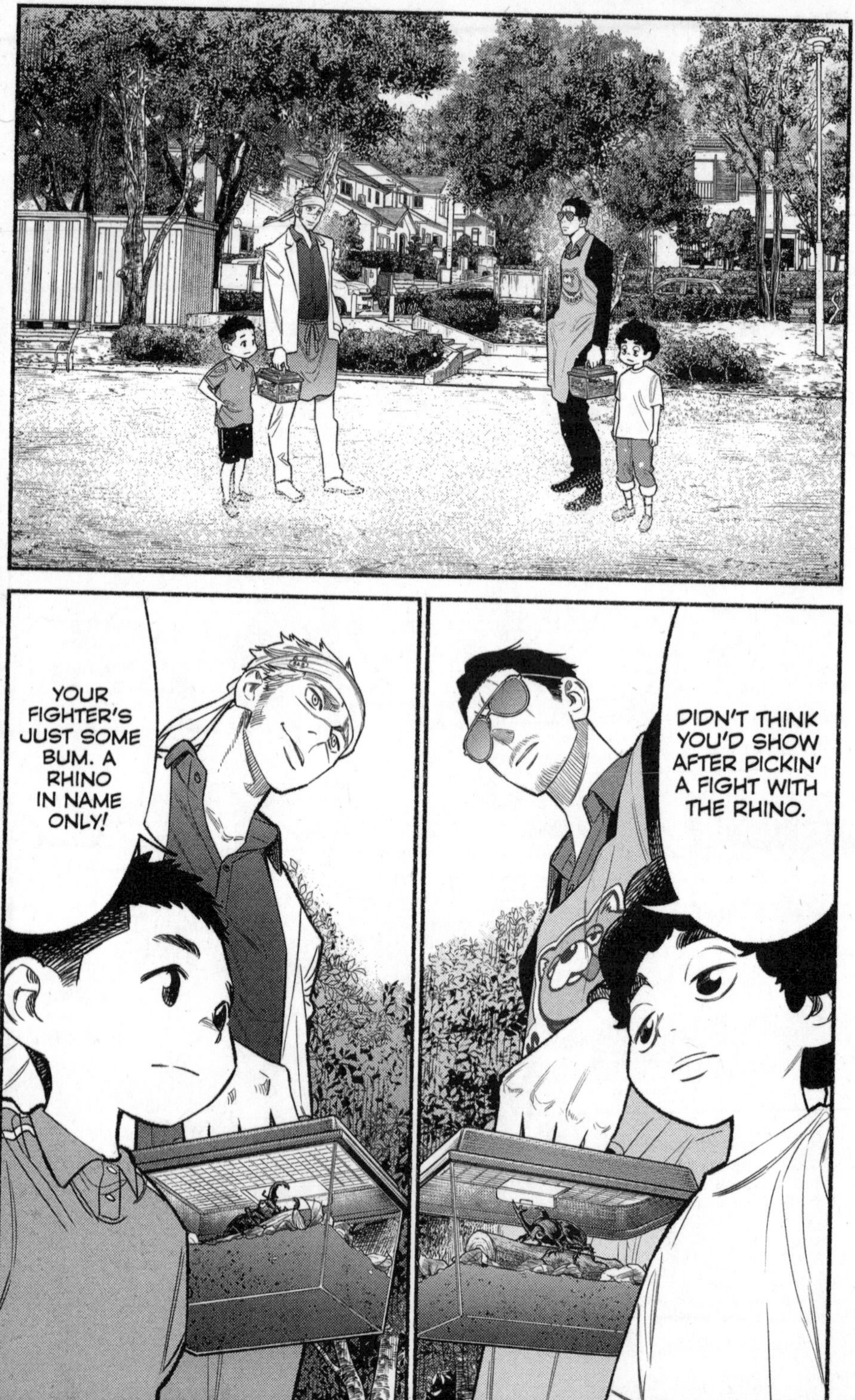
DIDN'T THINK YOU'D SHOW AFTER PICKIN' A FIGHT WITH THE RHINO.
YOUR FIGHTER'S JUST SOME BUM. A RHINO IN NAME ONLY!

WASTE 'IM, DAGGER!

SLICE 'IM IN TWO, BLADE!

READYYY...

...FIGHT!

IT'S A MIYAMA STAG BEETLE.

GEEZ, THESE GROWN-UPS HAVE A LOT OF ENERGY.

NICE!

SEND 'IM BACK TO THE CLINK!

THAT'S THE WAY! PUNCH HIS LIGHTS OUT!

SO WEIRD.

AH! THE STAG BEETLE CLIMBED ON TOP.

GRp

HA! GOT 'EM!

USE FINGER-CUTTING GUILLOTINE!

NOW! GO!

MAGNUM UNDERARM THROW!

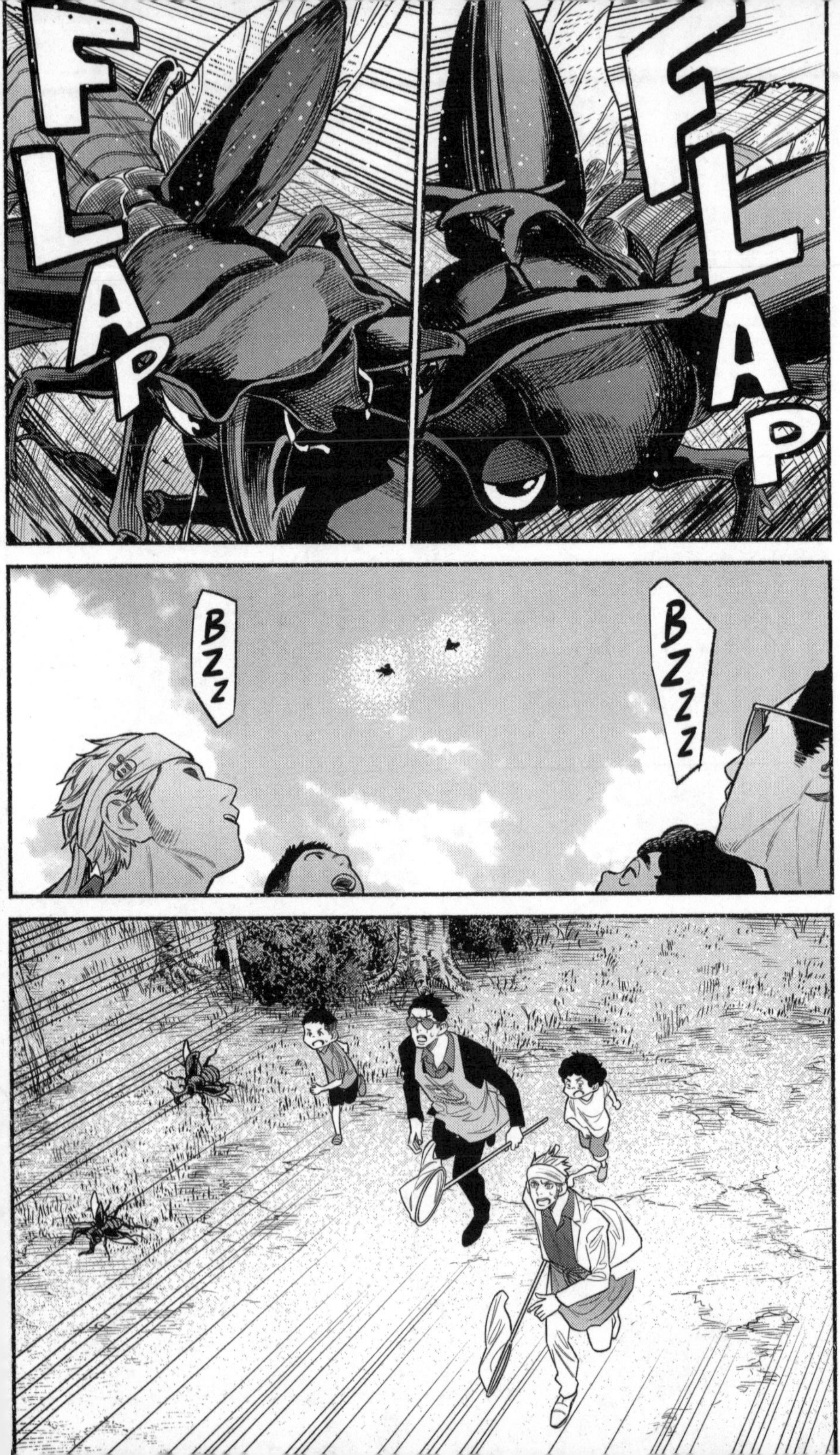
FLAP
FLAP
BZZZZ
BZZ

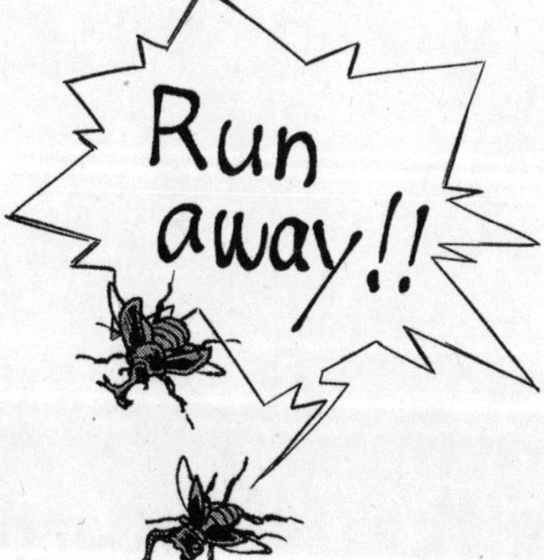
Run away!!

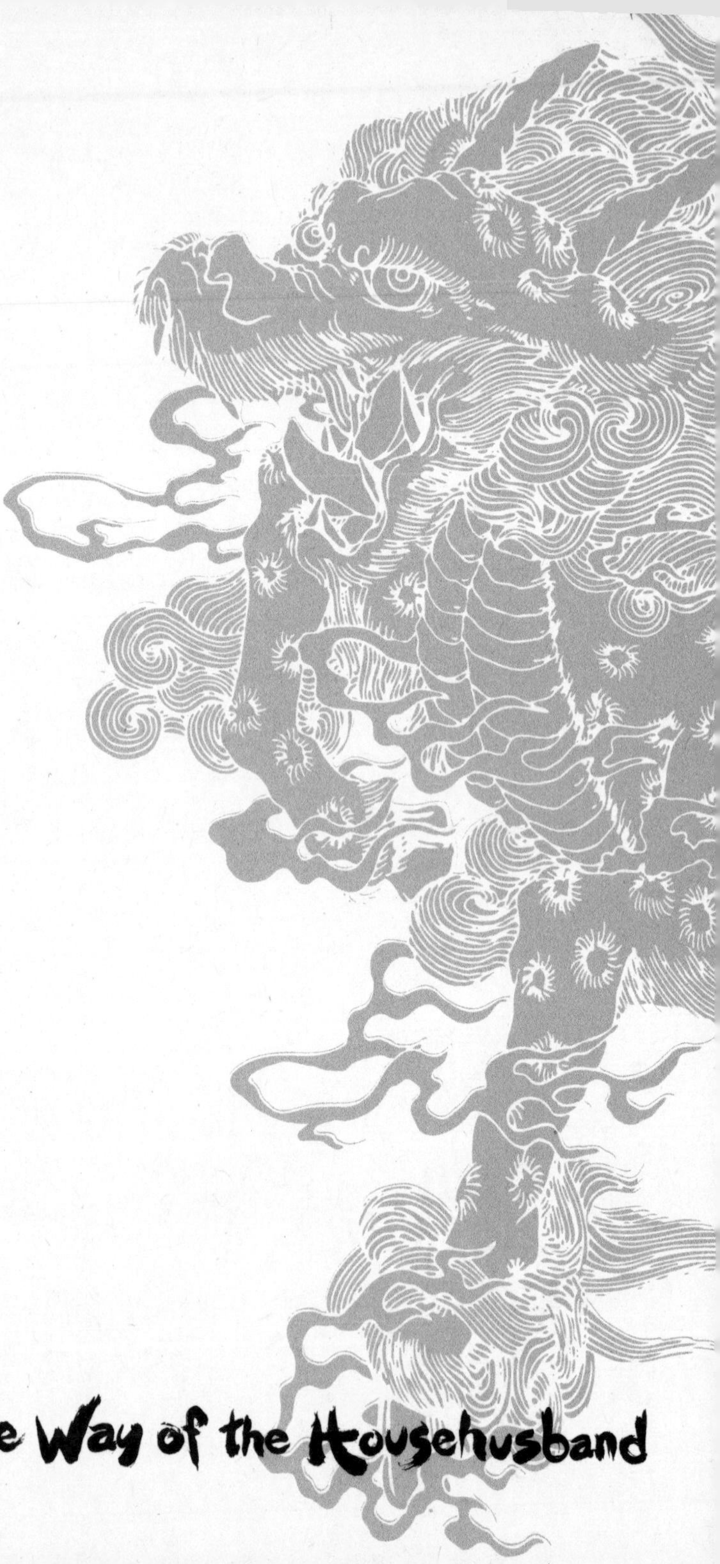

The Way of the Househusband

CHAPTER 80

METALWARE STORES LIKE MINE...

...ARE GETTING FEWER SHOPPERS THESE DAYS.

IT'S THE SAME AT MY WOMEN'S CLOTHING STORE.

WELL, YOU CAN BUY JUST ABOUT ANYTHING AT A SHOPPING MALL THESE DAYS...

IT'S A SIGN OF THE TIMES, I S'POSE.

THAT AIN'T RIGHT.

POPS, YOUR BLADES ARE THE BEST!

M-MR. TATSUP?! WHAT ARE YOU PLANNING TO DO?!

THEY'RE MUSCLIN' IN ON YER TURF. YA CAN'T TAKE THAT LYIN' DOWN!

I MAY NOT LOOK IT...

...BUT I DID DABBLE IN DEALIN' BACK IN THE DAY. THAT'S RIGHT...I WAS A STREET HAWKER!

THOK

STEP ON UP! DON'T BE SHY!!!

UNLESS YER IN A *HURRY*...

...I *SUGGEST* YA STICK AROUND AN' HAVE A LISTEN!!!

ANAMONO CORPORATION

HUH? WHAT? WHAT'S HE DOING?

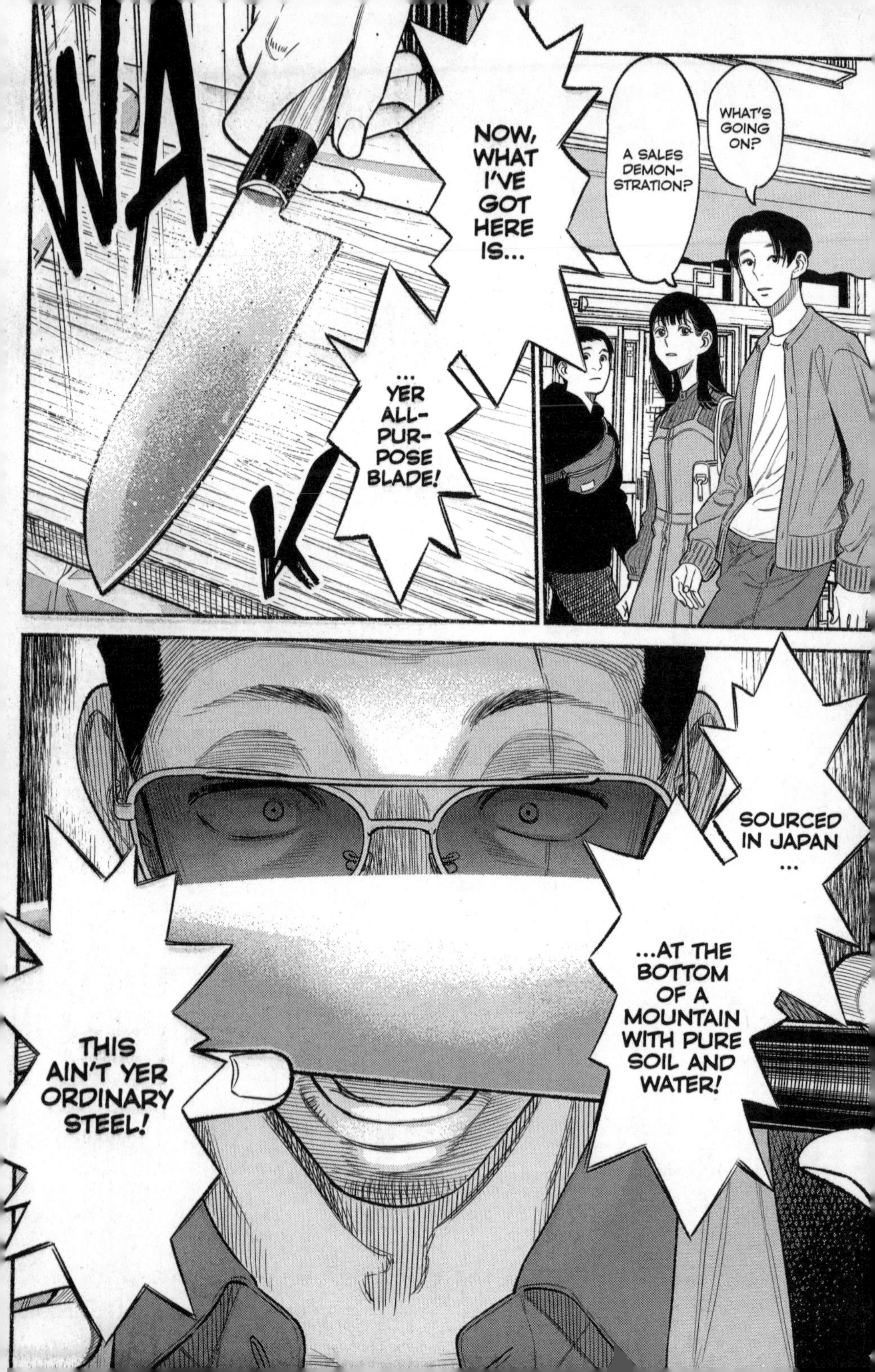
WHAT'S GOING ON?
A SALES DEMONSTRATION?
NOW, WHAT I'VE GOT HERE IS...
WAK
...YER ALL-PURPOSE BLADE!
SOURCED IN JAPAN...
...AT THE BOTTOM OF A MOUNTAIN WITH PURE SOIL AND WATER!
THIS AIN'T YER ORDINARY STEEL!

DULL BLADES HAVE SHARP TIPS AND A HEEL THAT WON'T CUT.

BUT A REAL BLADE CAN CUT THROUGH BAMBOO!

CH

OK

SCARY!

AND EVEN AFTER ALL THAT USE, THE TIP IS IN TIP-TOP SHAPE!

IT WON'T BEND!

IT WON'T BREAK!

TH UK

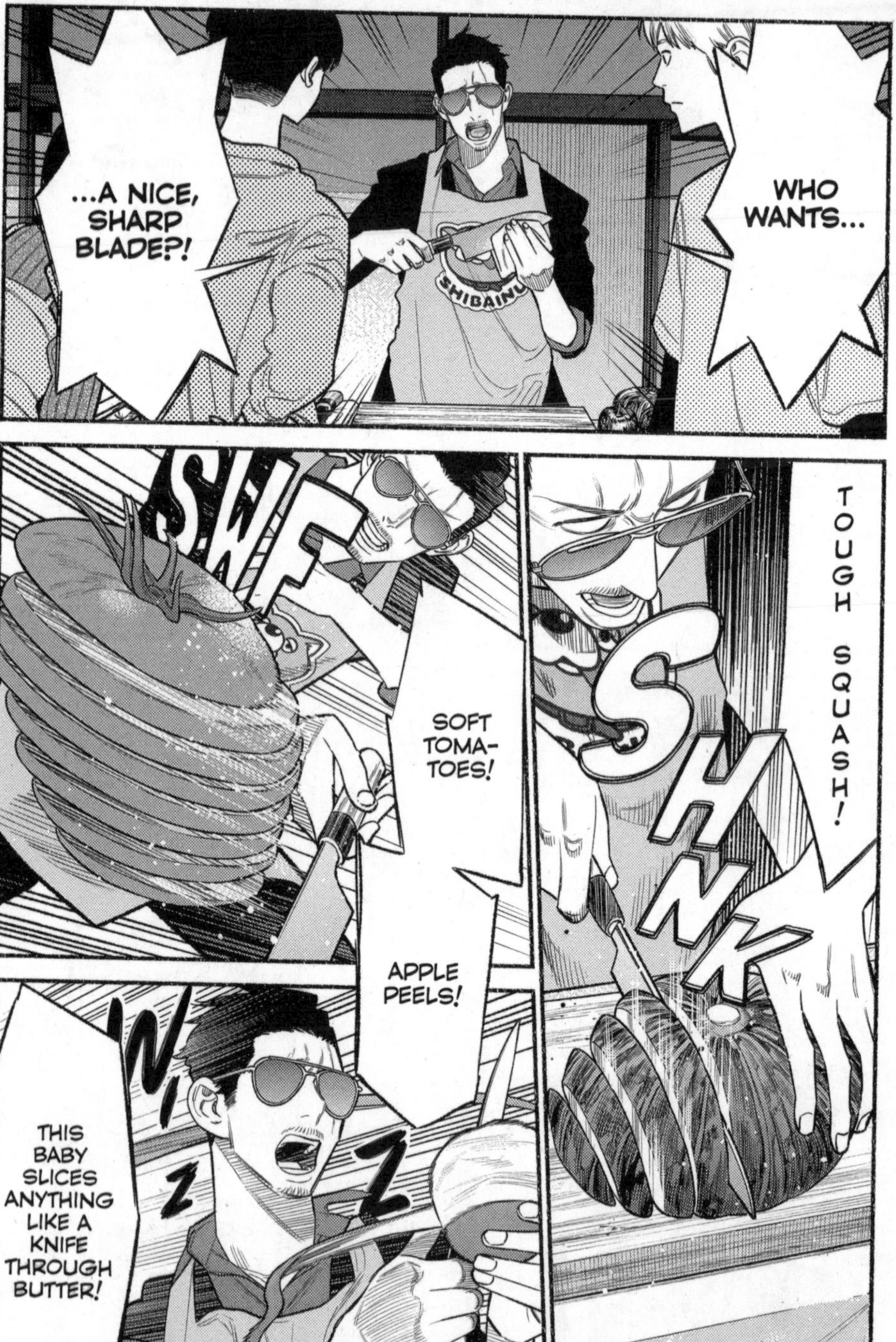
WHO WANTS...
...A NICE, SHARP BLADE?!
SHIBAINU
TOUGH SQUASH!
SHNK
SWF
SOFT TOMATOES!
APPLE PEELS!
THIS BABY SLICES ANYTHING LIKE A KNIFE THROUGH BUTTER!

IT'S PERFECT FOR FILLETIN' FISH!

YOU CAN EVEN USE IT FOR CHOPPIN' UP CHICKEN WITH THE SKIN STILL ON!

USE IT FOR YER NEXT HIT!

USE IT FOR ATONE-MENT!

I'LL TAKE ONE!

THERE WAS SOME SKETCHY STUFF MIXED IN THERE.

STEP ON UP AND TRY IT FOR YOUR-SELVES!

YOU'RE GONNA RUN ME OUTTA BUSINESS HAGGLIN' LIKE THAT, KID.

FUN FACT...

THE VERSION OF THE *POLICURE* SWEATER THAT DEPICTS THE NEW MAGICAL GIRL ALONE IS ACTUALLY A PRETTY RARE FIND DUE TO ITS LIMITED PRODUCTION RUN.

HEH!

AFTER IT PROVED MORE POPULAR THAN EXPECTED, ADDITIONAL SWEATERS WERE PRODUCED, BUT THEIR QUALITY DIDN'T MATCH UP TO THE ORIGINAL PRODUCT.

PLEASURE DOIN' BUSINESS!

CLASP

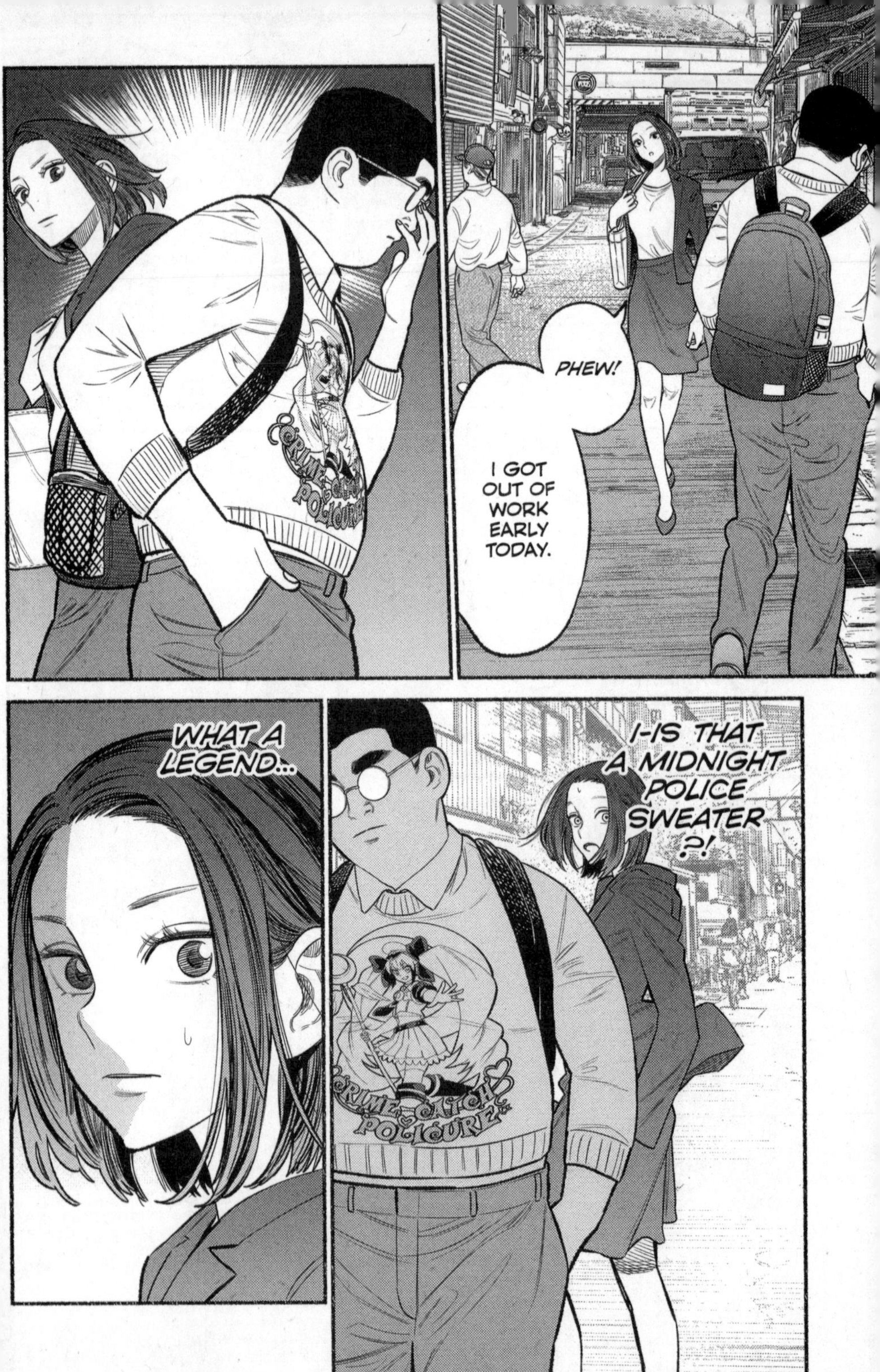
PHEW!
I GOT OUT OF WORK EARLY TODAY.
I-IS THAT A MIDNIGHT POLICE SWEATER?!
WHAT A LEGEND...

CRIME CATCH POLICURE

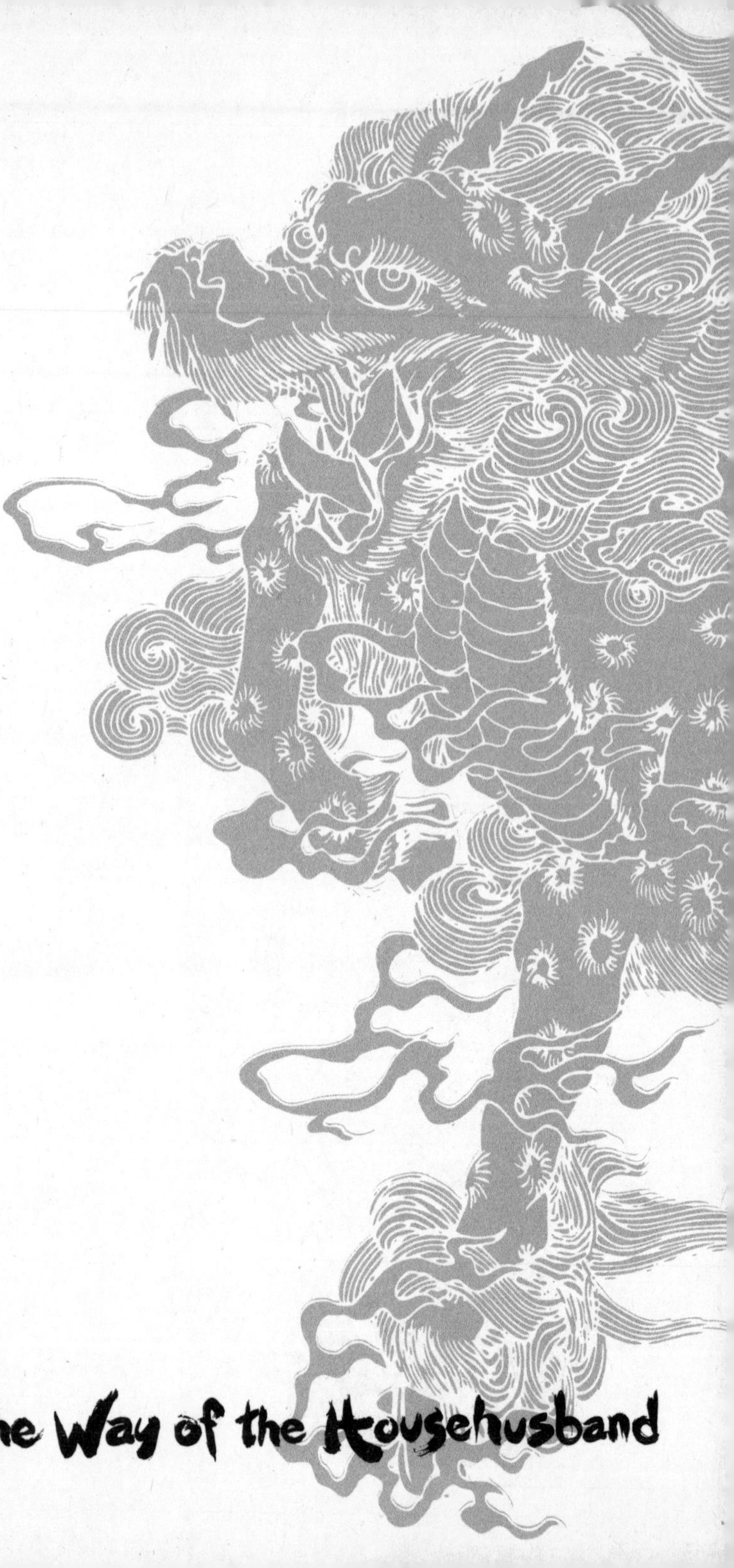

The Way of the Househusband

THIS IS WHAT THE YOUNG FOLKS ARE INTO THESE DAYS?

GOTTA KEEP APPRISED OF THE LATEST TRENDS TO PROTECT YER HUSTLE, BOSS.

CHAPTER 81

ONE LOVE BEAM OMELET RICE.

HERE YOU ARE!

... POWER!

M-MAGICAL MEOW-MEOW...

MAGICAL MEOW-MEOW POWER!

OKAY, MASTERS!

ARE YOU READY TO REPEAT THE MAGIC WORDS AFTER ME ?!

NN... MEOW MEOW?

NN... MEOW MEOW...

LOVE BEAM, LOVE BEAM, ACTIVATE!

LOVE MAKES FOOD TASTIER ON OUR PLATES!

SHIBAINU

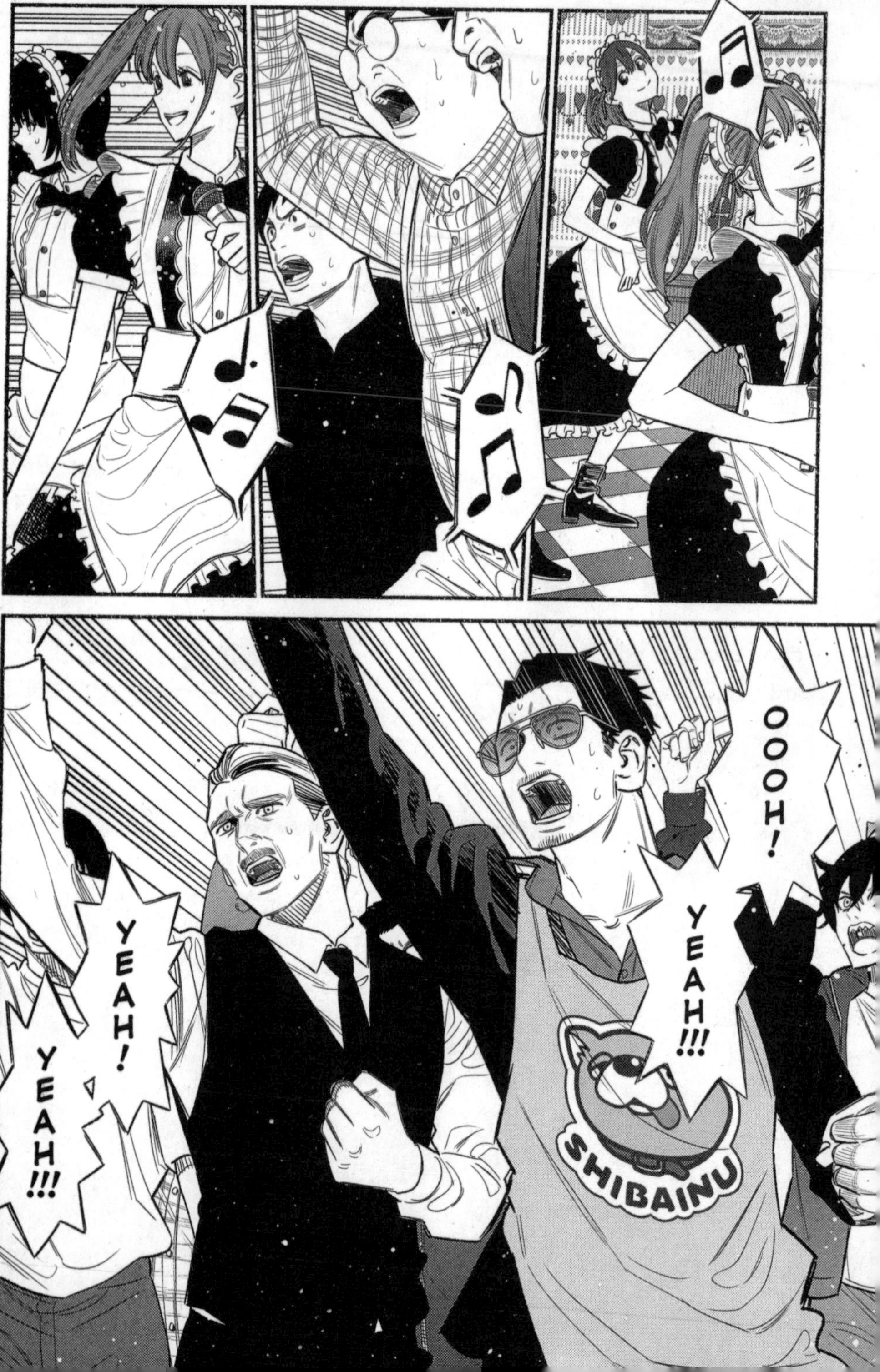
OOOH!
YEAH!!!
SHIBAINU
YEAH!
YEAH!!!

THEY
CALL
THAT LIVE
MUSIC,
BOSS.

HFF...
HFF...

WHAT
WAS THAT
PERFOR-
MANCE
ABOUT?

HFF...
HFF...

IT'S NOT
AS THOUGH I
KNOW ANYONE
I COULD ASK
TO PERFORM.

I DON'T
SEE HOW
JINGI
TEI CAN
COMPETE
WITH
THAT.

LIVE
MUSIC?

...I HAPPEN
TO KNOW A
GUY IN THE
MUSIC BIZ...

IF IT'S
CON-
TACTS
YOU
NEED...

JINGI TEI IS MY GO-TO LUNCH BREAK LOCATION.

IT'S MY TIME TO RELAX.

JINGI TEI
HOUSE OF HONOR

THE RETRO ATMOSPHERE.

LUNCH SPECIALS THAT NEVER LEAVE ME DISAPPOINTED.

THE POST-MEAL COFFEE IS PLEASING TOO...

BMM CHA BMM BMM CHA♪

HMM?

OMELET RICE.

ANY RECOMMEND-DATIONS YOU WANNA MAKE FO' US?

WITH HONOR EVER UNCHANGIN', THIS GENT'S BEEN FIGHTIN' AN' SLAYIN'. A DOPE REP HE NOW GAININ'.

TWO DECADES IN THE BIZ, DAMN, THAT'S HELLA TENACIOUS.

THE MEALS, THEY COME WITH COFFEE. A CUP TA LEND SOME COLOR TO YOUR STORY.

THIS OWNER, HE'S GONNA TURN 20 INTO 40!

AAAIGHT!

FLUFFY EGGS TO BRING OUT THAT MAGIC. THE PRESENTA-TION'S ALWAYS DYNAMIC.

OVERALL, THAT DISH IS JUST CLASSIC.

MAKE SOME *NOIIISE!*

CLAP CLAP

GODA. GODA.

CLAP

SMALL CHANGE OF PLANS.

COULD YOU SHOWCASE A NEW ADDITION TO THE MENU FOR ME TOO?

THE ADULT CREAMY PARFAIT.

YO, YO!

HUH? CREAM... PARFAIT?

THE NEW CREAMY PARFAIT'S, UH...THE DESSERT OF YOUR DREAMS.

UH...IT'S A PARFAIT WITH FRUIT AND...

...WHIPPED CREAM?

OH, ACTUALLY, IT DOESN'T HAVE ANY FRUIT.

HOMIE JUST DISHED UP A THEME. DUDE'S GOT THE BIGGEST BALLS I'VE EVER SEEN. MY HEART'S RACIN' AS I THINK UP MY NEXT RHYME SCHEME.

NO FRUIT... HUH? CAN YOU CALL THAT A PARFAIT?

UUUH... SO...ITS SWEETNESS WILL BLOW YOU AWAY.

FO' REAL... UH... BUY ONE TODAY.

ACTUALLY, IT ISN'T VERY SWEET EITHER.

NOW I CAN RELAX...

GREAT. WHATEVER *THAT* WAS SEEMS TO BE OVER.

I'M TAKIN' OVER THE MIC TO LAY DOWN MORE RHYMES.

THE NAME'S TATSU AND I WORK HERE PART-TIME.

I'M A FULL-TIME HOUSE-HUSBAND.

INTO BATTLE I WEAR THIS HERE APRON.

DAMN IT. HERE WE GO AGAIN.

SHIBAINU

OUR NEWEST ADDITION IS THIS CREAMY...

THE SECRET'S THIS WHITE STUFF, THE CREAM.

...ADULT PARFAIT.

IT'LL HAVE FAT STACKS OF CASH ROLLIN' INTO OUR CAFE.

ONE DOLLOP IS THE ACE UP OUR SLEEVE.

THESE PLANTS WILL HAVE YA FLYIN' HIGH.

THE MATCHA GREEN TEA. THAT'S WHAT I MEANT TO IMPLY.

IT'S SURE TA BE A HIT, SO GIVE IT A TRY.

WHAT? DON'T TELL ME THE OWNER'S GOING TO RAP TOO!

MAKE IT A COMBO WITH CAKE FOR A DISCOUNT.

AHEM... AS HE EXPLAINED...

I AP-PRECIATE YOUR SUPPORT BIG-TIME. MOROMI ENZYME.

...OUR NEW OFFERING IS A MATCHA-FLAVORED BITTER PARFAIT.

WE'RE JINGI TEI.

HYAY. AND WE'RE HERE TO STAY.

CHICKEN FILLET.

THE HEALTH DRINK?

THE WAY OF THE HOUSEHUSBAND ⑨ END

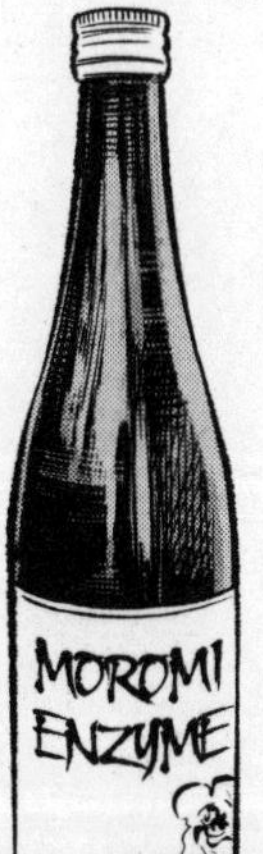
MOROMI
ENZYME

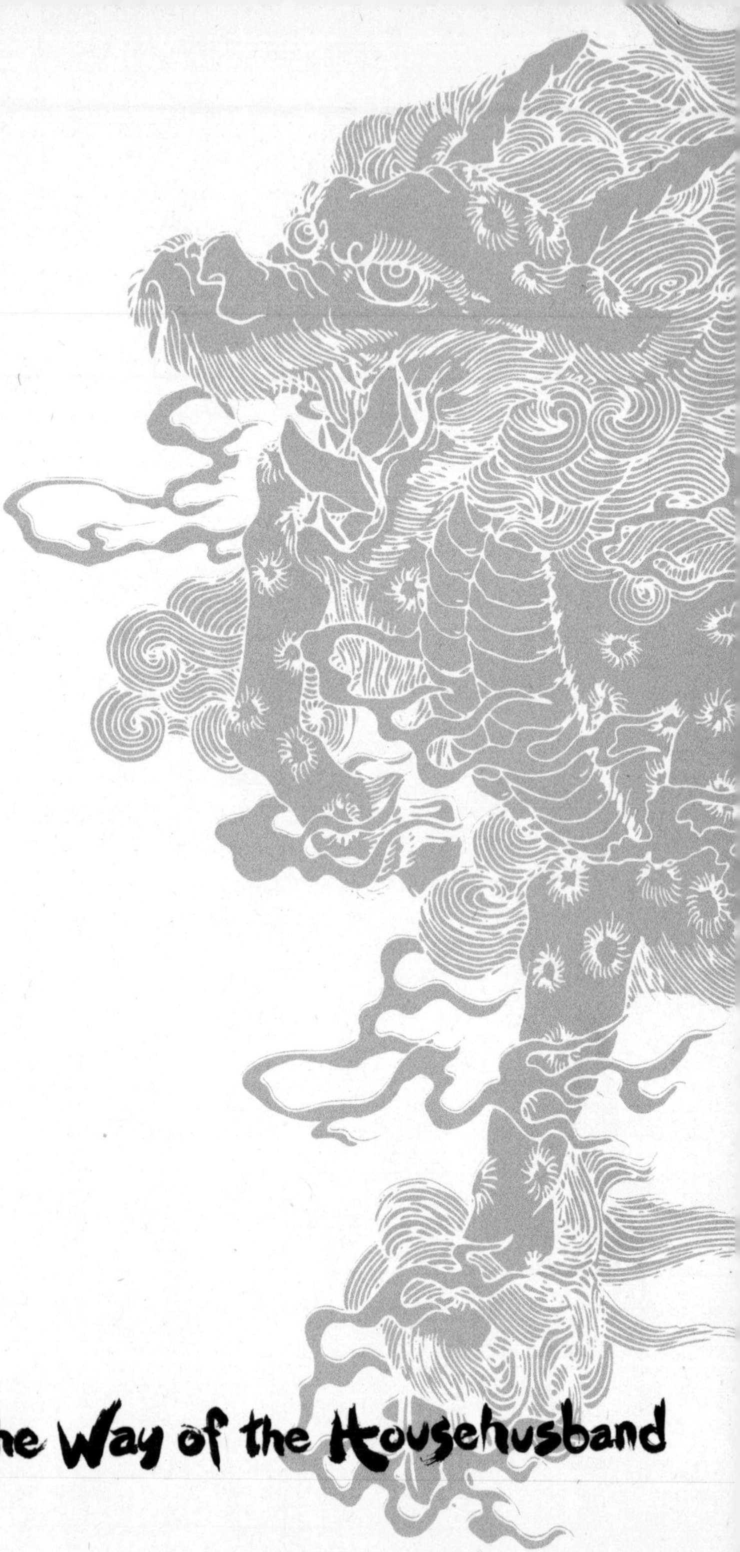

The Way of the Househusband

MORNING ROUTINE OF A TWENTYSOMETHING JOB-HOPPER

BRUSH
TEETH

4:05 P.M.

HE CAN TAKE IT SLOW
TODAY BECAUSE HE GOT
FIRED YESTERDAY.

WAKE UP

4:00 P.M.

A BIT OF A LATE RISER.

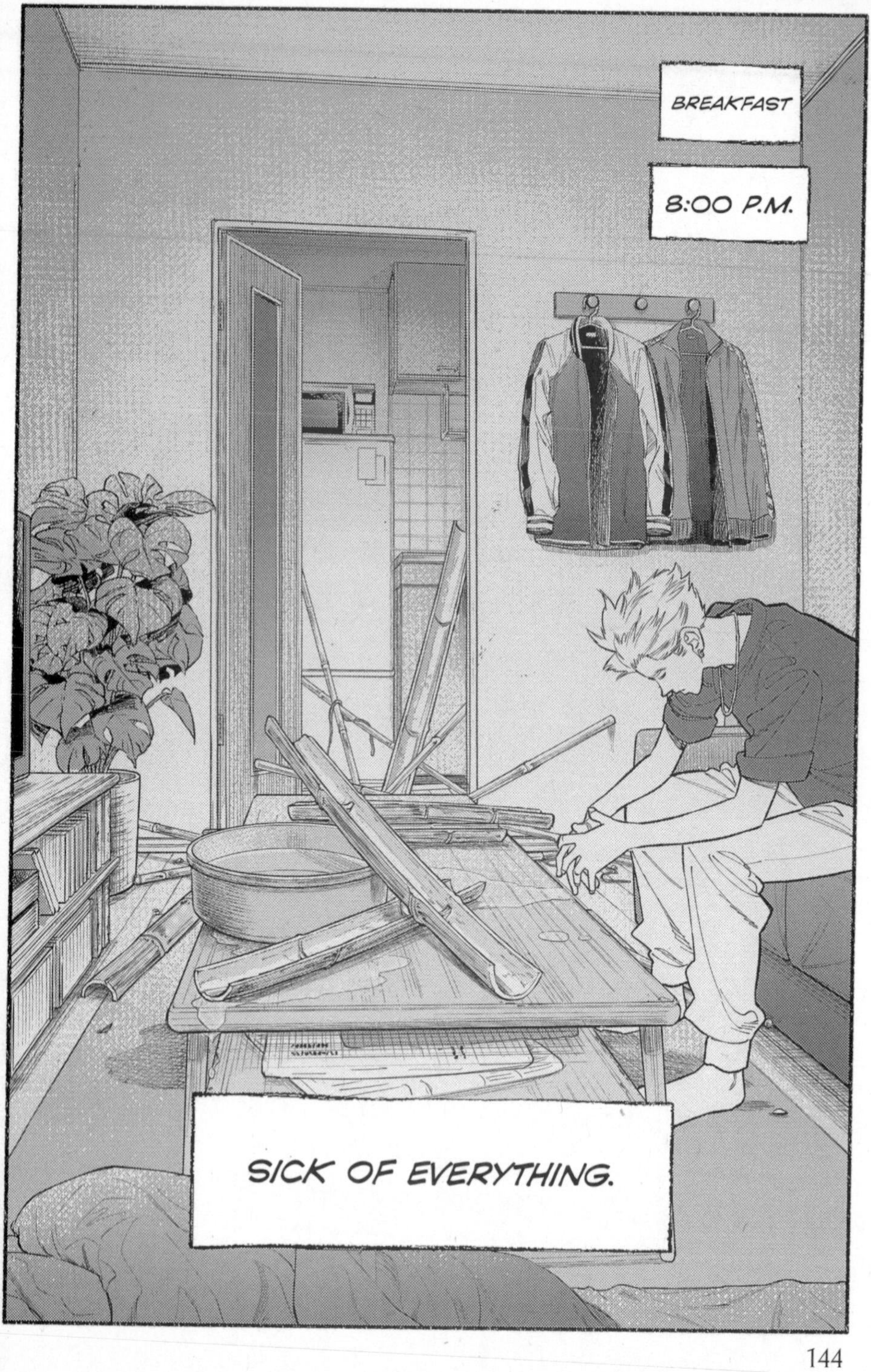
BREAKFAST
8:00 P.M.
SICK OF EVERYTHING.

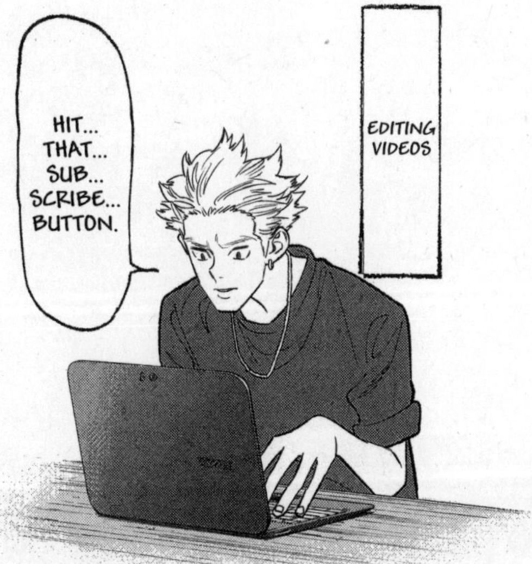
EDITING VIDEOS
HIT... THAT... SUB... SCRIBE... BUTTON.

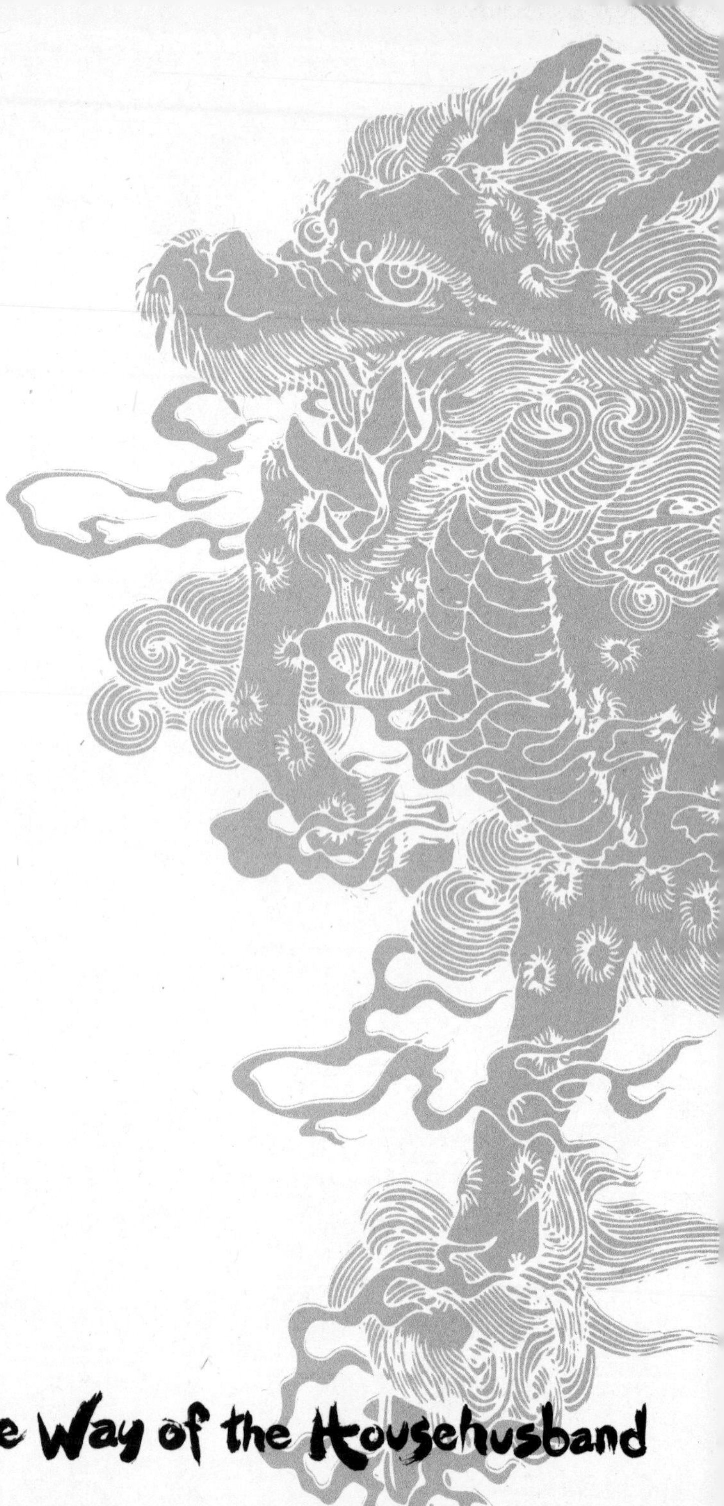

The Way of the Househusband

I SAW A BUNCH OF PEOPLE IN YUKATA ON MY WAY HOME FROM WORK TODAY.

OH, YEAH. THERE'S THAT FIREWORKS SHOW TONIGHT.

BOOM

!!!

I DON'T KNOW WHY SO MANY PEOPLE GO TO THEM.

THE CROWDS AT THOSE ARE SO EXHAUSTING.

SECURIN' A GOOD SPOT IS ALWAYS A BATTLE TOO.

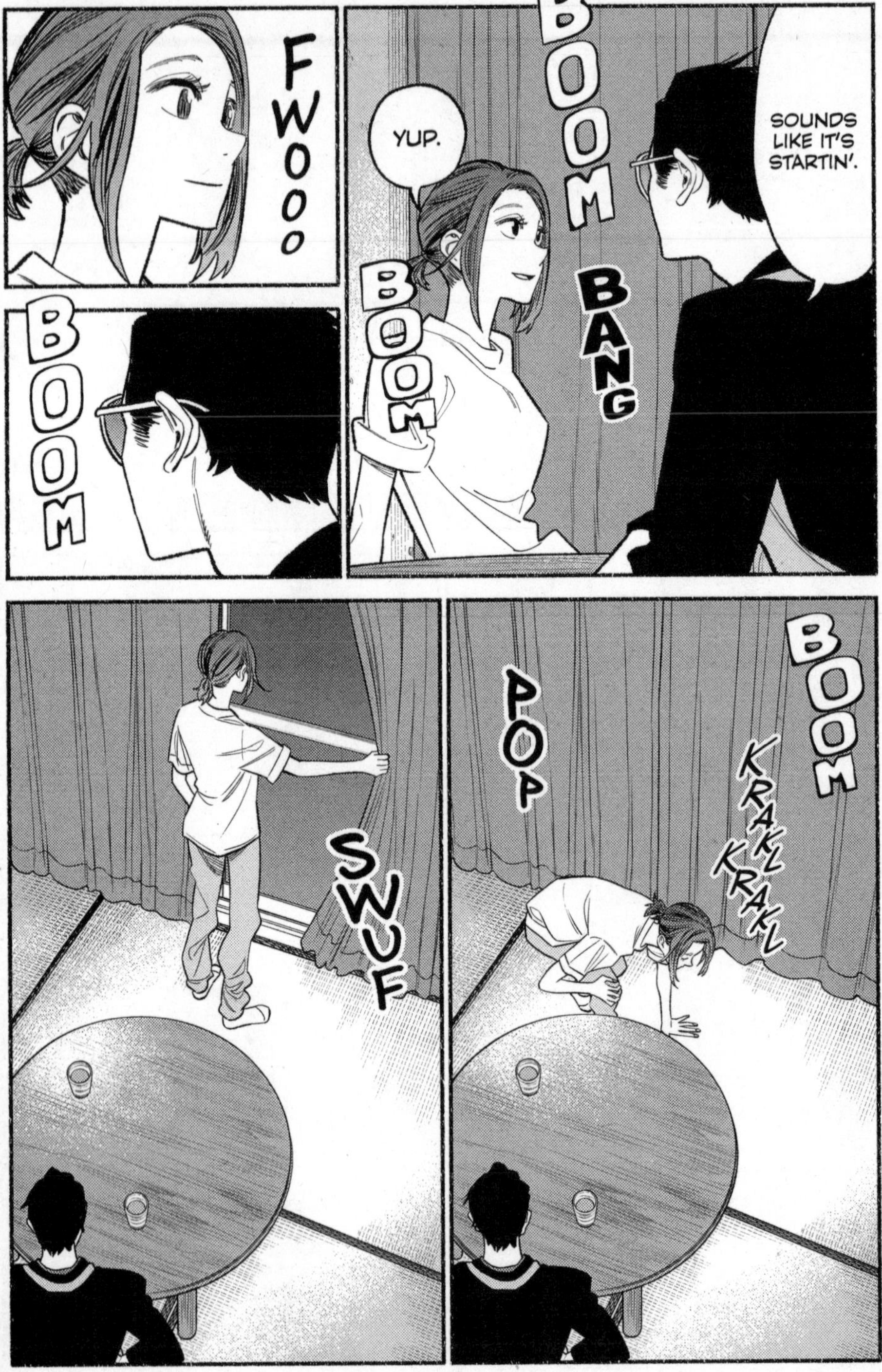
SOUNDS LIKE IT'S STARTIN'.
BOOM BOOM
YUP.
BANG
BOOM BOOM
FWOOO
BOOM BOOM
BOOM
KRAKL KRAKL
POP
SWUF

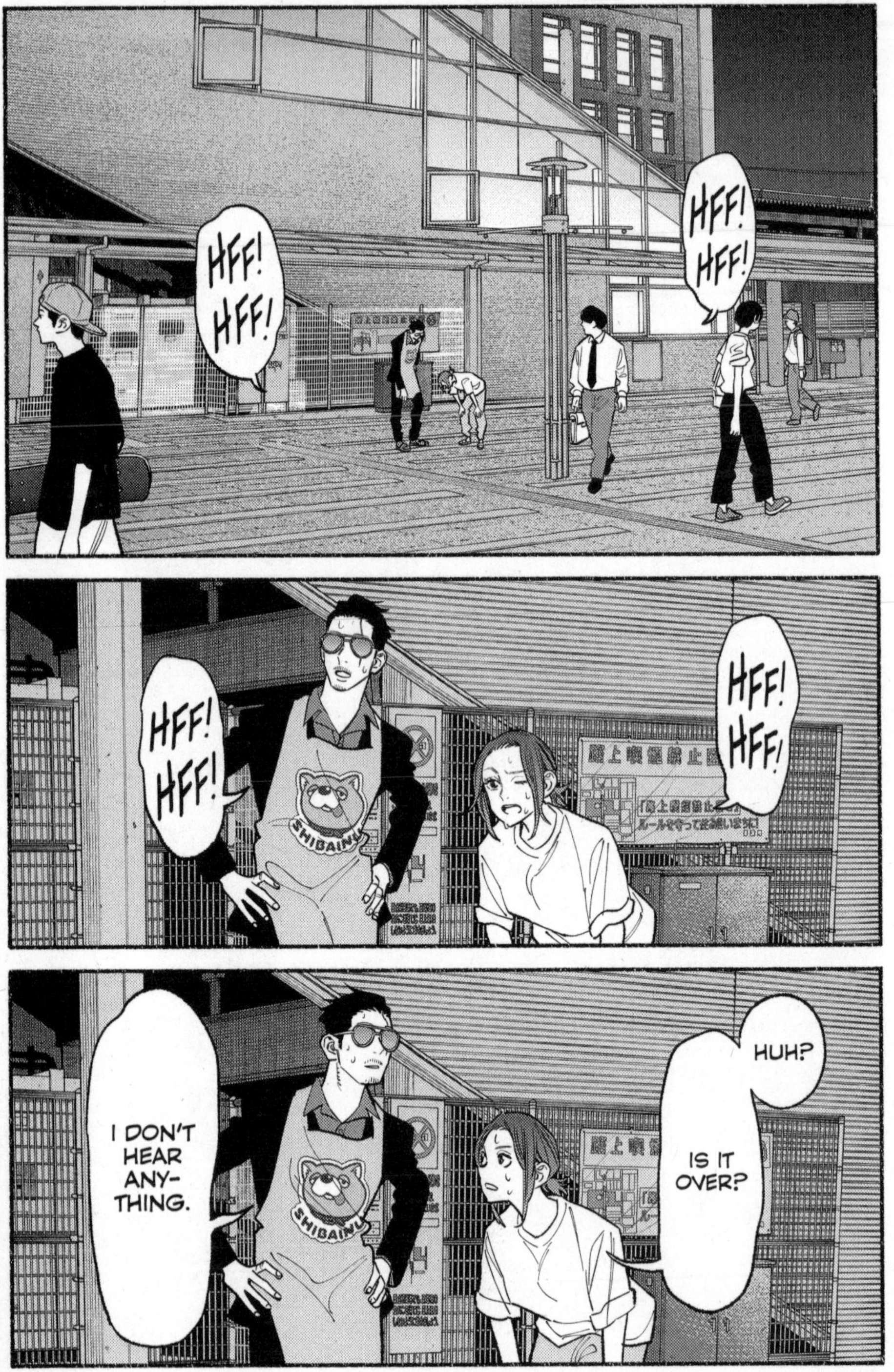
HFF! HFF!
HFF! HFF!
HFF! HFF!
SHIBAINU
HFF! HFF!
HUH?
IS IT OVER?
SHIBAINU
I DON'T HEAR ANY-THING.

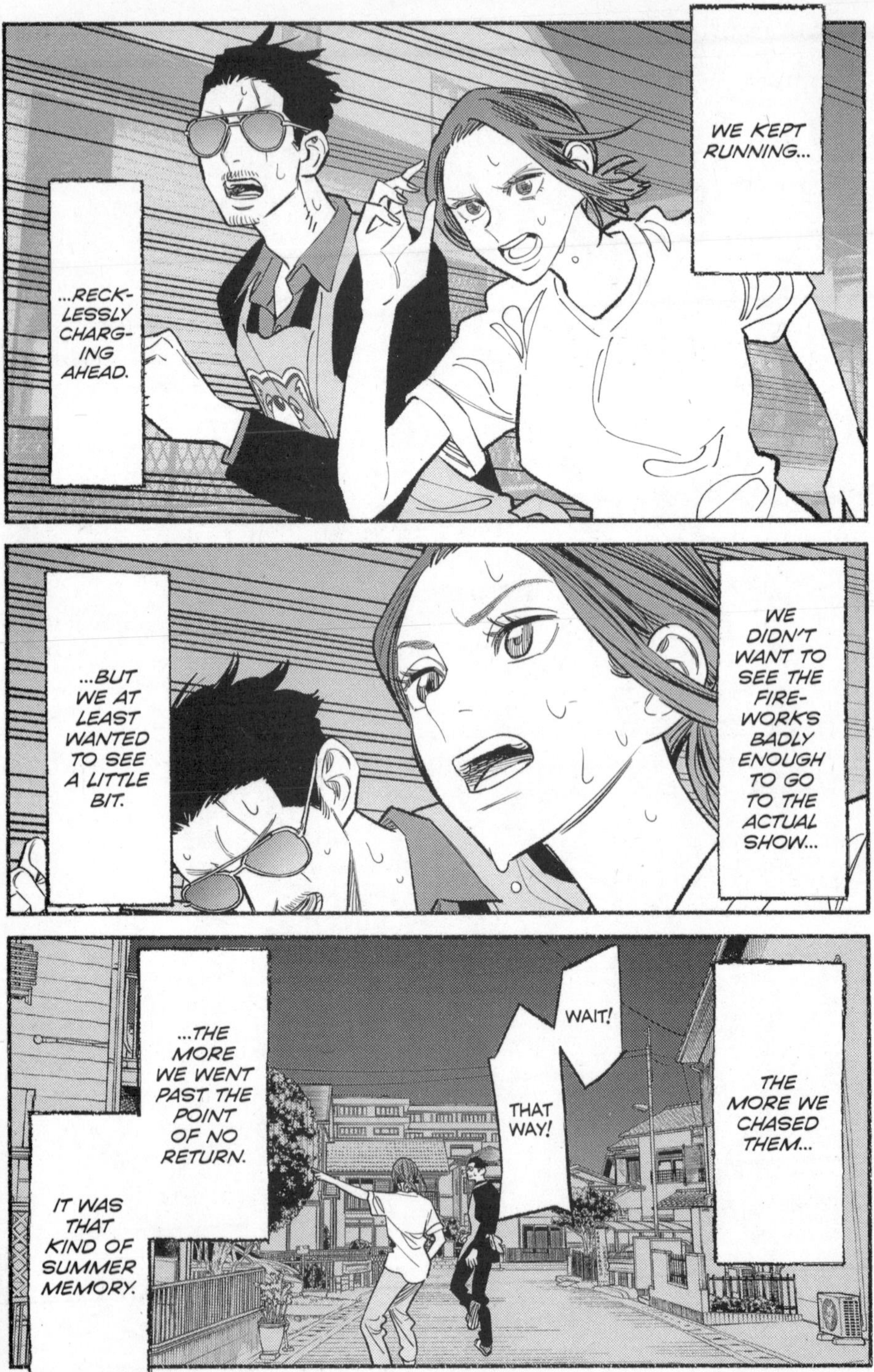
WE KEPT RUNNING...
...RECK-LESSLY CHARG-ING AHEAD.
WE DIDN'T WANT TO SEE THE FIRE-WORKS BADLY ENOUGH TO GO TO THE ACTUAL SHOW...
...BUT WE AT LEAST WANTED TO SEE A LITTLE BIT.
THE MORE WE CHASED THEM...
WAIT!
THAT WAY!
...THE MORE WE WENT PAST THE POINT OF NO RETURN.
IT WAS THAT KIND OF SUMMER MEMORY.

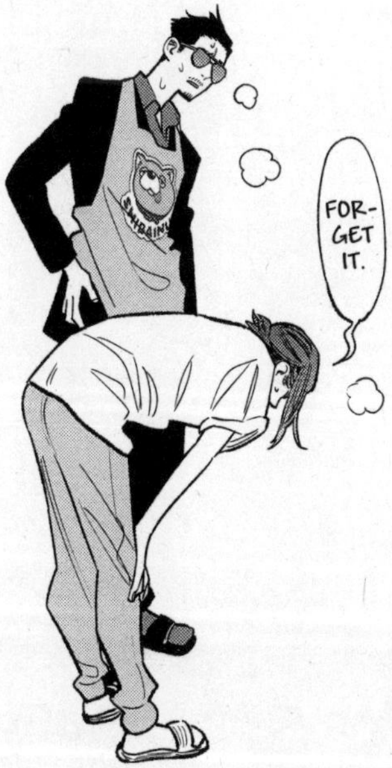
FOR-GET IT.

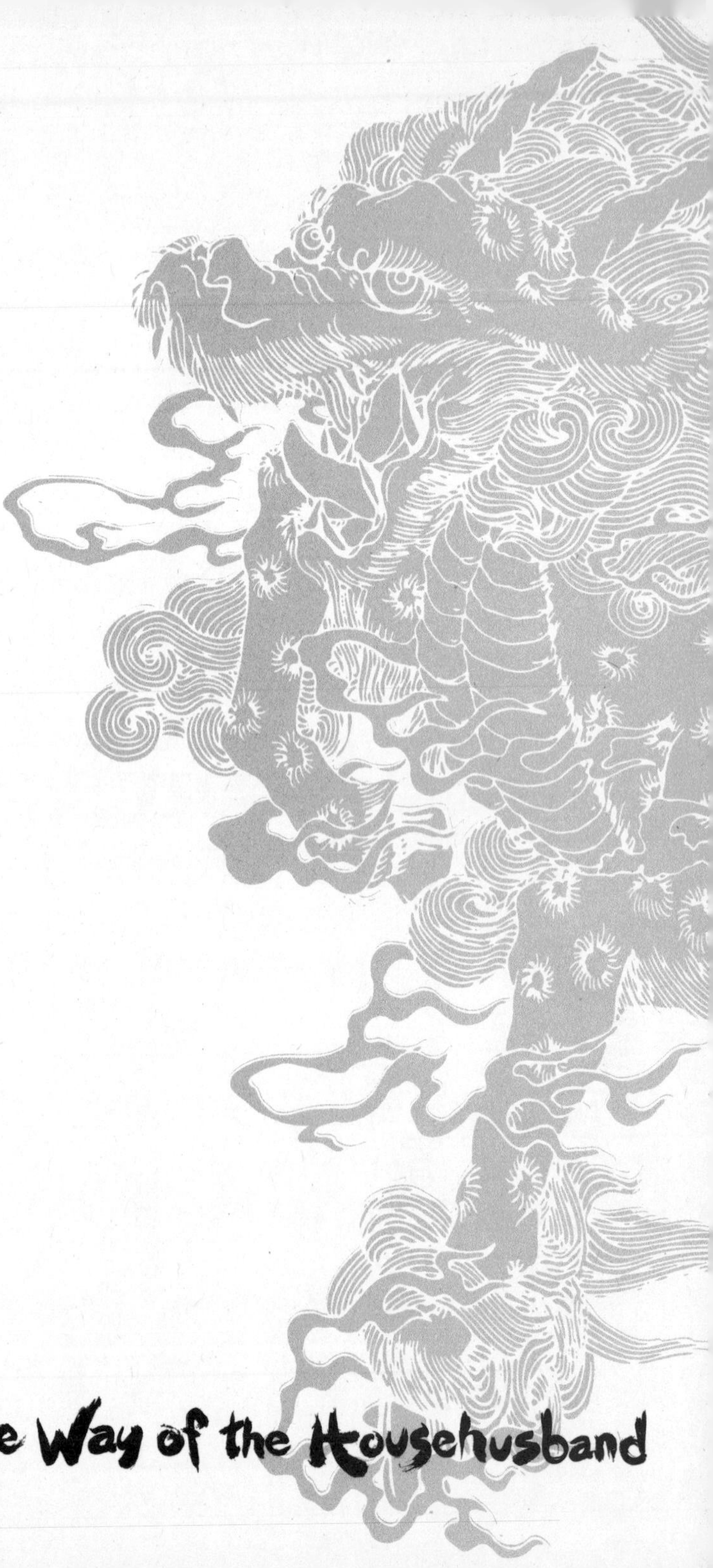

The Way of the Househusband

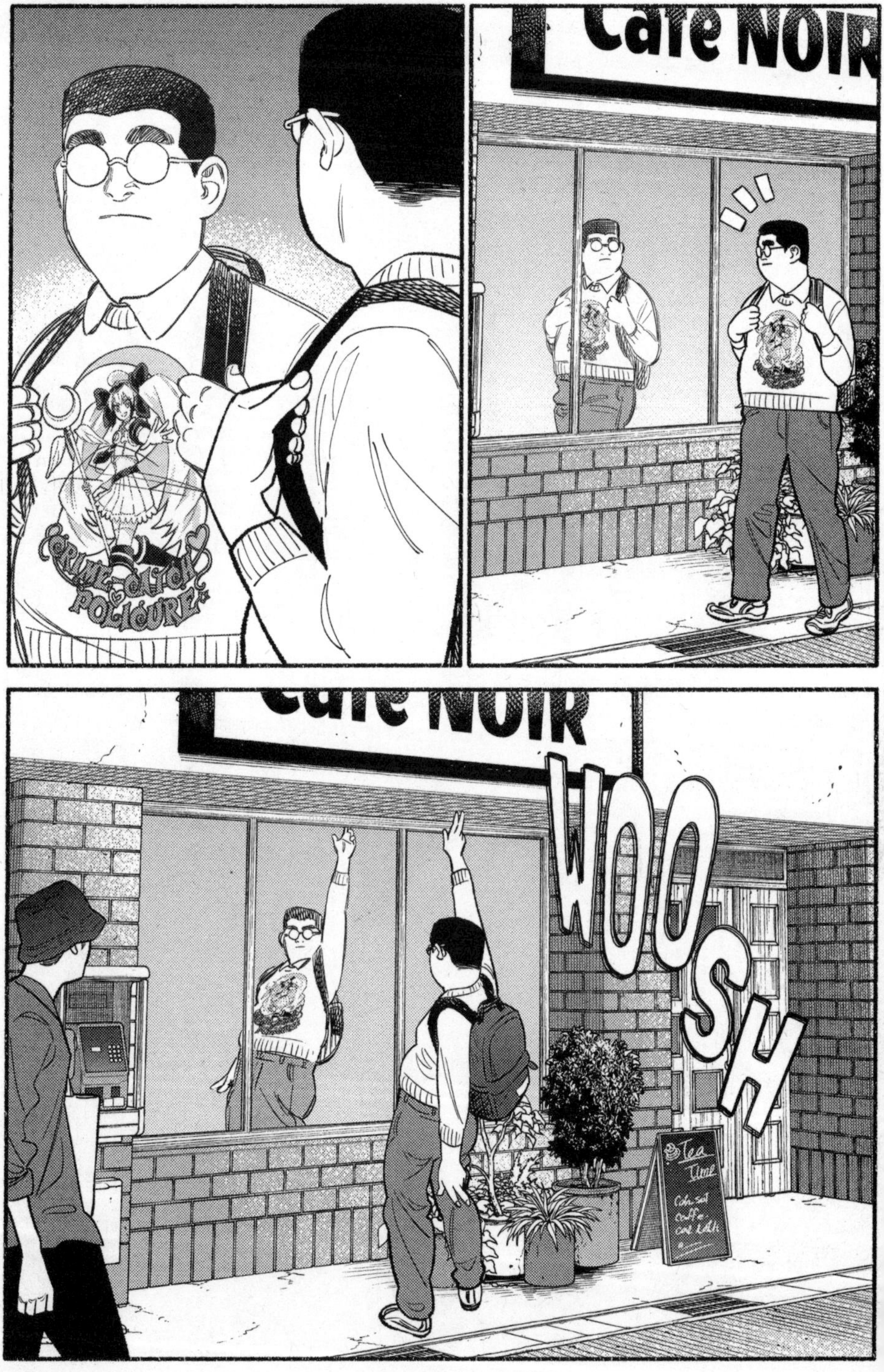
Cafe NOIR
CRIME-CATCH
POLICURE
Cafe NOIR
WOOSH
Tea Time

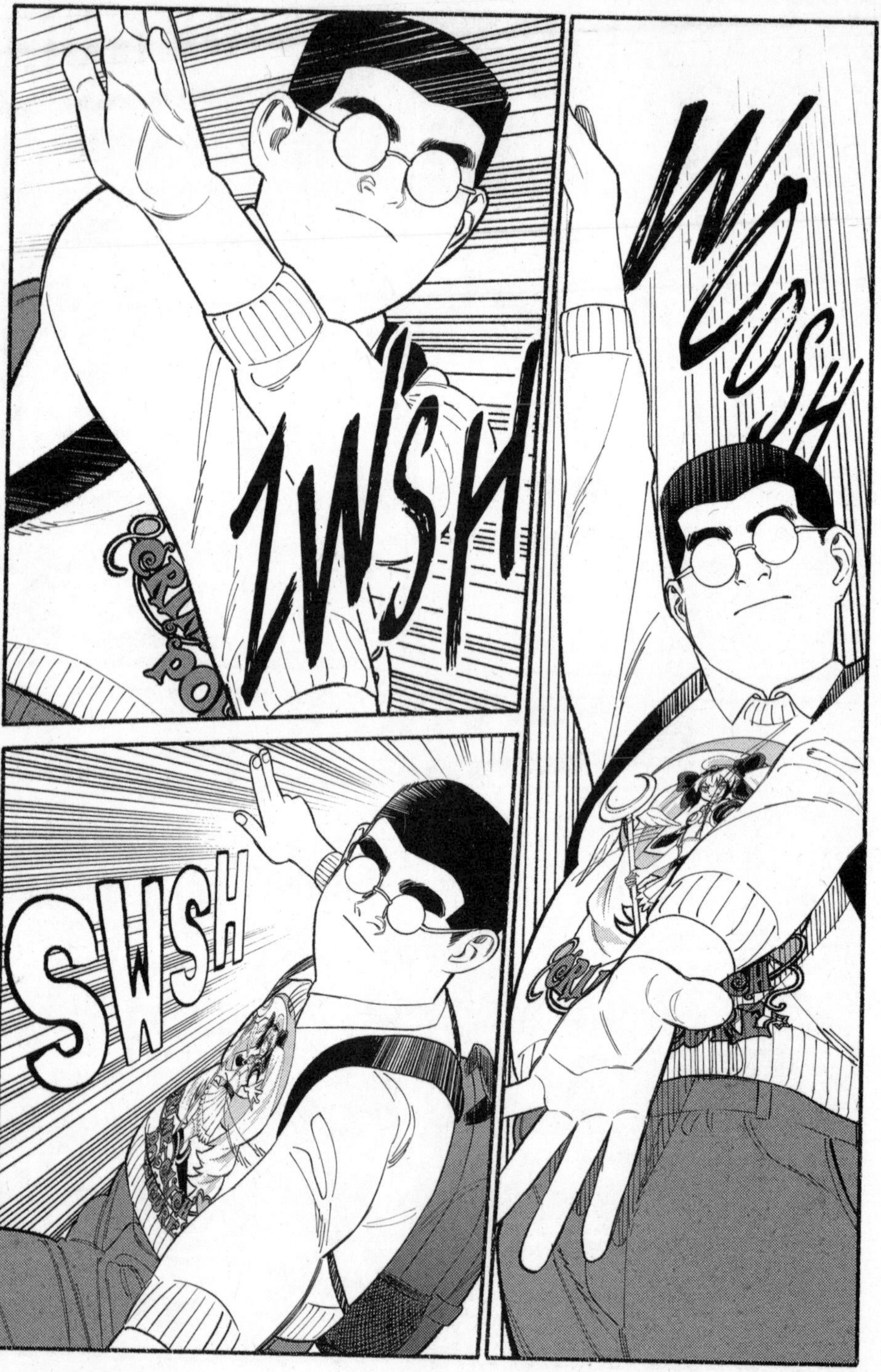
WOOSH
ZWSH
SWSH

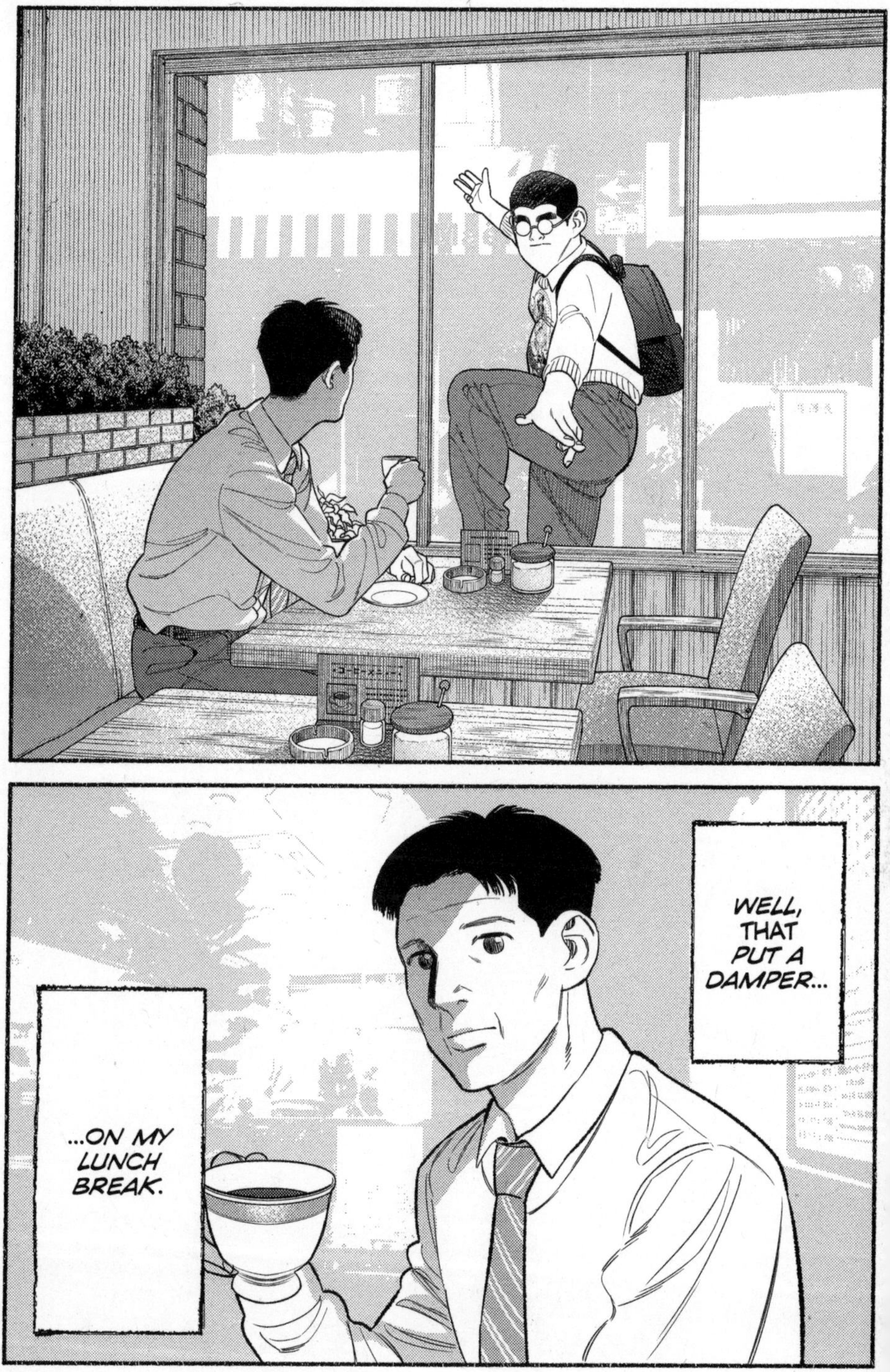
WELL, THAT PUT A DAMPER...
...ON MY LUNCH BREAK.

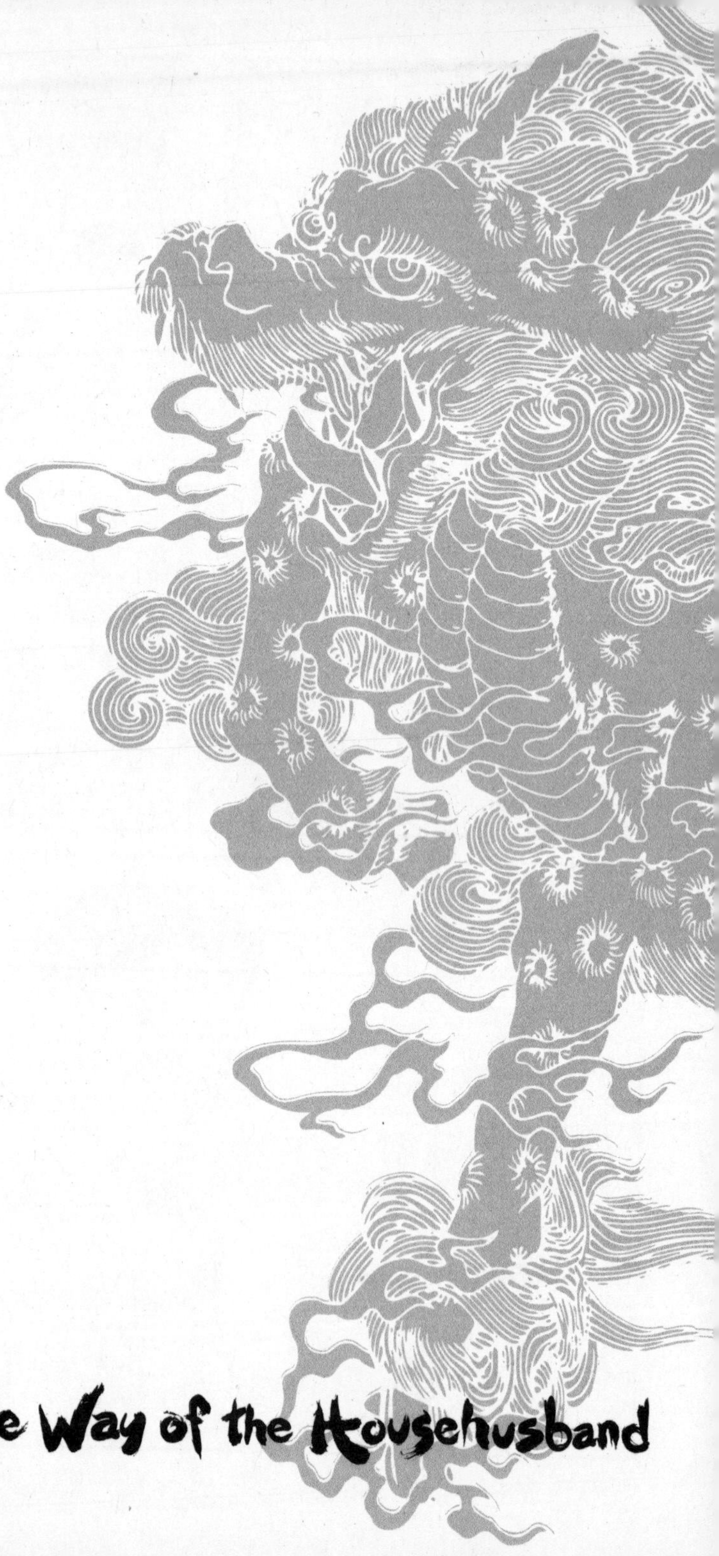

The Way of the Househusband

BONUS MANGA ④ SEEKING FREEDOM

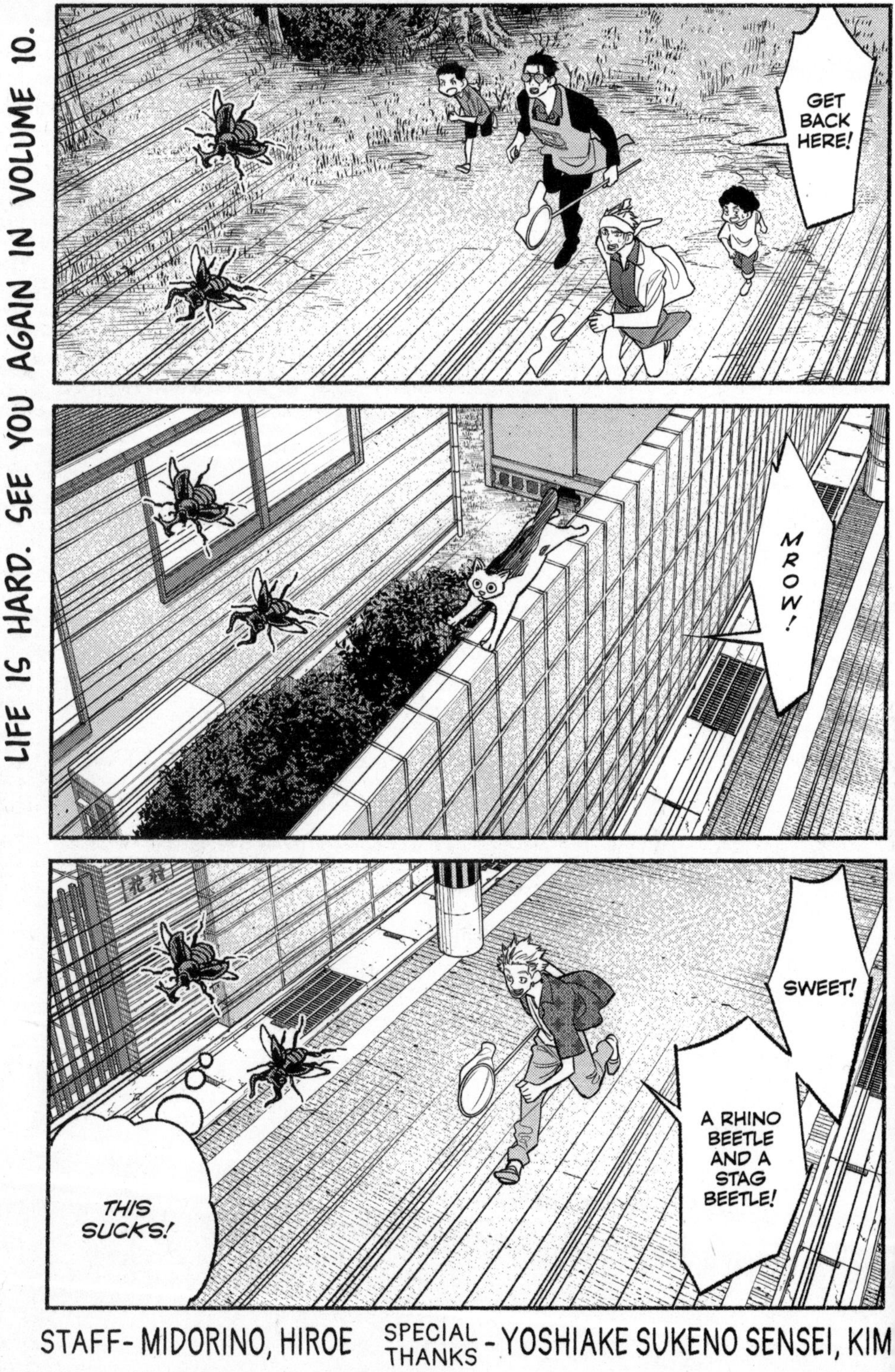
GET BACK HERE!
MROW!
SWEET!
A RHINO BEETLE AND A STAG BEETLE!
THIS SUCKS!

LIFE IS HARD. SEE YOU AGAIN IN VOLUME 10.

STAFF- MIDORINO, HIROE SPECIAL THANKS - YOSHIAKE SUKENO SENSEI, KIM

By the way, my pet Shiba
Inu's name is Daifuku,
after the Japanese sweet.
Because he's round like one.

KOUSUKE OONO

Kousuke Oono began his professional manga career in 2016 in the manga magazine *Monthly Comics @ Bunch* with the one-shot "Legend of Music." Oono's follow-up series, *The Way of the Househusband*, is the creator's first serialization as well as his first English-language release.

The Way of the House Husband

VOLUME 9

VIZ SIGNATURE EDITION

STORY AND ART BY
KOUSUKE OONO

TRANSLATION: Amanda Haley
ENGLISH ADAPTATION: Jennifer LeBlanc
TOUCH-UP ART & LETTERING: Bianca Pistillo
DESIGN: Alice Lewis
EDITOR: Jennifer LeBlanc

GOKUSHUFUDO volume 9
© Kousuke Oono 2018
All Rights Reserved
English translation rights arranged
with SHINCHOSHA Publishing Co., Ltd.
through Tuttle-Mori Agency, Inc., Tokyo

Printed in the U.S.A.

Published by VIZ Media, LLC
P.O. Box 77010
San Francisco, CA 94107

10 9 8 7 6 5 4 3 2 1
First printing, February 2023

VIZ MEDIA   *VIZ SIGNATURE*

viz.com   vizsignature.com

1

S'time to drop some beats. Jingi Tei, it's got good eats.
Fo' twenny long years, it's been on this street (hey yo).

With honor ever unchangin', this gent's been fightin' an' slayin'.
A dope rep he now gainin'.

Two decades in the biz. Damn, that's hella tenacious.
Any recommendations you wanna make fo' us?

"Omelet rice." Fluffy eggs to bring out the magic.
The presentation's always dynamic. Overall, that dish is just classic.

The meals, they come with coffee. A cup ta lend some color to your story.
This owner, he's gonna turn 20 into 40!

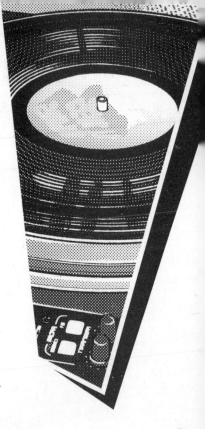

2

My list of its charms ain't complete. Jingi Tei, it's got good eats.
Fo' twenny long years, it's been on this street.

A menu that don't need changin'. Self-service water refills exchangin'.
Even the reviews got no complainin'.

Two decades in the biz, that's hella tenacious.
Any dope lunch recs you wanna make fo' us?

"Omelet rice." Lunch comes with a seasonal salad on the side.
Plus soup that'll have your eyes goin' wide.
If it's eggs ya want, he's happy to provide. (Damn straight!)

The meals, they come with coffee. A cup ta lend some color to your story.
This owner, he's gonna turn 20 into 40!

3

Runnin' out of things t' say, I'm on repeat. Jingi Tei, it's got good eats.
Fo' twenny long years it's been on this street.

This cafe's gonna go on unchangin'. Always stayin' cool and entertainin'.
Into the future, it'll be remainin'.

Two decades in the biz, that's hella tenacious.
Anythin' else you wanna say to us?

"Ahem, well then, I have to shout out a new addition to the menu.
It's called the Adult Creamy Parfait. It's a bitter parfait, and the
secret ingredient is matcha. Make it a combo with cake for a discount.
I hope you'll check it out. Also, completely unrelated, the shopping
district is holding its annual stamp rally again this year. If you have
a meal here, we'll stamp your sheet, so if you're interested in that,
please check it out as well."

Whoa, whoa, that's way too long. You gotta keep it short.

The meals, they come with coffee.
A cup ta lend some color to your story.
This owner, he's gonna turn 20 into 40!

Jingi Tei, it's got good eats.
Fo' twenny long years it's been on this street.

Lyrics: G Goda

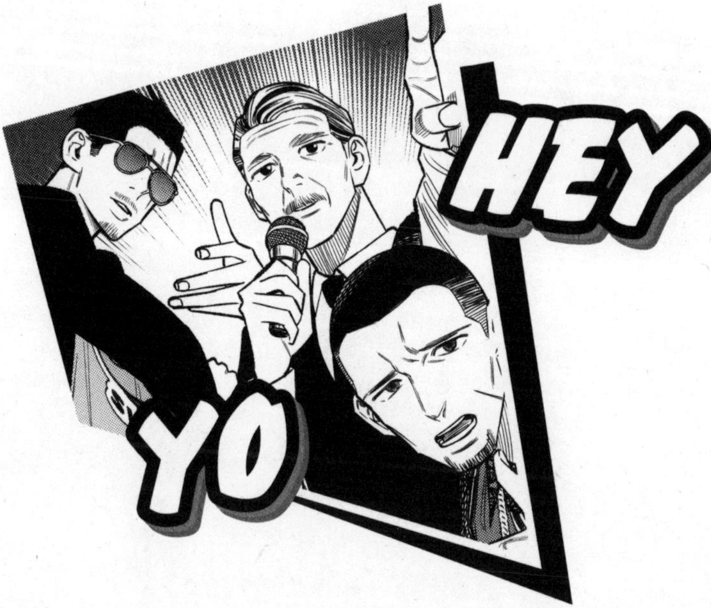
HEY
YO

Six short stories that set the scene for the best-selling *BEASTARS* series!

BEAST COMPLEX

Story and Art by Paru Itagaki

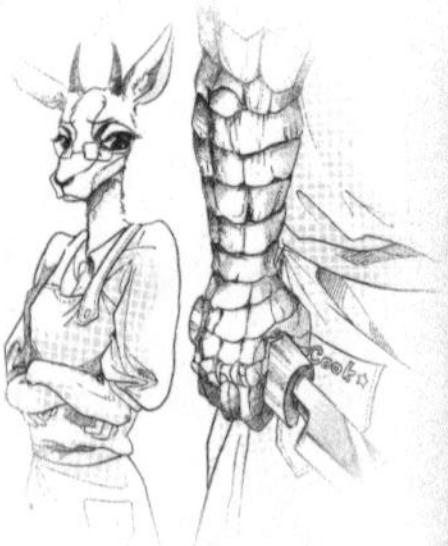

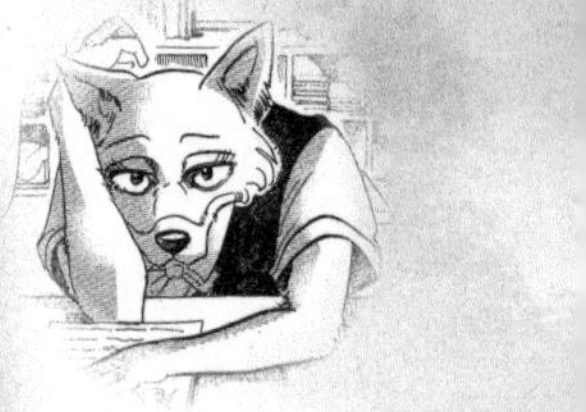

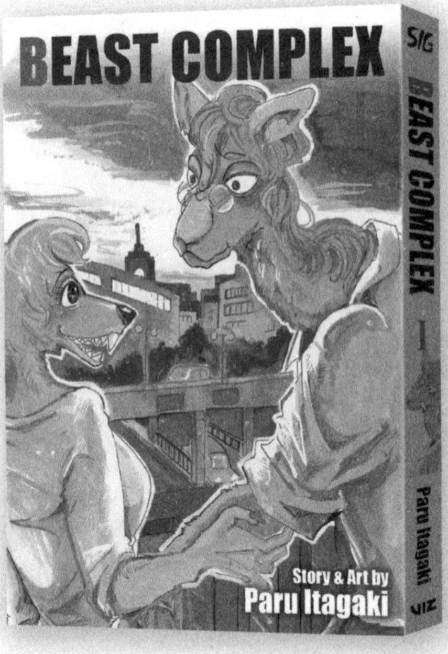
BEAST COMPLEX
SIG
BEAST COMPLEX
1
Paru Itagaki
Story & Art by
Paru Itagaki
VIZ

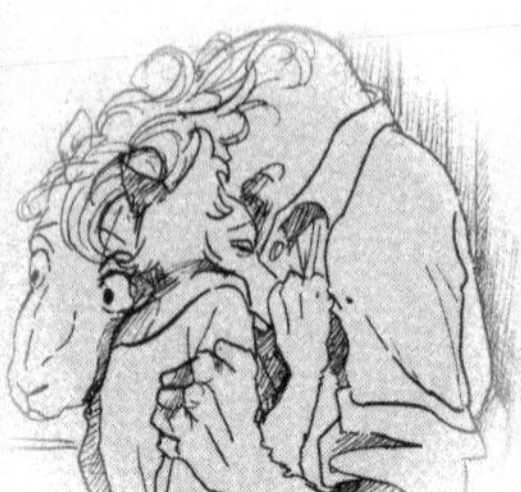

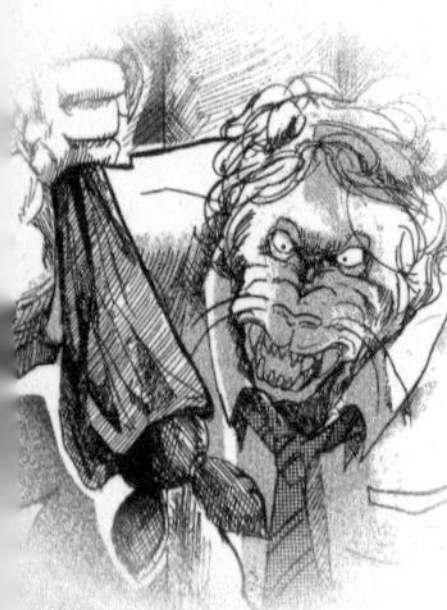

In these six stories from the creator of the Eisner-nominated, best-selling series BEASTARS, a menagerie of carnivores and herbivores grapple with conflicts based on their differences and—sometimes—find common ground.

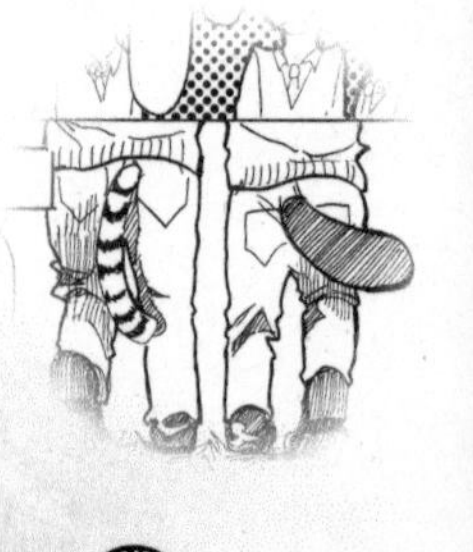

RATED T+ OLDER TEEN VIZ

TO STRIP THE FLESH

STORY AND ART BY
OTO TODA

Chiaki Ogawa has never doubted he is a man, although the rest of the world hasn't been as kind. When the burden of pretending becomes too great, Chiaki sets out to remake himself in his own image and discovers more than just personal freedom in his transition–he finds understanding from the people who matter most.

Stories that explore what must be stripped away to find the truth.

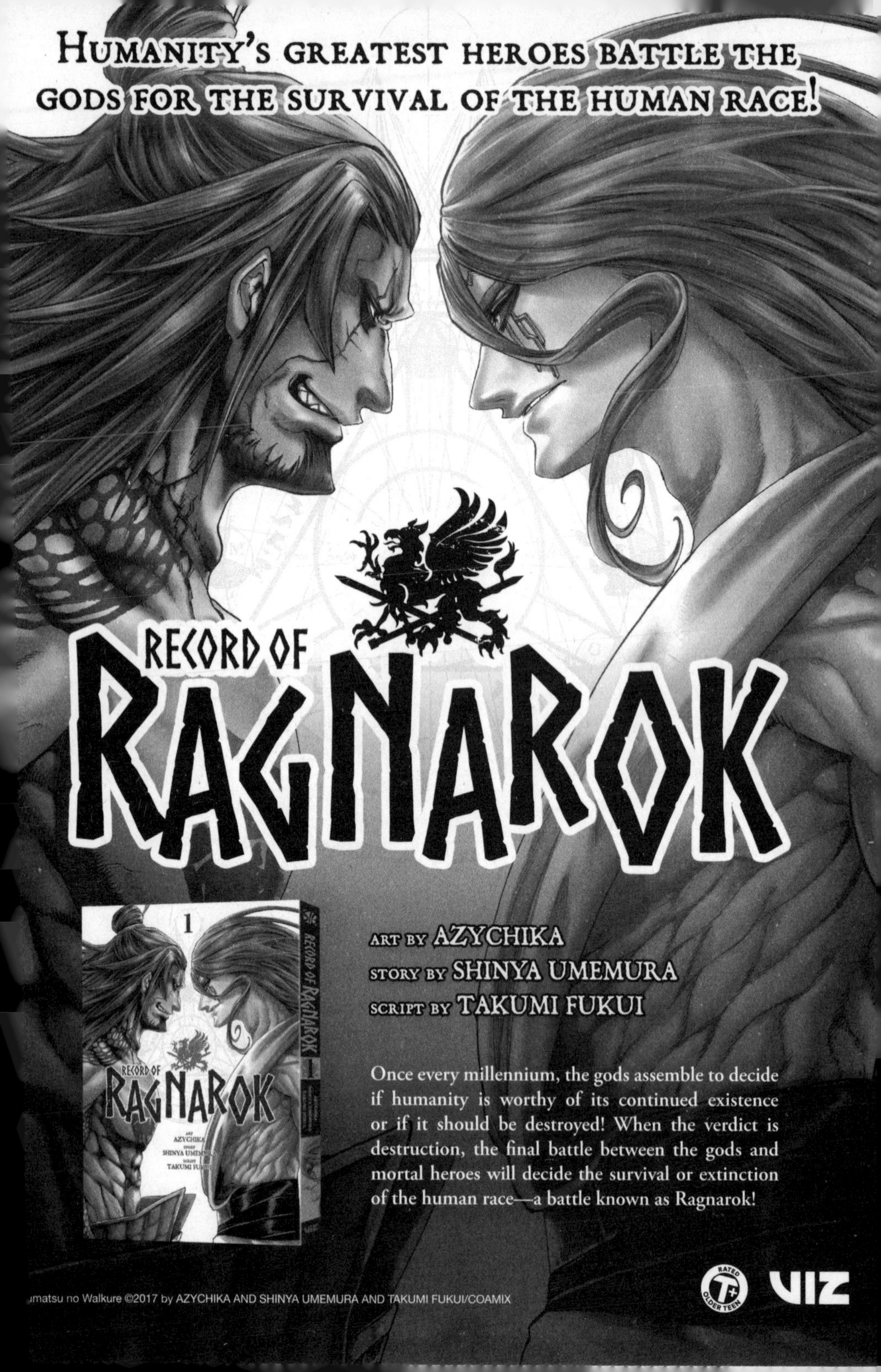

CHILDREN OF THE WHALES

In this postapocalyptic fantasy, a sea of sand swallows everything but the past.

In an endless sea of sand drifts the Mud Whale, a floating island city of clay and magic. In its chambers a small community clings to survival, cut off from its own history by the shadows of the past.

An unexpected love quadrangle comes between a group of friends!

Blue Flag

story and art by
KAITO

Love is already hard enough, but it becomes an unnavigable maze for unassuming high school student Taichi Ichinose and his shy classmate Futaba Kuze when they begin to fall for each other after their same-sex best friends have already fallen for them.